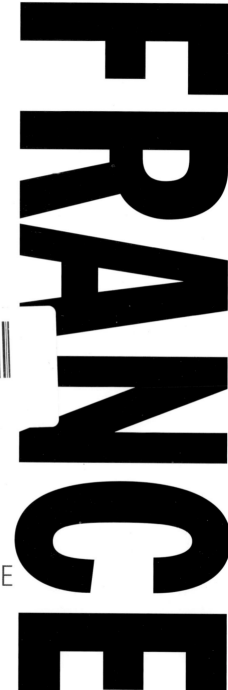

FRANCE

GW00602840

SPIRALGUIDE

AA Publishing

Contents

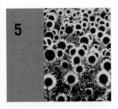

Compiled by Ann F Stonehouse
Revised and updated by Nick Inman

Project editor Sandy Draper
Project designer Alison Fenton
Series editor Karen Rigden
Series designer Catherine Murray

Published by AA Publishing, a trading name of AA Media Limited,
whose registered office is Fanum House, Basing View, Basingstoke,
Hampshire RG21 4EA. Registered number 06112600.

ISBN: 978-0-7495-6785-9

A CIP catalogue record for this book is available from the
British Library.

© AA Media Limited 2005, 2008, 2011
New edition 2011

Cover design and binding style by permission of AA Publishing
Colour separation by AA Digital Department
Printed and bound in China by Leo Paper Products

Find out more about AA Publishing and the wide range of services
the AA provides by visiting our website at theAA.com/shop

A04190
Maps in this title produced from cartographic data © Tele Atlas
N.V. 2005 Tele Atlas ◄ © IGN France with updates from mapping
© ISTITUTO GEOGRAFICO DE AGOSTINI S.p.A, Novara – 2010

The Magazine

A great holiday is more than just lying on a beach or shopping till you drop — to really get the most from your trip you need to know what makes the place tick. The Magazine provides an entertaining overview to some of the social, cultural and natural elements that make up the unique character of this engaging country.

Regional
SNAPSHOTS

Wherever you go in France, you will find yourself immersed in the rich French national culture but also surrounded by the distinctive trappings of the local region and its unique traditions, cuisine and, even, language.

Geography dictates the most obvious differences between the regions of France. Those of the north – Picardy, Champagne, Alsace and Lorraine – endure a colder climate and are distinctly closer to northern Europe. The north is also marked by its history of industrialization and war, having served as battlefields in two world wars. In contrast, the regions of the south, such as Provence, the Languedoc and Gascony, enjoy a warmer climate, and are more rural. They are noticeably remote from both Paris and the rest of Europe and influenced by their neighbours, Italy and Spain.

Along the French Coast
The peninsulas of Normandy and Brittany, to the west, are given character by their Atlantic coastlines and cooled by the sea breezes, while life in the centre and east of France is defined by the harsher mountainous terrain and climate of the Massif Central, the Jura and the Alps.

Sunflowers growing in the warm sunny climate of Provence (page 5); vineyards outside the medieval city of Carcassonne at sunset (below)

Discovering the *Pays*

To truly perceive the varieties of the country, however, you have to look beyond regions to *pays*. This is a word without an exact translation that delineates areas of France with a common heritage and a sense of self. A *pays* often has no precise extent and rarely coincides with local government boundaries but it is likely to have a prevailing agricultural tendency, a typical architectural style and a way of life that gives it unity and character, at least in the minds of its inhabitants. Nowadays, *pays* make convenient descriptions for tourist brochures.

You think you are visiting the *département* of the Dordogne but the locals will make it clear that you are in the Périgord or Quercy. And as you follow the Loire Valley downstream you will pass through Berry, Touraine and Anjou – all places linked by their role in history rather than by any modern political meaning.

MIND YOUR LANGUAGE

French is the universal official language of France – rigorously policed for its purity by the Académie Française – but it's only one of 20 tongues spoken in France. Catalan and Basque are making a vigorous comeback, although neither is as widely spoken as it is across the border in Spain. Breton, derived from Celtic languages, is spoken in Brittany. Alsatian (a mixture of French and German) is the everyday patois for many people of the northeast. Occitan (the Langue d'Oc), a Romance language, is used, mainly by older people and revivalists, across much of the south. Languages spoken by immigrant communities – especially Arabic and English – are commonly spoken in very localized areas.

Of Cabbages
and KINGS

Popular history may claim that France became a republic after the Revolution of 1789 and the *Terror* that followed, but when Louis XVI and his queen, Marie-Antoinette, lost their heads in 1793, the royal family still had another three reigns to serve. Proving that it takes more than a guillotine to get rid of a monarchy.

It is true that this literal severing of the major line of château-hopping, empire-building, style-inspiring royals marked a turning point in France's history. But perhaps surprisingly, it paved the way for an even more imperial chapter: that of Napoleon Bonaparte and his grand ideas for France, Europe and immortality.

No sooner was Napoleon forced to downsize his ambitions at the Battle of Waterloo (1815) than the Bourbon family was stepping back on the French throne. Louis XVIII worked out a new constitution and reigned from 1814, just 21 years since the declaration of "the end of the monarchy".

The "Citizen-King"
Ten years later, Louis' successor Charles X was foolish enough to try to bring back the grand old ways of his predecessors. The citizens of Paris did not appreciate a latter-day Sun King and revolted, forcing him to abdicate and introducing a regal compromise of a "Citizen-King", Louis Philippe, in 1830. This "monarch of the people" rode a tightrope of public opinion in a newly media-savvy age until the February Revolution of 1848 finally brought Republicanism back to stay.

Portrait of King Charles X (1757–1836) in Coronation Robes, 1827

France's natural instinct for continuity meant that in rejecting a king, the nation promptly elected to replace the head of state with another emperor, Napoléon III (1808–73). His charismatic blend of glamour and corruption kept political tempers on the boil as effectively as any previous monarch. In fact, it would not be until 1870, almost a century since the Revolution, that France finally shrugged off the tradition of being ruled by one man.

Divided Opinions

It is said that wherever you find two Frenchmen, you will find three opinions, so it is not surprising that, come the Revolution, France did not rise up with accord. Paris may have risen against the *ancien régime* in 1789 but the reaction around France was as varied as the landscape itself.

In Vendée, for instance, the staunchly royalist community signalled its counter-revolutionary tactics with semaphore-like turns of windmills. Provence, angered that Cardinal Richelieu had overridden the local parliament in Aix – in

> "Wherever you find two Frenchmen, you will find three opinions"

order to grab taxes for himself – took any opportunity to join the mob. Meanwhile, the folks of Marseille were comfortable with revolution, having already revolted against the King's great-great-grandfather, Louis XIV.

Marie-Antoinette at the guillotine, Place de la Revolution (Place de la Concorde)

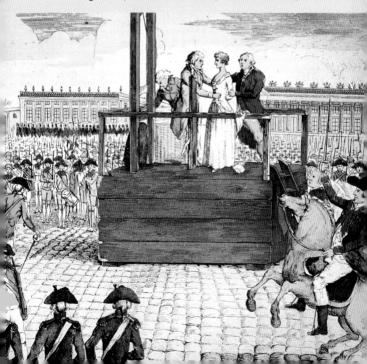

**Louis-Napoleon Bonaparte (1808–73);
Emperor of the French, 1852–70**

What's in a Name?

In a republic, everybody is equal – well, everyone who has not got an aristocratic "de" in his surname, at any rate. One of the great ironies of off-loading a monarchy is that snobbery loses its most obvious yardstick, and post-revolutionary France is riddled with local pretensions and anxieties regarding status. Noble families still receive overdue deference in local political arenas and when booking a table in restaurants. A former feudal lord is likely to hold at least one, if not several civic titles, whether mayor, councillor or even deputy.

Most telling of all, French Sunday tabloid newspapers are filled with stories and photographs of every other royal family in Europe, most notably that of Monaco, France's surrogate modern-day monarchy – if only for idle gossip.

Noblesse oblige – the concept that nobility entails responsibility – still exists, most notably in the line of the Comte de Paris, the leading pretender to the French throne. Prince Jean de France, the Duc de Vendôme and the modern Dauphin (heir apparent), has a resumé that includes studying philosophy at the Sorbonne, gaining an MBA in California and doing military service in the republican army.

MARIANNE

One of the symbols of the French Republic – along with the cockerel, the tricolour flag and the battle hymn of *the Marseillaise* – is Marianne, an allegorical young woman who personifies Liberty in the French Republic's motto "liberté, égalité, fraternité". She appears in portraits and busts, on coins and stamps, and in the government logo, in a variety of forms, but is always distinguished by her Phrygian cap. This kind of headgear is believed to have been worn by freed slaves in ancient Greece and Rome and was worn by people converging on Paris from the Midi during the Revolution, when Marianne made her first appearance. No one knows why the particular forename came to be chosen but it is probable that it was first used, perhaps disparagingly by counter-revolutionaries – to stand for the common people. Several uncommonly glamorous French women have served as models for Marianne in the recent past, including 1960s sex symbol Brigitte Bardot, film star Catherine Deneuve and supermodel Laetitia Casta.

The French have a word for it...

French wine has a very special principal ingredient: *Terroir*. It is what makes every wine different from its neighbour. *Terroir* is the indefinable ingredient that a wine gets from its soil, its town and the sweat and toil of the people whose lives are dedicated to nurturing the grape from the vine to wine.

The world-famous Châteauneuf du Pape is made from grapes grown in the Rhône Valley

Every region claims that its *terroir* makes its wines special. And, whether you are talking about a *grand cru* from the Bordeaux or a table wine from a co-op in the foothills of the Pyrénées, it will be special to the locals, since age-old family recipes will have been used to create its particular flavours.

While waiters in Paris and on the money-making strip of the Riviera might be tempted by snobbery or profit to nudge diners to overspend on the wine list, in other regions you can usually trust restaurant staff to recommend just the right accompaniment to the meal – and it generally pays to follow the local taste in wine. So, if you find yourself eating barbecued mussels at a Languedoc *brasucade* opt for a humble, local *vin de pays* rather than a pricier or more exotic Alsatian gewürztraminer. Likewise, stick with a good Burgundy with your *boeuf bourguignon*. The one exception to every rule is, of course, Champagne, which should be celebrated and drunk anywhere, any time and at every opportunity.

DESIGNER LABELS

French wine labels emphasize the region of production and also give the name of the producer and the date. They do not always give the grape variety, although this may be mentioned in the small print on the back of the bottle.

AOC (*Appellation d'Origine Contrôlée*) is the highest universally recognizable standard and indicates that the wine meets the strictest criteria before being allowed to be sold under the regional or vineyard name.

AOVDQS (*Appellation d'Origine Contrôlée Vin de Qualité Superieur*) is one gradation down from AOC status.

Indication géographique protégée (IGP) is a new name for what has always been called **vin de pays** to denote simple country wine from a defined area.

Vin de France or **Vin de table** is the cheapest variety of wine suitable for washing down your meal or a snack, but don't enquire too much about its family background, since it is often a blend from various regions.

Agriculture biologique indicates that the wine is from an organic wine grower.

Know Your Regions

Alsace: produces refreshing white wines. Unusually for France, bottles name the grape variety, perhaps Riesling (crisp), Pinot Gris (dry) or Gewürztraminer (more complex).

Beaujolais: nouveau may be a triumph of marketing over winemaking, but check out the *crus* – fruity red wines including Morgan, Moulin à Vent and Juliénas.

Bordeaux: arguably the greatest wines of France. Better known as claret, the classic reds such as Margaux or Petrus are for the wealthy, and come in various grades, with *premier cru* at the top of the range. White dessert wines from Sauternes include the famed Château d'Yquem. Neighbouring Bergerac provides good budget alternatives.

Burgundy: the Côtes de Nuits and de Beaune boast many of the world's most popular quality wines. Wines such as Nuits-St-Georges, Chablis and Mâcon are firm Burgundian favourites.

Champagne: top fizz any time, anywhere.

Jura: the yellow *vins jaunes* are full-flavoured treats.

Languedoc-Roussillon: France's biggest wine region, revived with many skills from the New World. The region now produces palatable everyday wines and some robust southern classics such as St-Chinian, Corbières and Fitou.

Loire: produces more than 100 wines, mainly white (such as the crisp Muscadet and sparkling Saumur), but also a famous Rosé d'Anjou and respectable red Gamay.

Provence: wine to enjoy on site rather than elsewhere. Good summery choices include Bellet rosé and whites.

Rhône: vineyards along the river from Avignon offer good local wines and reputable classics such as the quality red Châteauneuf du Pape.

Southwest: a disparate grouping of small wine regions covering vineyards from the Dordogne to the Basque Country and the Pyrénées.
Cognac: beautiful western wine region producing France's most famous distilled *digestif*.
Savoie: small wine region in eastern France beneath the Alps.

Crates of grapes picked from the local vineyards of the Haut Côte de Beaune

CHANGING HABITS

France's consumption of wine has been steadily declining for decades and there has been a quiet but seismic shift going on in society. Once there was always a cheap bottle of plonk on every dinner table at every meal and drinking wine was almost synonymous with being French. Now, many people simply don't drink wine unless it's a special occasion. The reasons for this are various. People certainly drink less for health reasons, because of strict drink driving laws and because there has been a lifestyle transition from manual labour to the service sector. The young, meanwhile, see wine as somewhat old fashioned and their preferences is for more stylish "designer" drinks.

Quality brands such as Bordeaux and Champagne have been more resilient to changing attitudes, although even they have had to compete in a world market in which high-quality New World wines are widely available.

Faced with the decline in domestic consumption, the government has to steer a delicate political course: while responsible for raising public awareness of health issues and promoting responsible drinking, with health warnings and drink driving campaigns, it also has to be seen to be concerned about the interests of producers, who claim that not only has their livelihood been damaged but also a part of French culture is under threat.

Living in a
COMMUNE

You can't understand France without appreciating the importance of a small, somewhat eccentric but stubbornly surviving – some would say anachronistic – unit of local government, the *commune*.

The country is divided into more than 36,500 of these quasi-autonomous political units, which are a hangover from the parishes and towns of the *ancien regime*. During the early days of the revolution, the National Assembly decided to organize affairs around them, giving local people power over their own affairs in place of the feudal arrangements that had just been overthrown. Nowadays, some central planners would like to abolish them in the interests of greater efficiency of public administration, but no government minister has yet dared tinker with the system.

Commune Populations
Communes usually comprise several villages, but vary enormously in size from Paris (population over 2 million) to several, isolated, depopulated villages that have only three, two or even one inhabitants. Six villages of the Meuse *département* even have no inhabitants at all: they have been left inhabited since 1916 as monuments to the destruction of World War 1.

Game of Boules (opposite); La Garde Freinet (left); Pernes le Fountaines (right)

Some *communes* are on the other side of the world in France's overseas territories. The furthest from the metropolis is 16,841km (10,526 miles) away on New Caledonia. While the average size of a commune covers an area of just a few kilometres, one, in Guyana, covers several thousand.

Government

Whether big, small or populous, each *commune* is essentially the same. It is governed by a directly elected mayor and his or her team of councillors. Together they are responsible for spending the slice of tax pie they are allocated and defending the *commune's* interests, which might, for instance, mean keeping the local school open when threatened by closure from the Ministry of Education.

The mayor is invariably a local personality, expected to be present at local events and to speak for the best interests of the *commune*. It is not always a rewarding job and, as a public figure, he is invariably criticized – usually in secret – by a segment of the population.

VILLAGE VOICE

Democracy doesn't get any simpler than in villages in France. You can vote for who you want, whether he or she has stood for election or not. You just cross out the names of the candidates you don't like on the ballot paper and write in the names you prefer. Every vote is officially recorded at the count, which is held in public. It is unusual, but not impossible, therefore, for a bashful local hero to win a seat on the council against his will.

Le "GRAND PROJET"

The French have always had the knack of dreaming up and executing big and bold building projects. Whether conceived for civil, religious or military reasons, to serve a function or simply intimidate and impress, the great buildings of France comprise an incomparable national architectural treasure.

You have only to stand in front of one of the great Gothic cathedrals, such as Amiens or Strasbourg, to marvel at the daring and dedication it must have taken to create such large and enduring monuments using the limited tools and technology of the 13th century.

The great chateaux of the Loire (▶ 122–131) and the palace of Versailles (▶ 66) are similarly examples of construction on a grandiose scale: the legacies of kings and aristocrats hoping to earn a bit of immortality for themselves from bricks and mortar.

Iconic Structures of Paris

Gustave Eiffel was following in the same tradition when he erected his ambitious industrial-age grid-iron tower (▶ 52–53) in the capital in 1889. It was initially scoffed at but later came to be adored, as much part of the city as the grand boulevards laid out 20 years before, which were also the subject of controversy. It is impossible to imagine the capital without

British-born Norman Foster's Millau motorway viaduct across the Tarn River Valley

either, or indeed without two other distinctive buildings: the "inside-out" Pompidou Centre (▶ 58–59) and, in a different way, the arch of La Defense (1989), a hollow cube of white marble and glass designed by the Danish architect Otto von Spreckelsen as a gateway to the modern skyscraper business district on the western outskirts of the city.

Architectural Landscape

Other grand building projects have added to the French landscape during the course of the 20th century. The postwar reconstruction of the port of Le Havre in a functional modernist style by Auguste Perret was considered to be worth certifying as a UNESCO World Heritage Site. Le Corbusier's striking chapel, Notre Dame du Haut (1954), at Ronchamp in eastern France is considered his masterpiece. And not far from Paris is another innovative religious edifice, a circular brick-built cathedral of Evry, designed by Swiss architect Mario Botta and opened in 1995.

Superstar Buildings

The country's great feats of engineering are also much admired, and one has even achieved superstar status. British architect Norman Foster's curved and sloping Millau motorway viaduct across the river Tarn in southwest France is considered a tourist attraction in its own right. At 343m (1,125ft) it is 19m (62ft) taller than the Tour Eiffel and the highest road bridge in the world.

French presidents, in the manner of French kings, also like to leave behind buildings to be remembered by, and Nicholas Sarkozy's contribution to the future is to be the "Grand Paris", an ambitious expansion of the capital, which is expected to be completed by 2030.

The cathedral of Evry, designed by the Swiss architect Mario Botta and opened in 1995

FICTIONAL FRANCE

France has always held its writers in high esteem and the country is littered with shrines to their lives and works. Taking a tour of the literary landscape, novel in hand, can be a great way to add another dimension to holiday sightseeing.

Paris is inevitably the most written about part of the country, and any number of authors offer themselves as guides to its streets. Two writers, however, stand out from all the rest. Jean-Paul Sartre and his lifelong companion Simone de Beauvoir may be buried in Montparnasse Cemetery but they still haunt the city's literary cafés and cast an indelible shadow on French intellectual life. One of Sartre's greatest works of fiction is *Les chemins de la liberté* (*The Roads to Freedom*, 1945–1949) in which he works out his influential existential philosophy against the brooding urban landscapes of Paris on the eve of war and under the Occupation.

Marcel Proust's home, now a museum (left); Françoise Sagan, photographed in November 1961, authoress of *Bonjour tristesse* (*Hello Sadness*, 1954) (right)

The romantic image of Notre-Dame and the statue of St Geneviève in silhouette at dusk

French Tales from Normandy

Normandy is another great stamping ground for novelists and the region is immortalized by two classics. Proust's monumental, semi-autobiographical *À la recherche du temps perdu* (*Remembrance of Things Past*) and *Madame Bovary* (1856) by Gustave Flaubert, a vividly told and gripping novel. It is the story of a provincial doctor's wife who yearns for a more exciting life. Her adultery ultimately leads to the destruction of herself and her family but Flaubert is at pains to show us the situation rather than to judge it – an apparently amoral stance that caused a scandal when the book was published and challenges modern readers to reach their own conclusions.

> "Flaubert is at pains to show us the situation rather than to judge it"

19th-century Literature

Another great 19th-century classic that explores universal themes of psychological and emotional conflict takes eastern France as its backdrop. Stendhal's *Le rouge et le noire* (*The Red and the Black*, 1830) takes its title from the career choice of the time: army or church. The protagonist, Julien Sorel, is born to a poor family in Verrières, a fictional village in the Franche-Comté. Driven by unflinching ambition, he tries to rise in a world stifled by the church and aristocracy, while preserving his own sense of sincerity, but his passion undermines his intellect and leads to ruin.

An altogether different drama is dealt with by Françoise Sagan's *Bonjour tristesse* (*Hello Sadness*, 1954), a bitter-sweet look at holidays and relationships set on the post-war French Riviera. It's a short, easy read about how 17-year-old Cécile tries to come to terms with her father's impending marriage while discovering her own awakening as a woman. The fact that the book became an overnight literary sensation for an author who was herself only 18 years old says much about the post-war, celebrity-hungry times it was written in.

Foodies'
FRANCE

It's a cliché, but true to say that the French love everything to do with food: buying it, preparing it, eating it and, most of all, talking about it. The favourite topic of conversation at mealtimes is either what's on the plate or some gourmet treat that someone around the table has recently enjoyed.

Fast food and hypermarkets may have made in-roads into French culinary culture but there is still a generalized preference for fresh, high-quality ingredients prepared with attention and flair. Not for nothing is the Michelin guide still the world's arbiter of good cooking.

Mealtimes for the French are not just about refuelling their stomachs, but eating well, even if this means a lengthy discussion with the waiter or restaurateur about the provenance of a piece of meat or the style of cooking. Don't be afraid to ask questions before you order or to send a dish back if it is not right.

Variety is the Spice

You can see the French love of food for yourself in any market set up in the main square or down the main street. Ask about some unusual cheese, jar of preserved snails or rare strain of garlic and you will be given an enthusiastic lecture on its history and how it is produced.

The variety of things to eat is almost infinite. De Gaulle is famously said to have remarked that it is difficult to govern a country that produces 246 kinds of cheese, but there are thought to be even four times as many as that today. Many of them are protected in the same way as wines with a zealously guarded *appellation d'origine contrôlée* (AOC). Many other local specialities are similarly protected to a greater or lesser degree, including white beans, cherries and oysters.

Regional Cuisine

There is a strong movement amongst restaurateurs to reclaim and promote the triumphs of their regional cuisine and the use of their local ingredients. Look out for the description *cuisine du terroir,* which is likely to be a sign of quality cooking.

The most exquisite restaurants and the finest ingredients cost money, but you don't have to fork out a fortune to eat well. Rural, small-town France is a picnicker's paradise. Get yourself a classic Opinel folding knife, a baguette from the *boulangerie*, a hunk of local cheese, a few slices of cured ham or a *saucisson*, a portion of paté, a scoop of marinated olives and a bottle of wine, and you can sit in the shade or sprawl by a river or canal bank and savour such delicacies at your leisure.

A *boulangerie* (bakery) in Le Marais; bread is usually bought fresh every day (above); eating al fresco; dining out and talking about food are part of life in France (opposite)

Pioneers of
Modern Art

For nearly 80 years, France was a crucible of artistic experimentation and the birthplace of every major artistic movement from the mid-19th to the mid-20th centuries.

The inception of modern art is often dated to 1863 when Edouard Manet first exhibited his controversial *Le déjeuner sur l'herbe* (*Lunch on the Grass*). This painting of two men and a naked woman picnicking shocked viewers at the time with what seemed to be its shameless voyeurism and assertion that an artist could choose to tackle any subject in any style.

   Claude Monet took a further step away from the rule book in 1872 when he set up his easel on the waterfront of Le Havre and recorded a blurry harbour view in swift brush strokes. He called his canvas *Impression, soleil levant (Impression, Sunrise)*, which led a sneering art critic to dismiss it as

mere "impressionism" – a name that was to become a mark of credibility for an entire artistic movement.

Monet's successors were similarly inspired to paint the world as it appeared to the artist's subjective eye not as staid academicians thought it should look. Edgar Degas and Henri Toulouse-Lautrec were both adept at catching the mood and moment of *belle-époque* Paris, including its low life.

Light and Colour

The intense outdoor light of the south, meanwhile, inspired the landscapes and portraits of Paul Cézanne, whose work initiated the artistic revolutions of the 20th century. Two other painters who found their muse in the sunshine and vivid colours of Provence were the primitivist Paul Gaugin and his unbalanced friend Vincent Van Gogh, who famously cut off his ear lobe after one of their violent arguments and later committed suicide.

Henri Matisse, André Derain and their associates, working in the first years of the 20th century, were dubbed the "*fauves*" ("wild beasts") for their expressiveness and use of colour. One of their number, Georges Braque, went on to collaborate with the expatriate Spaniard Pablo Picasso in the creation of Cubism, a way of disconcertingly dismantling reality before the viewer's eyes.

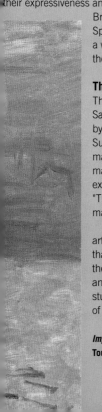

The Home of Modern Art

Three other influential foreign artists, René Magritte, Salvador Dalí and Joan Miró, were drawn to France by the next great wave of unbounded creativity, Surrealism, launched in Paris in the 1920s. Dalí, master of the one liner, could have been speaking for many artists of his own time, or for many during the explosion of modern art to come, when he declared: "There is only one difference between me and a madman: I am not mad."

France remained the unrivalled home of modern art up until 1939 but in the ruins and disillusionment that followed World War II, the initiative shifted across the Atlantic. Nevertheless, the country's museums and galleries, particularly in Paris and Provence, are stuffed with trailblazing works of art charting a fever of creativity unlikely to be repeated.

Impression, soleil levant by Claude Monet (left);
Toulouse-Lautrec's *L'anglais au Moulin Rouge* (above)

C'EST CHIC

Behind the Scenes on the Paris Catwalk

No matter what each year's fashion fad is, whether frivolous or enduring, it always contains one vital ingredient – the distinctive *je ne sais quoi* of French chic.

In the inimitable words of Coco Chanel, "fashions pass away; style lives on". It is always the household names – the Diors, the Yves Saint Laurents and the Jean-Paul Gaultiers of the fashion world, with their lavish haute-couture creations – who receive the praise. Yet their success depends, too, on *les petits mains* – the devoted teams of seamstresses, button- and bead-makers, lace-makers, embroiderers and countless other rarely acknowledged artisans who create the vital accessories. Their names are known only to a privileged few. François Lesage is one such name that is more widely known.

> "Haute couture caters for a clientele of a mere 2,000 or so women"

His Paris workshop of pearls and beads in rue St-Honoré was founded by his father in 1924, and he claims, "I was born on a pile of pearls". The painstakingly detailed work of his embroidery school graces the designs of Dior, Balmain, Lacroix and Gaultier.

Feathers, Flowers, Hats and Shoes

Another great name is André Lemarié, whose firm in Faubourg St-Denis specializes in feathers and silk flowers for the likes of Chanel, Mugler, Nina Ricci, Valentino and Dior. It was founded in the days of Charles Frederick Worth and has played a major role in haute couture ever since.

THE INVENTOR OF HAUTE COUTURE

Ironically, it was an Englishman, Charles Frederick Worth, who founded French haute couture. Having moved to Paris from London in 1845, aged 20, he worked in a draper's shop until he could afford a shop of his own, 13 years later, at 7 rue de la Paix. He specialized in well-cut clothes, and not only radically changed the female silhouette but also introduced the rhythm of the seasons to fashion by preparing his collections in advance. Another of his innovations was the use of live models for fashion shows.

Gérard Lognon's family business, which specializes in pleating, operates in an apartment in rue Danielle-Casanova; Patrice Wolfer at the renowned Michel in rue Ste-Anne, an ancient street of milliners, is the principal supplier of haute couture hats; while Raymond Massaro, at 2 rue de la Paix, is the most celebrated shoemaker in Paris, and creator of the famous Chanel-style shoe.

Extraordinary Fashion

Perhaps the most extraordinary aspect of haute couture is that it caters for a clientele of a mere 2,000 or so women. In fact, haute couture constitutes only six per cent of a fashion house's turnover. An average outfit requires at least 100 hours' work with three or four fittings and costs around €8,000 while an evening dress can cost four times this amount.

These extravagant and prestigious creations, the result of months of work, are presented, together with the less exclusive ranges, at the fashion shows staged at the Carrousel du Louvre every January and July, before 2,000 journalists and celebrities and 800 buyers. The atmosphere is electric, and tickets are like gold dust. Some of the seats are reserved for *les petites mains* – who can watch their handiwork come alive as the world's top models step out on to the catwalk to rapturous applause.

French embroider François Lesage examines a piece of fine embroidery (far left); the famous Chanel store in Paris (left); Raymond Massaro, shoemaker (below)

Hooked on CARTOONS

Tintin and Asterix may still be the leading international ambassadors of the *bande dessinée* – the comic book or graphic novel – but there is a lot more to this genre of art, which is taken extremely seriously in France.

Dip into any bookshop anywhere in France and it's hard not to notice the amount of shelf space given over to *bande dessinées,* or BDs for short.

They are the product of a feverish Franco-Belgian publishing industry that may be partly inspired by American comic book art but which has been steadfastly going its own way since the 1960s, giving an outlet to authors and artists who are feted at home but unheard of abroad.

Popular Culture

While some BDs are for children and others are meant to be humorous, most are intended as serious adult reading. They deal with a range of themes, including history, war, sci-fi and fantasy, but perhaps the most interesting of them are those that tell everyday stories depicting familiar French towns and landscapes in lavish colour in a hyper-realistic style.

Browsing or reading is one thing, but if you want to see the life behind *bande dessinées* you'll need to visit the Festival international de la bande dessinée d'Angoulême (www.bdangouleme.com), which has acted as a rallying point for artists, writers, readers and publishers since 1974. This festival is at once a celebration of past achievements – attracting the VIPs of the *band dessinée* world – and an opportunity to allow new talents to emerge.

Jean Giraud, known as "Moebius", speaks at a symposium on France's *bande dessinées;* the cobbled winding streets of the picturesque town of St Émilion (page 27)

Finding Your Feet

First Two Hours

France has international gateways all around its national borders, which are shared with Belgium, Luxembourg, Germany, Switzerland, Italy, Spain and Andorra. In addition, there is ready access through the northern coastal ports, such as Calais, via rail routes including the Eurotunnel and Eurostar links with the UK, and to numerous airports.

Arriving in Paris
By Air
- Most international flights arrive into **Roissy–Charles de Gaulle Airport** (tel: 3950, in France; www.adp.fr), 23km (14 miles) from the centre of Paris. There are three terminals at the airport, with information desks, a variety of shops, several restaurants, banks, bureaux de change and car-rental firms.
- **Taxis** to the city centre take 30 minutes to 1 hour, and cost around €50.
- **Trains** into the city centre (Gare du Nord, Châtelet or St-Michel), on RER line B, are the cheapest option at round €8.50. They operate between 5:30am and 12:15am and take 35 minutes.
- Air France **shuttle buses** run from T1 and T2 to Montparnasse, Gare de Lyon and the Arc de Triomphe (€16.50, 45 minutes to 1 hour). A Roissybus goes from all terminals to Opéra, between 6am and 11pm (€9.10, 50 minutes).
- **Orly Airport** (tel: 3950, in France; www adp.fr) is 14km (8.5 miles) south of the centre, and deals with domestic and some international flights. It has two terminals, with the usual facilities. A **taxi** into Paris will cost around €35 and take 15 to 30 minutes. The Orlyval **train** connects to RER line B at Antony; the fare to the centre is €9.60 and the journey time 35 minutes. The Orlybus links to the **Métro** at Denfert-Rochereau (€6.30, 30 minutes), while the Air France **shuttle bus** takes you to Les Invalides and Montparnasse (€11.50, 30 minutes).
- **Beauvais Tillé Airport** (tel: 0892 682 066; www.aeroportbeauvais.com) is 56km (35 miles) north of Paris, and used by low-cost airlines. The distance means a **taxi** into Paris will cost around €140, and the journey takes 1 hour 20 minutes. There is **no train** link into the centre, but there is a **bus** to Porte Maillot (€14, 1 hour 15 minutes).

By Train
- **Eurostar** direct trains depart from London (in UK tel: 08705 186 186; www.eurostar.com) arrive in Paris's Gare du Nord station. A **taxi** from the train station into the centre costs around €15. The station is also on the Métro lines 4 (purple) and 5 (orange), and on the RER railway lines D (green) and B (blue).

- **Paris City Centre Tourist Office** ✉ 25–27 rue des Pyramides, 75001 ☎ 08 92 68 30 00 (€0.34 per minute); www.parisinfo.com 🕐 Jun–Oct daily 9–7; Nov–May Mon–Sat 10–7, Sun 11–7 🚇 Métro: Pyramides

Arriving in Marseille
- **Marseille-Provence Airport**, also known as Marseille-Marignan (tel: 04 42 14 14 14; www.marseille.aeroport.fr), lies 30km (18.5 miles) northwest of the city, with the usual facilities.

■ A **taxi** into Marseille will cost around €40 and takes 30 minutes. There's **no rail** link, but **buses** run every 15 minutes to the Gare St-Charles railway station in the city (€8.50, 30 minutes).

■ **Marseille Tourist Office** ✉ 4 La Canebière, Marseille
☎ 04 91 13 89 00; www.marseille-tourisme.com ◷ Mon–Sat 9–7, Sun 10–5 (longer hours in peak season)

Arriving in Toulouse

■ **Toulouse-Blagnac Airport** (tel: 08 25 38 00 00; www.toulouse.aeroport.fr) lies 8km (5 miles) northwest of Toulouse, with all main facilities.
■ A **taxi** into the city costs around €23, and the journey takes 20 minutes. There is **no rail** link, but **buses** into the city run regularly every 20 minutes (€4, 20 minutes).

■ **Toulouse Tourist Office** ✉ Donjon du Capitole, 31080 ☎ 05 61 11 02 22; www.toulouse-tourisme.com ◷ Jun–Sep Mon–Sat 9–7, Sun 10–1, 2–6:15; Oct–May Mon–Fri 9–6, Sat 9–12:30, 2–6, Sun 10–12:30, 2–5

Arriving in Strasbourg

■ **Strasbourg Airport** (tel: 03 88 64 67 67; www.strasbourg.aeroport.fr) is 12km (7.5 miles) southwest of the city, with all main facilities.
■ A **taxi** into the city costs around €25 and takes 15 minutes. The airport is a five-minute walk from the Gare Entzheim, from where you can catch a **train** into the city centre (5am–9pm, 15 minutes). The **TRAM+TER** service allows passengers to travel on public transport, including trams and buses, between the airport and the city centre. Once stamped, the ticket is valid for 90 minutes (€3.60).

■ **Strasbourg Tourist Office** ✉ 17 place de la Cathédrale, 67082
☎ 03 88 52 28 28; www.ot-strasbourg.fr ◷ Mon–Sat 9–7, Sun 9–6

Arriving in Lyon

■ **Lyon St-Exupéry Airport** (tel: 08 26 80 08 26 in France, 33 426 007 007 outside France; www.lyon.aeroport.fr) lies 28km (17 miles) east of Lyon, with all main facilities.
■ A **taxi** into the city centre will cost around €40, and the journey takes 30 minutes. There is **no rail** link, but **buses** leave every 20 minutes for the centre (€8.90, 40–50 minutes).

■ **Lyon Tourist Office** ✉ place Bellecour, 69002
☎ 04 72 77 69 69 ◷ Daily 9–6

Arriving in Calais

■ **Ferries and catamarans** from Dover arrive at Calais. The main *autoroutes* from here are the A16/E40 north towards Dunkerque, then the A26/A1/ E15 towards Paris; and the A16/E40 south down the coast.
■ The **Shuttle** train from Folkestone, travelling via the Eurotunnel (from UK tel: 08443 35 35 35; www.eurotunnel.com), delivers cars and their passengers to Calais/Coquelles. Main routes are as above.

■ **Calais Tourist Office** ✉ 12 boulevard Clemenceau, 62100
☎ 03 21 96 62 40; www.ot-calais.fr ◷ Apr–mid-Jun daily 10–7; mid-Jun–mid-Sep 9–7; mid-Jun–Mar Mon–Sat 10–6

Getting Around

France is a big country, but an excellent network of fast trains and *autoroutes* (motorways/expressways) means that you can usually travel between regions quickly and easily.

Domestic Air Travel

■ France's national airline is **Air France** (in UK tel: 0870 142 4343; www.airfrance.co.uk; in US tel: 1 800 237 2747; www.airfrance.com) operates flights across a wide network of towns, linking 16 to Paris Roissy–Charles de Gaulle and 14 to Paris Orly. The longest flight takes around 1 hour. For information on regional airports, see www.aeroport.fr.

Trains

■ Train services within France are run by the state railway company, the Société Nationale des Chemins de Fer (**SNCF**, tel: 3635; www.voyage-sncf com), and are generally fast, comfortable and efficient.

■ The **TGV** (*Train à Grande Vitesse*) high-speed train links major towns and cities at speeds of up to 300kph/186mph. A journey from Paris to Bordeaux or Marseille takes around 3 hours. **CORAIL** trains provide regular long-distance services (*Grandes Lignes*), and the **TER** (*Transport Express Régional*) provide the local service (*Lignes Régionales*).

■ There are many **overnight sleeper trains** between major cities, offering reclining seats (in second class only), *couchette* berths (four or six to a compartment) or a sleeper car (two or three to a compartment). *Auto-Trains* can also take your car at the same time – the most useful services link Calais with Brive, Toulouse, Narbonne, Avignon and Nice.

■ **Buy tickets** at the railway stations, at SNCF offices or through some travel agents. **Ticket machines** can also be used to collect tickets ordered in advance on the Internet or by telephone or Minitel. It is essential to **reserve tickets for TGV trains** in advance, and **book ahead** for any rail travel in the peak season (June to mid-September) to be sure of your place. Most trains have first and second class options, and fares are split into normal (blue) and peak (red) times. **You must stamp your ticket** in the orange machine on the platform before boarding the train at the start of your journey, to validate it.

■ Under-26s can get a 25 per cent **discount on travel** (*Carte 12–25*), and discounts are also available for older people (*Carte Senior*) and by booking well ahead. A variety of discount rail passes is available for travel within France, or within the whole of Europe, and should be bought before arrival in France from travel agents or Rail Europe (in the UK www.raileurope.co.uk; in the US www.raileurope.com).

■ The **SNCF luggage service** will pick up your luggage from your hotel and deliver it to your final destination for you. Request this service when you make your reservation at a SNCF office or tel: 3635 and request *service pratique* and then *service bagage*. You will also need to provide the name and address of your accommodation and details of your destination.

Buses

■ **Long-distance bus routes** within France are generally slightly less expensive than the trains, but much slower. You'll usually find the **bus station** (*gare routière*) close to the railway station (*gare SNCF*). **Eurolines** (tel: 08 92 89 90 91; www.eurolines.fr) operates services between major towns and cities within France and to other destinations within Europe. **SNCF** (tel: 3635) also runs services as extensions to rail links.

Taxis

- **Taxis** are a convenient way to get around, but generally an expensive option. You'll pay a pick-up charge and a charge per kilometre, plus extra for items of luggage and travel in the evening or on Sundays. All taxis use a **meter** (*compteur*), and **taxi stands** in towns and cities are marked with a square blue sign.
- Some taxis accept bank cards, but it is best to **have cash available**. It is usual to give a **tip** of around 10 per cent.

Driving

- An excellent system of **motorways/expressways** (*autoroutes*, marked A on maps and road signs) fans out from Paris, making it straightforward to drive between destinations. **Tolls are charged** on most *autoroutes*, so have some cash, as foreign credit cards are not always accepted. Key routes include the A1 north, the A13 to Normandy and the northwest, the A4 east, the A6 to the Alps and the Riviera, and the A10 west and southwest.
- There's a comprehensive network of other roads across the country, including main highways (*route nationale*, marked N), lesser highways (*route départementale*, marked D), and minor country roads. Surfaces are generally good at all levels.
- **Driving in Paris** is a nightmare so avoid it if possible, especially during the rush hour (7–9:30am and 4:30–7:30pm, weekdays). Bear in mind that a car can be a positive hazard in some other big cities, with congested traffic, confusing one-way systems and expensive parking.
- If **bringing your own car** to France, you must always carry the following documentation in addition to your passport: a full, valid national driver's licence, a certificate of motor insurance and the vehicle's registration document (plus a letter of authorization from the owner if it is not registered in your name). Third-party motor insurance is the **minimum requirement**, but fully comprehensive cover is strongly advised. Check that your **insurance** covers you against damage in transit, and that you have adequate **breakdown cover** (for information visit the AA at www.theAA.com, or your own national breakdown organization). You must also display an **international sticker** or distinguishing sign plate on the rear of the car by the registration plate. **Headlights** of right-hand-drive cars must be adjusted for driving on the right. Carry a hazard warning triangle and fluorescent waistcoat/jacket in case of a breakdown.

Driving Know-How

- Drive on the **right-hand side** of the road (*serrez à droite*).
- Drivers must be aged **18 years or over**, and you'll need to be aged **20 or over to hire** a car.
- **Speed limits** are 50kph (31mph) on urban roads, 90kph (56mph) outside built-up areas (80kph/49mph in rain), 110kph (68mph) on dual carriageways/divided highways and non-toll motorways (100kph/62mph in the rain), and 130kph (80mph) on toll motorways (110kph/68mph in the rain). Visiting drivers who have held a licence for less than two years must follow the wet-weather limits **at all times**, even when it's dry. Drivers who exceed the speed limit by more than 30kph (18mph) will have to appear in court and will be fined.
- **Yield** to vehicles coming from the right (*priorité à droite*). At roundabouts/traffic circles with signs saying *Cédez le passage or Vous n'avez pas la priorité*, traffic already on the roundabout has priority. On roundabouts without signs, traffic entering has priority.
- **Do not overtake** where there is a solid single line in the centre of the road.
- The **blood alcohol limit** is 0.5 per cent (US blood alcohol content 0.05). If you drink, don't drive.

- **Fuel** (l) comes as unleaded (95 and 98 octane), lead replacement petrol (LRP or *supercarburant*), diesel (*gasoil* or *gazole*) and LPG. Many filling stations **close on Sundays** and at 6pm during the week.
- Before you take to the road, familiarize yourself with the **French highway code** on www.legifrance.gouv.fr. For information on **road signs**, visit www.permis-enligne.com.

Renting a Car

- Cars can be rented by **drivers over 20** who have held a full driver's licence for a year, but some companies require a minimum age of 21 or 25. The average maximum age limit is 70.
- Most major **car rental firms** such as Europcar, Avis and Hertz have outlets at airports, main railway stations and in large towns and cities throughout France. Most car rental firms will let you return your car to other cities and even countries, but agree this ahead, because there may be a surcharge for this service.
- Most rental cars in France are manual, so **if you want an automatic**, make sure you specify this and reserve ahead.

Urban Transport

- You can walk around the main sights in most French cities; historic centres are usually small, many are pedestrianized, and walking gives a great "feel" for any new place. Several cities have métro systems or trams, including Paris, Lyon, Marseille, Toulouse and Lille, and all towns have efficient bus services.

In Paris

- The **Métro and buses** use the same tickets and travel cards, which are also valid for RER trains within the city centre. **Buy them** at Métro stations, on buses (one-way tickets only) and some news-stands. Children under four travel free, and age four to nine, half price. The city is divided into **fare zones**, and most of the major sights are in Zone 1.
- The **Métro** underground train runs from Sun–Fri 5:30am–1:15am, Sat 5:30am–2:15am, and is a fast, efficient way of getting around. Lines are **colour-coded** and numbered on maps (free), and stations are identified by a large M. Maps show the suburban RER train lines too, which are lettered and usually run off the map; www.ratp.fr.
- **Buses** are a great way to see the city as you go. Most run from 7am to 8:30pm, with some late services until 12:30am. Remember to **stamp your ticket** in the machine next to the driver, to validate it.
- **RER** (*Réseau Express Régional*) trains provide a local service around the Paris suburbs, with five main lines named A to E. Trains run from around 6am to 12:30am.
- The **Batobus** is a river shuttle boat, with regular services between February and November 10–7, and to 9:30 in midsummer. Stops include the Tour Eiffel, Musée d'Orsay, Notre-Dame and the Louvre.
- **Urban transport** website www.ratp.fr.

Admission Charges
The cost of admission for museums and places of interest mentioned in the text is indicated by the following price categories.
Inexpensive under €6   **Moderate** €6–€10   **Expensive** over €10

Accommodation

There's a wide variety of accommodation available to visitors throughout France, and you should find something to suit your budget and your taste. The international hotel chains such as Best Western, Hilton and Holiday Inn are well represented in France, but there are plenty of luxury hotels if you want to stay in style. For a more authentic experience of France, you may like to try a campsite, a rented *gîte* or perhaps a family-run *auberge*.

Types of Accommodation

Hotels

■ Hotels in France are regularly inspected and are **classified into six categories**, from no stars (at the bottom) to four stars and four-star luxury hotels. **Charges** are usually **per room** rather than per person, and breakfast is generally charged separately. If you're travelling with a family on a budget, note that for a little extra, many hotels will put another bed in your room.

■ Family-run inns and small hotels, the **Logis de France,** usually offer some of the best accommodation if you're exploring on a budget. All have a basic standard of comfort, and some are in particularly charming locations. Most have their own restaurant, serving good local food. If you are on a hiking or cycling holiday **luggage can be transported** between Logis for you. As well as star gradings, Logis also have their own chimney symbol of classification to help visitors find the perfect accommodation. Find them listed on the website www.logis-de-france.fr or get a complete list from the tourist office.

■ There are some great **luxury hotels** to choose from in France, if you want to treat yourself to a very special experience. The Paris Ritz is one of the best-known, and the traditional *belle-époque* hotels of the Riviera have a cachet that is hard to beat. For something with a more modern twist, take a look at some of the French designer hotels such as the Hi-Hotel in Nice, where rock pools and plasma screens are part of the fun. Boutique hotels – small but chic – are becoming more popular. And if you fancy staying in a luxurious château setting, contact Relais & Châteaux (tel: 08 25 32 32 32; www.relaischateaux.com).

Bed-and-Breakfast

■ **Chambres d'hôtes** offers a taste of life in a real French household, whether it is on a farm or in a château. Ask at the tourist office for local availability. Many of the best are affiliated to the Gîtes de France organisation, which grades them with one to four ears of corn (*épis*) according to the level of comfort and facilities.

■ For the **top end** of the scale – a room in a privately owned Loire château – contact Bienvenue au Château (Centre d'Affaires Les Allizés, La Rigourdière, 35510 Cesson Sevigne; www.bienvenueauchateau.com).

Self Catering (*Gîtes*)

■ Self-contained cottages, villas and apartments (*gîtes*) are widely available in towns, villages and country areas throughout France, offer flexible accommodation and are particularly good value for families. They are usually **rented by the week or fortnight**, and facilities may range from simple and basic (bring your own linen) to more elaborate, with swimming pools and other facilities included in the price.

Finding Your Feet

■ Many *gîtes* are administered through the **Gîtes de France** organization, which also inspects and grades them according to comfort and facilities (www.gites-de-france.fr). Local tourist offices also generally hold this information for their area.

Youth Hostels

■ There are around 200 youth hostels (*auberges de jeunesse*) across France, which are open to members from other countries if they have a membership card with photo. For a complete list and details, contact the **Fédération Unie des Auberges de Jeunesse**, 27 rue Pajol, 75018 Paris (tel: 01 44 89 87 27; www.fuaj.org).

Camping

■ This is hugely popular in France, with a roll-call exceeding **9,000 fully equipped campsites**, plus around 2,300 farm campsites. Sites are **inspected and graded** with a star system like that of the hotels, and range from basic (electricity, showers, lavatories) to luxurious, with swimming pools and other family sports activities, restaurants and bars, and kids clubs. You don't even have to take your own tent – many have **pre-pitched tents and mobile homes** on site, complete with cooking equipment, fridge and beds.

■ Expect to **book well ahead**, especially in high season, which runs from May to September in the north, and April to October in the south. For more information, contact the **National Federation of Campsites** (tel: 01 42 72 84 08; www.campingfrance.com).

■ Note that camping or overnight parking of caravans and motorhomes is **not permitted** on the beach or at the roadside. If you get caught out and need to find a campsite, the local tourist office should be able to advise you, and, in case of an emergency, police stations can also let you have a list of local campsite addresses. Many communes have *aires de service* offering free or low-cost overnight camping for motorhomes.

Finding a Room

■ If you haven't booked ahead, visit the **local tourist office**, as they will have a list of accommodation with prices. In towns or villages without a tourist office, head for the main square or centre of town, where you're likely to find the greatest concentration of hotels.

■ When you **check in**, you'll need to complete a registration form and show your passport. Ask to see the room first, especially in cheaper accommodation.

■ **Check-out times** are usually around 10 or 11am.

Seasonal Rates

■ Accommodation prices are likely to **vary throughout the year**, according to the season. In the resort areas of southern France, higher prices may be charged between April and October, while in northern France the summer season is generally shorter – July to September. Paris hotels often charge lower rates during July and August, when the sticky heat of the city coincides with the mass-exodus of Parisians on annual holiday.

Accommodation Prices
Expect to pay per night for a double room.

€ under €120	€€ €120–€220	€€€ over €220

Food and Drink

Few nations enjoy their food with quite the pride and relish of the French. Eating out is one of the "must do" experiences on any French holiday, and there's no better way to discover the wealth of local dishes and culinary twists than at a local bistro. You'll discover that by sampling the regional specialities you'll enjoy an insight into the local area too. Fine dining is also fun to try, and you'll also find top-class restaurants in many towns and cities, not just the capital.

Regional Menus

■ Around **Brittany, Normandy and the Loire**, *crêpes and galettes* (buckwheat pancakes), both sweet and savoury, are the fast-food of choice, freshly prepared with fillings such as chocolate or ham and cheese. *Moules marinières* (mussels in white wine) are delicious, and other seafood treats include *coquilles St-Jacques* (hot scallops in a creamy sauce topped with melted cheese or breadcrumbs, served in the shell), *langouste* (crayfish), *crevettes* (prawns) and *huîtres* (oysters). Look out, too, for **châteaubriand** (thick, tenderloin steak cooked with a white wine, herb and shallot sauce) and pork cooked in a *sauce normande* (cider and cream). Desserts include the upside-down apple pie, *tarte tatin*.

■ In the **north and Alsace Lorraine**, the influences are more Germanic, with hearty dishes such as *choucroute garnie* (pickled cabbage cooked in wine with pork, sausage and smoked ham, served with boiled potatoes), and meaty stews such as *bäeckeoffe* (cooked in wine) and *carbonnade flamande* (in beer and spices). It's also the home of *quiche Lorraine* (egg custard tart with bacon, onion and herbs) and the *salade de cervelas* (cold sausage in vinaigrette sauce).

■ Around **Burgundy and the northern Rhône** area, sample different meats cooked in red wine, from *boeuf bourguignon* (beef with onions and mushrooms) to *coq au vin* (chicken with mushrooms and onions). *Escargots à la bourguignon* are snails served in garlic and parsley butter, and local sausages include *boudin* (blood pudding/sausage).

■ Throughout **Jura and the Alps**, try a fondue, either *au fromage* (bread cubes are dipped into melted cheese mixed with wine) or *bourguignonne* (meat cubes are cooked in oil then dipped into various sauces). *Gratin dauphinois* (potatoes, sliced and baked with cream and nutmeg) and *gratin savoyard* (sliced potatoes with cheese, cooked in stock) are also favourites of this region.

■ In the **Pyrénées and the southwest** you'll taste dishes cooked *à la landaise* (in goose fat with garlic), *à la bordelaise* (with red wine sauce and mixed vegetables), *à la périgourdine* (with a truffle or *foie gras* sauce or stuffing) and *à la basquaise* (with Bayonne ham, **cèpe** mushrooms and potatoes). Duck is a particular favourite, with *magret de canard* (boned duck breast, grilled or fried), *confit de canard* (salted duck pieces cooked and preserved in their own fat) and of course, *foie gras* (the enlarged liver of maize-fed ducks or geese, served in slices hot or cold).

■ The flavours in the **southeast and around the shores of the Mediterranean** are those of the sunny climes, from the classic *salade niçoise* (any combination of tomatoes, green beans, anchovies, olives, peppers and boiled egg) to *ratatouille* (a stew of tomatoes, onions, courgettes/zucchini, aubergines/eggplant and garlic in olive oil). Stewed meats include *cassoulet* (a thick, rich stew of haricot beans and garlic with goose and pork sausage), and the ultimate fish stew – *bouillabaisse*.

Where to Eat

- You'll find a decent **restaurant** or several in every town, where the glasses are polished and the linen and waiters starched, and where the locals will go for a special occasion, a formal encounter or a top treat. Expect to **reserve your table in advance, dress smartly, and allow plenty of time** for the full gastronomic experience. Michelin stars and Gault et Millau *toques* help to identify the top eating places. If the dinner price is beyond your budget, look out for better-value set menus at lunchtime. The *menu dégustation* offers a selection of the restaurant's signature dishes with accompanying wines at a fixed price. Logis de France hotels are also associated with good local restaurants.
- **Brasseries** are **informal** establishments, generally open long hours, where you can sample local dishes alongside staples such as *steak-frites* (steak with chips/fries) and *choucroute* (sauerkraut).
- **Bistros** tend to be **small, informal, family-run** restaurants serving traditional and local dishes, with a modest wine list.
- Most French people eat their main meal at midday, so lunchtime menus often offer the **best value**, when a *menu du jour* (daily menu) of two or three courses with wine is likely to cost much less than an evening meal. *Prix-fixe* meals of three or four courses also generally offer good value.
- Restaurants mostly keep to **regular opening hours**: noon–2:30 and 7–10, although some may stay open longer during a holiday period. They generally **close** at lunchtime on Saturday and Monday, and Sunday evening. Some Paris restaurants may close completely in July and August, and those along the south coast may shut between November and Easter.
- **Service** is usually **included in the bill** (*l'addition*) – look for the words *service compris*, or *s.c.* If the service is exceptional, you may like to leave your loose change or a tip of around five per cent.

Where and What to Drink

- Relaxing in a **café** and watching the world go by is one of the pleasures of France. As a rule, you'll pay more for your drink if you're sitting outside on the terrace. Cafés and bars serve coffee, soft drinks, alcohol, snacks and often traditional and herbal teas.
- Cafés and bars sometimes open as early as 7am to serve breakfast, and may close any time between 9pm and the early hours of the next morning. Licensing hours when alcohol may be sold vary according to the individual establishment.
- A *citron pressé* (freshly squeezed lemon), to which you add your own sugar, can be particularly refreshing on a hot day. Bottled water (*eau*) comes as *gazeuse* (carbonated) or *non-gazeuse* (still). Beer (*bière*) is usually the light European-style lager, and cider (*cidre*) is found particularly around the apple-growing areas of Normandy. White and red wine (*vin blanc, vin rouge*) is widely available, and it is worth seeking out the local wines (► 11–13). If in doubt, try the house wine (*vin ordinaire* **or** *vin de table*).
- There is also a wide variety of regional liqueurs and spirits to try, including Benedictine, Calvados, Cognac, Armagnac and Chartreuse.
- The **legal age** for buying alcohol is 18.

Restaurant Prices
Expect to pay per person for a meal, excluding drinks.
€ under €30   €€ €30–€60   €€€ over €60

Shopping

Shopping in France can be a real pleasure, whether it's hitting the boutiques for haute couture, choosing the chocolatiest cake in the *pâtisserie*, conversing with the small-scale cheese producers in the *marché* (market), or strolling through the varied delights of a *hypermarché* (hypermarket). Prices may not be cheap, but quality is usually high.

Opening Hours

- **Opening times** vary according to the type of shop, the season and the location, and there are no hard and fast rules. For example, many **smaller shops** often **close at lunchtime** between noon and 2:30, but this may extend to 4pm in the south during summer, with later opening into the evening to compensate.
- **Department stores** and larger shops are usually open from Monday to Saturday, 9 to 6:30.
- **Food shops** usually open from Tuesday to Saturday, between 8 or 9 and 6:30 or 7:30, and may close for lunch. Some may open on Monday afternoons, and they may open on Sunday mornings. *Boulangeries* (bakers) usually open on Sunday morning.
- **Supermarkets and hypermarkets** generally open from 9 to 9 or, occasionally, 10 in the evening, Monday to Saturday; the main names include Carrefour, Auchan, Champion and E. Leclerc.
- Daily and weekly **markets** are a feature of cities and towns, and usually operate from around 8 to noon. Often the people who produced or grew the food are the people selling it, too, and can tell you about their range of cheeses or whatever.

Payment

- Shops in towns and major tourist areas usually accept payment by **credit or debit card**. For markets and smaller outlets, carry euros **in cash**.
- Visitors from outside the European Union can **reclaim tax** on certain purchases if they spend more than €175 in the same shop on the same day. You'll need a *détaxe* form from the shopkeeper, which must be shown with the receipts and stamped at customs, then returned to the shop by post for a refund.

What to Buy

- France is known world-wide for its stylish **fashion**, which is by no means limited to the capital. Check out the chic clothes stores in any of the bigger cities, and in resorts such as Cannes, Biarritz and Chamonix.
- France is also the heart of a fabulous **perfume** industry, with names such as Dior and Chanel. You'll find fragrances and soaps in shops all across the country; Grasse, in Provence, is where much of it originates.
- It is difficult to come away from France without a shopping bag or two of your favourite **food**, whether it's *galettes* (buttery biscuits) from Brittany, *saucisson* (sausages) from the northeast, *pâté* and sugared walnuts from the Dordogne, or *fromage* (cheese) from just about anywhere.
- There are various options for buying **wine**. Hypermarkets usually stock a wide range of excellent French wines. Go for a tasting at a vineyard and you will probably want to buy at least one bottle – and, of course, more if you find something you really like. And in wine-growing districts, ask in the tourist offices about co-operatives, where you can sample the locally produced AOC (*Appellation d'Origine Contrôlée*) wines.

Entertainment

France's rich cultural heritage means that you're rarely far from a venue for music, theatre and cinema, whether that's a small, intimate club, a 15,000-seat Roman amphitheatre or something a little more conventional. Performances are likely to be in French, but some cinemas show movies in their original language; look for the symbol "VO" (*version originale*). From top sporting events to outdoor opera extravaganzas, tourist offices can usually tell you what's on and how to obtain tickets.

Music and Dance

■ Paris is naturally the centre of **high culture**, including the famous **Comédie Française** theatre group (www.comedie-francaise.fr) and the Opéra de Paris ballet company (www.operadeparis.fr). Several other cities have ballet companies, and contemporary dance finds a focus at Montpellier's **Centre Choréographique National** (www.mathildemonnier.fr).

■ France lacks a world-class national orchestra, but top-class recitals of **classical music** by smaller ensembles such as the **Orchestre de Paris** (www.orchestredeparis.com) are held across the country, often in historic settings such as châteaux and cathedrals.

■ More than 300 **music festivals** are held around the country every year. They include the famous **International Celtic Festival** of folk music in Lorient, Brittany, at the start of August (www.festival-interceltique.com).

■ **Jazz** has a great following in France, with annual festivals in Paris, Nice, Antibes, Vienne and Grenoble.

Nightlife

■ Inevitably, the quality and quantity of nightlife varies according to where you are. In **Paris** you'll be spoilt for choice, with cabaret revue shows, bars and clubs galore. Other big cities such as **Marseille, Lyon and Toulouse** also have a vibrant night scene. Particularly in rural districts, however, you may find that the pool table in the local café-bar is as exciting as it gets.

■ **Casinos** are part of the French entertainment scene: most resorts have them, and the most famous of them all is in **Monte Carlo** (➤ 164).

■ For some of the best **gay and lesbian nightlife**, head for the Marais district of Paris. Other lively spots are found along the Côte d'Azur and around St-Tropez – check out local listings magazines for details.

Sports and Outdoor Activities

■ France is a great **winter sports destination**, with resorts in the Alps, the Massif Central and the Pyrénées. Chamonix and Courcheval are the places to be seen, but there are plenty of more affordable options.

■ The sport of **cycling** is a national obsession, which reaches fever pitch around the time of the gruelling annual **Tour de France**, a race around the country held over three weeks in July. Renting bicycles for **leisure cycling** is also popular – they are available from more than 200 railway stations, at a cost of around €12 per day.

■ **Motor racing** fans will look forward to the **Le Mans** 24-hour rally (www.lemans.org), and the glamorous Formula One **grand prix** races at Monte Carlo (www.acm.mc) and Magny Cours (www.magnyf1.com).

■ **Walkers** can head for the hills or stride the plains on more than 30,000km (18,600 miles) of footpaths, marked on maps as *Grandes Randonnées* (long-distance) and *Petites Randonnées*.

Paris and the Île de France

Getting Your Bearings

The Arc de Triomphe and the place de la Concorde, at either end of the broad, straight avenue des Champs-Élysées, are the twin traffic hubs of this vibrant capital. Through its heart curves the River Seine.

The Left Bank, or Rive Gauche, is the southern sector and contains many of the best-known attractions, including the Musée d'Orsay and the Tour Eiffel. East of here, the Quartier Latin is a bohemian student district. The mid-river Île de la Cité was home to the earliest settlers, the *Parisii* tribe (hence the city's name), and here you'll find Notre-Dame. North of the Seine, the area around the Louvre has elegant squares and fashion emporia. Head northwest for the Jardin des Tuileries, the Arc de Triomphe and La Défense. East of this lies the Beaubourg district, with Les Halles shopping centre and the eccentric Centre Georges Pompidou. Overlooking all is Montmartre, which retains its village identity.

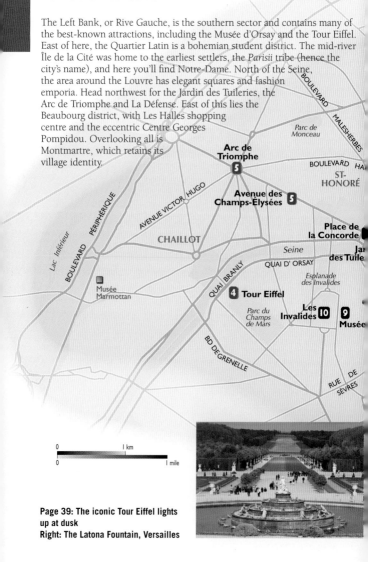

BOULEVARD MALESHERBES

Parc de Monceau

Arc de Triomphe 5

BOULEVARD HA
ST-HONORÉ

AVENUE VICTOR HUGO

BOULEVARD PÉRIPHÉRIQUE

Avenue des Champs-Élysées 5

CHAILLOT

Place de la Concorde

Seine

Jar des Tuile

QUAI D' ORSAY

QUAI BRANLY

Lac Intérieur

Esplanade des Invalides

Musée Marmottan

4 Tour Eiffel

Parc du Champs de Mars

Les Invalides 10 **9 Musée**

BD DEGRENELLE

RUE DE SÈVRES

0   1 km
0   1 mile

Page 39: The iconic Tour Eiffel lights up at dusk
Right: The Latona Fountain, Versailles

★ Don't Miss

At Your Leisure

MONTMARTRE

La Villette 12

HALLE

BOULEVARD FAYETTE

RUE LA

Canal St-Martin

BD DE SÉBASTOPOL

MAGENTA

Parc de Belleville

RÉPUBLIQUE

AV DE LA RÉPUBLIQUE

LES HALLES

RIVOLI

Centre Georges Pompidou 7

Musée Picasso 13

Cimetière du Père-Lachaise 15

BOULEVARD VOLTAIRE

6 Musée du Louvre

LE MARAIS

Sainte-Chapelle

Conciergerie

1 Île de la Cité

14 Place des Vosges

Notre-Dame

Île St-Louis

Germain Prés

STMICHEL

Musée National du Moyen Age

BASTILLE

Jardin du Luxembourg

RUE ST-JACQUES

2 Quartier Latin

Jardin des Plantes

QUAI D'AUSTERLITZ

BOULEVARD DIDEROT

BOULEVARD ARAGO

Further Afield

In Three Days

If you're not quite sure where to begin your travels, this itinerary recommends a practical and enjoyable three days exploring Paris and Île de France, taking in some of the best places to see using the Getting your Bearings map on the previous page. For more information see the main entries.

Day 1

Morning
Take the métro to Cité to explore **❶ Île de la Cité** (➤ 44–46). Be first in line to climb the 387 steps of the tower of **Notre-Dame** cathedral (➤ 44–45) for fantastic views of Paris and the roof gargoyles. Relish the blacker side of Parisian history in a guided tour of the **Conciergerie** (➤ 45) before crossing the Pont de l'Archevêché for lunch at **La Rôtisserie du Beaujolais** (➤ 45).

Afternoon
Walk south through **❷ Quartier Latin** (➤ 47–49) heading for the **Musée National du Moyen Âge–Thermes de Cluny** (➤ 47) to see some of Paris's finest early treasures. Go for a stroll or chill out afterwards in the nearby **Jardin du Luxembourg**.

Evening
Stroll back towards the river through the bohemian district of **❽ St-Germain-des-Prés** (below; ➤ 60) and pick out a restaurant for dinner.

Day 2

Morning
Start the day at the **3 Musée d'Orsay** (left; ➤ 50–51), a magnificent art gallery on the south bank of the Seine. In summer, catch the **Batobus** (➤ 32) west to the **4 Tour Eiffel** (➤ 52–53), and take the lift to the top for outstanding views. Dine in the **café** on level 1 or the **restaurant** on level 2 (➤ 53).

Afternoon
Take a taxi across the river to the **5 Champs-Élysées** (➤ 54–55), making sure the driver includes a circuit of the **Arc de Triomphe** (➤ 54–55) before dropping you off on the famous avenue for some leisurely shopping or people watching at a café.

Evening
Book ahead for a glamorous night out at a **dinner and cabaret show** (➤ 72), maybe at the **Moulin Rouge** in **Montmartre** (➤ 184).

Day 3

Morning
Get to the **6 Musée du Louvre** (➤ 56–57) as it opens to beat the crowds, and check out the *Mona Lisa* (right). If there's time, catch the métro to the **7 Centre Georges Pompidou** (➤ 58–59), for the contrast of modern art.

Afternoon
Take a picnic and eat it on the train on the way to **20 Versailles** (➤ 66). Spend the afternoon exploring the gardens and admiring the gilded interior.

Evening
Head back into town and seek out one of the great views of **Paris by night** – from the **Tour Eiffel** (➤ 52–53), perhaps.

0 Île de la Cité

The history of this small, boat-shaped island in the Seine is the history of Paris. Here, in around 300BC, the Parisii tribe settled, and it was here two centuries later that the Romans built the town of Lutetia, meaning "settlement surrounded by water". This was to become the seat of the ancient kings of France, the centre of political power, and the home of the church and the law. There's lots to see, and you can easily spend a whole day here, enjoying attractive parks and the flower market (Marché aux Fleurs), which on Sundays becomes a bird market (Marché aux Oiseaux).

Notre-Dame-de-Paris

Despite the inevitable crowds of tourists, the grandeur of this landmark cathedral, with its impressive sculpture-encrusted facade, its distinctive flying buttresses and its soaring nave, never fails to inspire.

The sculpted facade of Notre-Dame-de-Paris

Notre-Dame is one of the world's most beautiful examples of early Gothic architecture. The **facade** seems perfectly proportioned, with its two towers narrower at the top than at the base, giving the illusion of great height. Look closer, however, and you will notice the north (left) tower is wider than the south tower and that each of the three main entrances is slightly different in shape. On a sunny day, the nave is bathed in multi-coloured light, filtered through the superb **stained-glass windows**.

In the early 12th century the Bishop of Paris decided to build an immense church here, on a site where the Romans had earlier built a temple to Jupiter. It took over 150 years to complete (1163–1345). Over the centuries, the cathedral has fulfilled many roles, serving as a place of worship, a community hall, and even the setting for lavish banquets and theatrical productions. At one point it was abandoned altogether but, thanks largely to Victor Hugo's Hunchback of Notre-Dame, it was finally restored under Napoleon III.

Sainte-Chapelle

Sainte-Chapelle is surely Paris's most beautiful church – a veritable Sistine Chapel of **shimmering stained glass**, and a remarkable fusion of art and religion. The chapel is split into two levels, and the most striking feature of the **upper chapel** is its transparency. It seems as though there are no walls – only glowing stained-glass windows and clusters of slender columns rising to the vaulted ceiling. The **gigantic rose window** is best seen at sunset.

The church was built in 1248 by Louis IX to house the Crown of Thorns and a fragment of the Holy Cross. He had paid the outrageous sum of 1.3 million francs (the chapel itself cost only 400,000 francs) for these relics. He wanted the edifice to have the light, lacy aspect of a reliquary, and the result, in just five years, was this bejewelled Gothic masterpiece.

The Conciergerie

The imposing buildings, stretching the entire width of the island at its western end, were once **a royal palace**, and house the city's law courts. The Conciergerie occupies part of the lower floor. Originally a residence, it served as a prison between 1391 and 1914. **Guided tours** make the most of its history and include the Salle de la Toilette, where prisoners were prepared for the guillotine. During the Revolution, 2,780 people were guillotined in place de la Révolution (today's place de la Concorde), including Marie-Antoinette, who spent 76 days in a cell here before losing her head in 1793.

NOTRE-DAME: DID YOU KNOW...

- The **interior** is 130m (430ft) long, 48m (160ft) wide and 35m (115ft) high.
- **387 spiral steps** lead to the top of the 75m (245ft) high north tower.
- **12 million people visit** each year, of whom 6,000 attend services.
- The main bell, the "Emmanuel", rang out in 1944 to **celebrate the liberation** of France.

TAKING A BREAK

Cross the Pont de l'Archevêché to enjoy a traditional French meal at **La Rôtisserie du Beaujolais**, 19 quai de la Tournelle (tel: 01 43 54 17 47, closed Mon).

PLACE DU PARVIS NOTRE-DAME

Île de la Cité is the heart of the city and of France. Set into the pavement on the square outside the main portal of Notre-Dame, a bronze star marks the *point zéro des routes de France*, from which all distances are measured to and from Paris throughout France.

Detail of a stained-glass window in Sainte-Chapelle depicting biblical scenes

✚ 204 C2 🔘 Cité

Notre-Dame

✚ 209 D2 ✉ 6 place du Parvis Notre-Dame ☎ 01 42 34 56 10; www.monum.fr 🕐 Daily 8–6:45pm; sacristy: Mon–Sat 9:30–5:30 💶 Free; sacristy inexpensive; tower moderate 🔘 Cité 🚉 RER St-Michel–Notre Dame

Sainte-Chapelle

✚ 208 C3 ✉ 4 boulevard du Palais ☎ 01 53 40 60 80; www.monum.fr 🕐 Mar–Oct daily 9:30–6; Nov–Feb 9–5 (last entry 30 mins before closing). 🔘 Cité/St-Michel 🚉 Châtelet–Les-Halles, St-Michel–Notre-Dame 💶 Moderate (combined Ste-Chapelle/Conciergerie ticket is available)

The Conciergerie

✚ 208 C3 ✉ Palais de la Cité, 2 boulevard du Palais ☎ 01 53 40 60 80; www.monum.fr 🕐 Mar–Oct daily 9:30–6; Nov–Feb 9–5 💶 Moderate 🔘 Cité 🚉 Châtelet

ÎLE DE LA CITÉ: INSIDE INFO

Top tips Visit Notre-Dame early in the morning, when the cathedral is **at its brightest and least crowded.**

■ If you plan to climb the tower of Notre-Dame to admire the gargoyles and the views, **remember to wear sensible shoes** and be prepared to queue (Apr–Sep daily 10–6:30; Oct–Mar10–5.30).

■ For a wonderful and atmospheric tour of the cathedral, you can visit Notre-Dame **at night** during the summer (Jul–Aug Sun 10–11).

■ For a magical experience, attend one of the **regular candlelit chamber music concerts** at Sainte-Chapelle. Ask for details at the ticket office or tourist information office.

■ For security reasons, visits to the towers are cancelled in bad weather.

■ The **flower market** (Marché aux Fleurs) on place Louis-Lépine is a wonderful place to spend a couple of hours. On Sundays it becomes a bird market (Marché aux Oiseaux, daily 8–7).

One to miss Don't bother with the **lower chapel of Sainte-Chapelle.** It pales into insignificance beside the upper chapel.

2 Quartier Latin

Quartier Latin, the district surrounding the 750-year-old Sorbonne, has long been the vibrant, artistic, student heart of Paris. A warren of atmospheric streets, lined with cafés, boutiques and ethnic shops, are bordered by the Boulevard St-Michel, which spills down hill from the Panthéon to the left bank of the River Seine opposite Notre-Dame. Its most visited attraction is the Musée National du Moyen Âge.

Musée National du Moyen Âge – Thermes de Cluny contains many medieval treasures

Musée National du Moyen Âge–Thermes de Cluny

Even if you're not a fan of medieval art and history, this outstanding museum, with **exhibits spanning 15 centuries**, is a must, if only for the remarkable building, which in itself is the architectural embodiment of this period.

The collections are housed in two adjoining buildings. Around AD200, the guild of Paris boatmen built a complex of Roman baths here. The remains of the well-preserved *frigidarium* form a kind of basement gallery, exhibiting Roman items. In the 15th century, monks of the abbey of Cluny in Burgundy built a mansion here to house visiting abbots. With its **ornate turrets, gargoyles and cloistered courtyard**, it's the finest example of medieval civil architecture in Paris.

Its treasures reflect the richness and diversity of life in the Middle Ages, including furnishings, stained glass, jewellery, statuary, carvings, illuminated manuscripts, paintings and, most famous of all, the *Dame à la licorne* (*Lady and the Unicorn*) tapestries. This exquisite series of **six embroidered panels** portraying a lady flanked by a lion and a unicorn, set against a pink flower-strewn background, provides a reflection of the chivalrous world of courtly love.

Panthéon

This neo-classical 18th-century church was begun under the *ancien régime* and completed during the French Revolution. Since then, the Panthéon has served as a **mausoleum** to the illustrious men and women of French history buried there, including Joan of Arc, Marie Curie, Voltaire, Rousseau, Victor Hugo and Zola.

Boulevard St-Michel

Known familiarly to young Parisians as the **"Boul' Mich"**, this grand avenue is, together with the Boulevard Saint Germain, one of the two principal arteries of the Left Bank, laid out in the 19th century as part of Baron Haussman's restructuring of the city's street plan. Boulevard Saint Michel runs from Port Royal, past the Jardin du Luxembourg to the river bank at Place St Michel and separates the 5th *arrondissement* (Quartier Latin) from the 6th (St-Germain-des-Prés). Today it is always busy with traffic, and pedestrians visiting its many **bookshops, boutiques, restaurants and cafés**. It is hard to imagine that for a brief, but historic, period in May 1968 it was blockaded and turned into a battleground in which student protesters from the Sorbonne confronted the police.

The Sorbonne

In international shorthand, the name "Sorbonne" is used as if there were a single University of Paris. In the early 1970s, however, the city's higher education faculties were split into thirteen separate but linked educational institutions. Four of these contemporary universities share the famous Sorbonne name and the historic complex of Baroque buildings that dominate the Quartier Latin.

The Sorbonne was founded in 1253 as a college for theology students and named after the confessor of Louis IX, Robert de Sorbon. Over the centuries, it grew to be one of the **world's most famous universities**, a haven of intellectual fervour attracting the brightest brains from all over Europe. Its main facade looks over the Place de la Sorbonne, just off the Boulevard St-Michel, but the university buildings can be visited only by pre-arrangement on a **guided group tour**.

People sitting by the fountains at Place de la Sorbonne

treet stalls
n Boulevard
t-Michel,
nown as the
Boul' Mich"

TAKING A BREAK
Have lunch at one of the area's ethnic restaurants, mainly found on rue Severin and rue de la Harpe. If you want a traditional French bar-restaurant try **Café de la Nouvelle Mairie**, an old-fashioned café at 19 rue des Fossés Saint-Jacques (tel: 01 44 07 04 41).

➕ 209 D1

Musée National du Moyen-Âge–Thermes de Cluny
➕ 208 C2 ✉ 6 place Paul Painlevé ☎ 01 53 73 78 00; www.musee-moyenage.fr 🕐 Wed–Mon 9:15–5.45. Closed Tue, public holidays 🎫 Moderate 🚇 St-Michel, Cluny–La Sorbonne 🚉 RER B or C St-Michel–Cluny-Sorbonne

Panthéon
➕ 208 C1 ✉ Place du Panthéon ☎ 01 44 32 18 00; http://pantheon.monuments-nationaux.fr 🕐 Apr–Sep 10–6:30, Oct–Mar 10–6 🎫 Moderate, under 18s free 🚇 Maubert–Mutualité, Cardinal–Lemoine

Sorbonne
➕ 208 C1 ✉ Rectorat de Paris, 47, rue des Ecoles, 75005 ☎ 01 40 46 22 11; www.sorbonne.fr 🕐 Guided tours by pre-arrangement, applications via email to visites.sorbonne@ac-paris.fr

MUSÉE NATIONAL DU MOYEN-ÂGE: INSIDE INFO

Top tips Even if you don't have time to visit the museum, **step inside the courtyard** to admire its ornate turrets, gargoyles and friezes.
■ Pick up a leaflet at the ticket desk which **details the key sights** and provides a plan of the floors of the museum.

Must-sees As well as the **Roman baths**, *Lady and the Unicorn* tapestry and the monks' **chapel**, don't miss:
■ **Statues of the Kings of Judaea** from Notre-Dame's facade (ground floor, room 8).
■ The Flamboyant Gothic **chapel of the monks of Cluny** (first floor, room 20).

3 Musée d'Orsay

If you visit only one art gallery during your stay, make it the Musée d'Orsay, a feast of 19th-century art and design, including a hugely popular collection of Impressionist paintings. The originality of this amazing museum lies in its presentation of a wide range of different art forms – painting, sculpture, decorative and graphic art – all under the lofty glass roof of a former Industrial Age railway station.

The museum occupies the former Gare d'Orsay, built by Victor Laloux on the site of the **Palais d'Orsay**. The station was inaugurated in 1900 but ceased operating in 1939 with the dawn of electric trains. It was subsequently used as an auction room, then as a theatre, and was saved from demolition in 1973, to be finally converted into a museum in 1986. Much of the original architecture has been retained.

The gallery is housed in a vast former railway station

Seeing the Museum

The art collections span the years from 1848 to 1914, conveniently starting where the Louvre (▶ 56–57) leaves off and ending where the Centre Georges Pompidou (▶ 58–59) begins. They are organized chronologically on three levels, with additional displays throughout.

Vincent Van Gogh's moving "self portrait" (1889) at the museum

The skylit upper level houses a crowd-pulling, dazzling collection of **Impressionist and post-Impressionist treasures**. It would be impossible to list all the star attractions, but favourites include Monet's *Coquelicots (Poppies)* and *La Rue Montorgueil – Fête du 30 juin 1878*, Renoir's *Danse à la ville (Town Dance)* and *Danse à la campagne (Country Dance)*, Van Gogh's *La Chambre à Arles (Room at Arles)* and Matisse's pointillist *Luxe, calme et volupté*. Montmartre fans will especially enjoy Renoir's *Bal du Moulin de la Galette*, Degas' *L'Absinthe* and Toulouse-Lautrec's *Danse au Moulin Rouge*.

The close juxtaposition of **paintings and sculptures** on the ground floor illustrates the huge stylistic variations in art from 1848 to 1870 (the key date when Impressionism first made its name). Look out in particular for Courbet's *L'Origine du monde (Origin of the World)* and early Impressionist-style works such as Boudin's *La Plage de Trouville (The Beach at Trouville)*.

The middle level has objects reflecting the **art nouveau movement**, which display the sinuous lines – epitomized in jewellery and glassware by Lalique – that led the French to nickname the movement *style nouille* (noodle style). And throughout the museum you will find priceless sculptures at every turn, with works by Rodin on the middle floor and Degas on the top floor.

🔲 207 F3 ✉ 1 rue de la Légion d'Honneur ☎ 01 40 49 48 14; www.musee-orsay.fr 🕐 Tue–Sun 9:30–6 (Thu until 9:45). Ticket sales stop 45 mins before closing time 💰 Moderate. Free on first Sunday of the month 🍴 Self-service cafeteria; café; restaurant 🚇 Solférino 🚉 RER Musée d'Orsay

MUSÉE D'ORSAY: INSIDE INFO

Top tips Be sure to **pick up a plan of the museum** as the layout is not clearly signed and can be rather confusing.
■ Buy a copy of the excellent *Pocket Guide*. It provides a succinct outline of the most important works of the collection. For a more comprehensive look at the collection, the beautifully illustrated *Guide to the Musée d'Orsay* is a must for all self-respecting art-buffs.
■ If you are pressed for time, **ignore the lower floors** and head straight to the upper level to see the famous Impressionists on the river side of the gallery.

Tickets and tours Tickets for the permanent exhibits are valid all day, so **you can leave and re-enter** the museum as you please.
■ **English-language tours** (charge: moderate) begin daily (except Sun and Mon) at 11:30. Ask for a ticket at the information desk.
■ **Audioguides** – tours (charge: inexpensive, available in six languages from just beyond the ticket booths on the right) – steer you round the major works. The audiotours and the English-language tours are both excellent.

4 Tour Eiffel

Strange to think that Gustave Eiffel's famous tower, the universally beloved symbol of France, was considered a hideous eyesore when it was constructed over 100 years ago. Yet since its inauguration in 1889, more than 200 million people have climbed the tower, and today the "iron lady" attracts 6 million visitors annually, making it one of the world's premier tourist attractions.

The lacy wrought ironwork of this masterpiece of engineering is amazing, and most visitors find soaring skywards in a **double-decker glass lift** both exciting and alarming. No visit to Paris is complete without seeing this awesome structure of gleaming metal, and **the views** from the top are unforgettable.

In 1885, Paris held a competition to design a 300m (985ft) tower as the centrepiece for the Centennial Exhibition of 1889. Gustave Eiffel, nicknamed the **"magician of iron"**, won the contest with his seemingly functionless tower, beating

Looking up at the enormous structure of the Tour Eiffel

VITAL STATISTICS
WEIGHT: 7,000 tonnes
TOTAL HEIGHT:
320m/1,050ft (15cm/6 inches higher on hot days due to metal expansion)
NUMBER OF METAL SECTIONS: 18,000
NUMBER OF RIVETS: 2.5 million
NUMBER OF RIVET HOLES: 7 million
NUMBER OF STEPS: 1,710
Visibility from the top: 75km (47 miles)
Maximum sway at the top: 12cm (5 inches)

107 other proposals, including one for a giant sprinkler and another for a monster commemorative guillotine. It took less than two years to build, and for years the finished product remained **the world's tallest building** (until New York's Chrysler Building of 1930), but it was not without its critics. Local residents objected to this "overpowering metal construction" that straddled their district, fearing it would collapse onto their homes. Author Guy de Maupassant was a regular at the second-floor restaurant, swearing that it was the only spot in Paris from which you could not see the tower! He launched a petition against its erection, describing it as a "monstrous construction", a "hollow candlestick" and a "bald umbrella". On the other hand, playwright Jean Cocteau described it as the "Queen of Paris".

The tower was designed to stand for 20 years. Fortunately, its height was its salvation – the tall iron tower proved to be a marvellous antenna. The first news bulletin was broadcast from Tour Eiffel in 1921, and the first television broadcast in was made 1935.

TAKING A BREAK
There are restaurants on level 1, *58 Tour Eiffel* (tel: 08 25 56 66 62) and level 2, *Le Jules Verne* (tel: 01 45 55 61 44). Buffets at ground level and levels 1 and 2, serve fast food and snacks to eat in or take away (www.restaurants-toureiffel.com).

➕ 206 A2 ✉ quai Branly ☎ 01 44 11 23 23; www.tour-eiffel.fr 🕐 Sep to mid-Jun daily 9:30am–11pm; mid-Jun to Aug 9am–midnight. Last access 30 mins before closing 🛗 By elevator: 1st floor (57m/185ft) inexpensive; 2nd floor (115m/375ft) moderate; 3rd floor (276m/905ft) expensive. On foot (1st & 2nd floors only) inexpensive 🍴 Café (Level 1); Jules Verne restaurant (Level 2) 🚇 Bir-Hakeim 🚆 RER Champ-de-Mars

TOUR EIFFEL: INSIDE INFO

Top tips Visit early in the morning or late at night to avoid the worst of the queues. **For the best views**, arrive one hour before sunset.
- **Forget the third level** unless it's an exceptionally clear day – the views can be disappointing as you're very high up and Paris is so flat.
- The tower itself looks at its **best after dark** when every girder is illuminated.
- Get your postcards stamped with the famous **Eiffel Tower postmark** at the post office on level one (daily 10–7:30).

Fast track Skip the long queues for the lifts and **climb the stairs to the first level** (it takes about 5 minutes and isn't as tough as it looks). Catch your breath in the cineiffel (a short film recounts the tower's history), then walk or take the lift to level two. Tickets for both stages are available at the ticket office at the bottom of the southern pillar – Pilier Sud.

5 Champs-Élysées and Arc de Triomphe

The Arc de Triomphe rises majestically at the head of the city's most famous avenue, the Champs-Élysées. Planned by Napoléon I as a monument to his military prowess, the colossal arch was not finished until 15 years after his death, in 1836. The Tomb of the Unknown Soldier beneath the archway makes it also a place of remembrance.

Arc de Triomphe

Two hundred and eighty-two steps up a narrow spiral staircase will lead you to the 55m (180ft) terrace. Here, the **breathtaking view** highlights the city's design – the Voie Triomphale from the Louvre to La Défense, and the 12 avenues radiating out from the arch itself like the points of a star (hence the name place de l'Étoile, which stubbornly persists despite it having been changed officially to place Charles-de-Gaulle).

It is hard to believe that the broad and busy thoroughfare of the **avenue des Champs-Élysées** was just an empty field before André Le Nôtre converted it into parkland as an extension of the Tuileries. For centuries it was a popular strolling ground, reaching its zenith in the mid-1800s, when a constant flow of horse-drawn carriages paraded up the street in order to allow ladies to show off their finest fashions. Today, with its brash shops, cinemas and fast food joints, the avenue that was once the "most beautiful street in the world" has lost much of its magic, glamour and prestige, yet it still retains an aloof grandeur and unique appeal.

The Tomb of the Unknown Soldier at the Arc de Triomphe

Street Celebrations

The avenue des Champs-Élysées has always been associated with **grand parades and parties**. In 1810 Napoléon I organized a lavish procession here (complete with life-size mock-up of the Arc de Triomphe, then under construction) to celebrate his marriage to his second wife, Marie Louise.

The avenue's patriotic status was confirmed by the World War I victory parade of 14 July 1919. Twenty-five years later, Charles de Gaulle followed the same triumphal route at the end of World War II. It remains the venue for national

The iconic image of the Arc de Triomphe lit up at night

celebrations – the last leg of the Tour de France cycle race every July ends here, and it is the scene of great pomp on **Bastille Day (14 July)** and **Armistice Day (11 November)**.

TAKING A BREAK

Have lunch or dinner at the bar or terrace of **Le Fouquet's** – the place to see and be seen – well placed at 99 avenue des Champs-Élysées (tel: 01 47 23 50 00).

Arc de Triomphe

🚩 206 A5 ✉ place Charles-de-Gaulle-Étoile ☎ 01 55 37 73 77; www.monum.fr 🕐 Apr–Sep daily 10am–11pm; Oct–Mar 10am–10:30pm 🚇 Charles-de-Gaulle-Étoile 💷 Moderate

Avenue des Champs-Élysées

🚩 207 D4 🚇 George V, Franklin D Roosevelt, Charles-de-Gaulle-Étoile

CHAMPS-ÉLYSÉES AND ARC DE TRIOMPHE: INSIDE INFO

Top tips The best time to visit the Arc de Triomphe is early in the day, when the **morning light emphasizes the details** of the sculptures, or late afternoon as the sun sets over the roof-tops. Glittering lights map out the city on an evening visit.

■ **Don't attempt to cross the road** to reach the arch. Access is via a subway at the top of the Champs-Élysées.

■ Don't forget your camera as the **views are stupendous**. An orientation table at the top of the arch makes spotting the key landmarks easy.

■ Wear **comfortable shoes** because the **stroll down the avenue** is much longer than it looks on the map.

One to miss The small museum at the top of the arch tracing its history is not particularly inspiring.

6 Musée du Louvre

The centuries-old Musée du Louvre contains one of the largest, most important art collections in the world – more than 35,000 works of art are displayed. Whether you find your visit here breathtaking, overwhelming, frustrating or simply exhausting, one thing's for sure – you would need a lifetime to see everything. The key to a successful visit is to pace yourself, be selective and enjoy: you can always return tomorrow for more. Allow at least half a day, and be patient.

The museum buildings were originally a **12th-century hunting lodge**, which later became a royal residence and a succession of rulers improved on and enlarged the complex. François I replaced the imposing keep with a Renaissance-style building and also started the Louvre's collections with **12 stolen Italian works of art**, including Leonardo da Vinici's iconic *Mona Lisa*.

One of the more recent additions to the Louvre is the glass pyramid entrance

STAR ATTRACTIONS

■ Leonardo da Vinci's *Portrait of Mona Lisa*, also called *La Gioconda* (1503–6, Denon, first floor, room 13, then room 6).

■ *The Lacemaker* by Jan Vermeer (1669–70, Richelieu, second floor, room 38), an exquisite portrayal of everyday domestic life in Holland.

■ Michelangelo's *The Slave* (1513–15, Denon, ground floor), sculpted for the tomb of Pope Julius II in Rome.

■ The unrivalled *Venus de Milo* (second century BC, Sully, ground floor, room 74), found in 1820 on the Greek island of Milo.

■ The *Winged Victory of Samothrace* (190BC, Denon, first floor), poised for flight.

In the 17th century, Louis XIV added further works by Leonardo da Vinci, Raphael and Titian, and Napoleon filled the palace with artworks looted during his victorious years. The art collections were first opened to the public after the Revolution, in 1793.

Recent architectural additions include the **glass pyramid entrance** by architect Ieoh Ming Pei (1989), and Richelieu wing renovation (1993). With an exhibition space of 60,000sq m (645,900sq ft), the Louvre is the largest museum in the world.

The Wings – Finding Your Way

The collections are divided between **three wings** – the Sully, the Richelieu and the Denon. Each has four levels, on which are arranged seven departments, each represented by a colour: yellow for Near Eastern Antiquities/Islamic Art; pale blue for Egyptian Antiquities; blue for Greek, Etruscan and Roman Antiquities; red for Paintings; pink for Prints and Drawings; purple for Decorative Arts; light brown for Sculpture; dark brown for the History of the Louvre/ Medieval Louvre.

TAKING A BREAK

The **Café Marly** at the Louvre makes a pleasant lunch stop.

✚ 208 B4 ✉ 34–6 quai du Louvre ☎ 01 40 20 51 51 (recorded message); 01 40 20 53 17 (information desk); www.louvre.fr 🕐 Wed–Mon 9–6; evening opening Mon (part of the museum only) and Wed and Fri (the whole museum) until 9:30pm. Closed Tue 💷 Moderate (reduced rate after 6pm Wed and Fri). Free first Sun of the month 🚇 Palais Royal-Musée du Louvre, Louvre Rivoli

---

MUSÉE DU LOUVRE: INSIDE INFO

Top tips Your ticket will get you into any of the wings **as many times as you like** during one day.

■ To avoid the queues, visit **early in the morning**, or Monday or Wednesday evening. Avoid Sunday, when the museum is at its most crowded.

■ If you have a Museum Pass or buy your ticket in advance on the website or from one of the city's FNAC or Virgin stores, you can **enter the fast track** at the Richelieu passage, Porte des Lions or Galerie du Carrousel entrances. You can also buy tickets online at www.louvre.fnacspectacles.com, www.parismuseumpass.com or www.ticketnet.fr.

■ If you don't already have a ticket, go in by the **Carrousel entrance**: the queues are usually shorter here.

Getting In There are **four entrances** – via the pyramid, via the Richelieu passage (off the rue de Rivoli), via the Porte des Lions, by the Seine, or via the Carrousel du Louvre (closed Friday).

7 Centre Georges Pompidou

Known to Parisians as "le Beaubourg", the avant-garde Centre Georges Pompidou is one of the city's most distinctive landmarks and one of its most visited attractions. An X-ray-style extravaganza of steel and glass, striped by brightly coloured pipes and snake-like escalators, it looks as if someone has turned the whole building inside out. What's more, it contains one of the largest collections of modern art in the world.

It was in 1969 that President Georges Pompidou declared "I passionately want Paris to have a **cultural centre** which would be at once a museum and a centre of creation." The building caused an outcry when it was opened in 1977, in the heart of the then run-down Beaubourg district, and it has been the subject of controversy ever since, but it is generally acknowledged as one of the city's most **distinctive landmarks** – a lovable oddity, and far more popular as a gallery than anyone anticipated.

Before you go inside, pause to admire the centre's **unique external structure**, designed by Richard Rogers and Renzo Piano. Glass predominates, giving the entire edifice a transparency that abolishes barriers between street and centre. Steel beams cross-strutted and hinged over the length and width of the entire building form an intriguing external skeleton. Inside, walls can be taken down or put up at will, enabling the interior spaces to change shape for different displays.

On the outside, the building reveals all its workings by way of **multicoloured tubes**, ducts and piping in "high-tech" style. Far from being merely

The avant-garde Georges Pompidou

FINDING YOUR WAY AROUND

There are six main floors:

- The **1st and 2nd floors** house a reference library and a cinema.
- The **4th and 5th** floors house the permanent collections of the Musée National d'Art Moderne (MNAM). Works from 1905 to 1960 – the Collection Historique – are on the 5th, with the 4th reserved for more recent art – the Collection Contemporaine (1960–present) – and a room for viewing video-art. (Note that to reach the 5th floor you must enter the museum on the 4th floor.)
- The **1st and 6th** floors are for temporary exhibitions.
- The **basement and remaining floors** are used for all types of shows, films, meetings and documentation.

decorative, they are carefully colour-coded: green for water, blue for air-conditioning and yellow for electricity.

Musée National d'Art Moderne

The Centre Georges Pompidou's main crowd-puller is its **collection of over 50,000 works** of contemporary art (of which about 2,000 are on display at one time), starting from the early 20th century, where the Musée d'Orsay (➤ 50–51) leaves off. Among the artists represented are Matisse, Derain, Chagall, Braque and Picasso. The collection also includes futurists, surrealists and minimalists.

Displays change annually, so if there's a particular piece you're eager to view, visit the website to check that it's on show.

TAKING A BREAK

There is a **café** on the 1st floor, and the ultra-cool restaurant, **Georges**, with sweeping views over the roof-tops of Beaubourg, on the 6th floor.

Views, art and architecture is a crowd-pulling combo

➕ 209 D4 ✉ 19 place Georges-Pompidou ☎ 01 44 78 12 33; www.centrepompidou.fr 🕐 Wed–Mon 11–10; MNAM and exhibitions close at 9 (11 Thu), box office at 8 💰 MNAM and exhibitions: expensive 🚇 Rambuteau, Hôtel de Ville

CENTRE GEORGES POMPIDOU: INSIDE INFO

Top tips If you are limited by time, stick to the exhibits on the **4th floor**, which tend to be the more frivolous, outrageous and highly entertaining works.
- **L'Espace Nouveaux Médias** (New Media Collection), on **Level 4**, offers one of the world's largest collections of videos, CD-Roms, websites, installation art and sound documents by artists specializing in the media. A place to get inspired for your own personal or family website?

Hidden Gem *Josephine Baker* by sculptor Alexander Calder (1898–1976) is an early, elegant example of the mobile – a form that he invented.

At Your Leisure

8 St-Germain-des-Prés

St-Germain is the literary and artistic heart of Paris, bursting with ambient cafés, restaurants, antique shops, art galleries and fashion boutiques, and is peopled by students, arty types, the wealthy socialist intelligentsia, and the simply rich, who come here to sample bohemian life. The area is now a luxury shopping district, with a spotlight on fashion, and such designers as Giorgio Armani, Christian Dior and Christian Lacroix have moved in from the Rive Droite.

The main artery, boulevard St-Germain, stretches from the Quartier Latin to the government buildings of the Faubourg St-Germain. Between the two world wars, just about every notable Parisian artist, writer, philosopher and politician frequented three cafés on boulevard St-Germain – the Café de Flore (No 172), Brasserie Lipp (No 151) and Les Deux Magots (6 place St-Germain-des-Pres). The Benedictine Abbey of St-Germain-des-Prés was founded in the sixth century, but only the Romanesque church – the oldest in Paris – survived the Revolution.

✚ 208 B2 🚇 St-Germain-des-Prés

Musée Rodin, housed in Hôtel Biron, the mansion where Rodin once lived

9 Musée Rodin

There is nowhere in Paris more pleasurable on a sunny day than the sculpture-studded gardens of this stunning open-air museum dedicated to the best-known sculptor of the modern age.

Auguste Rodin (1840–1917) lived and worked in the adjoining elegant mansion – Hôtel Biron (1730), now the Musée Rodin – alongside Cocteau and Matisse. Inside are 500 superb sculptures, including such masterpieces as *The Kiss*, and *The Age of Bronze*, whose realism so startled the critics at the time that they accused Rodin of having imprisoned a live boy in the plaster. See Rodin's most celebrated work, *The Thinker*, in deep contemplation, in the garden he loved.

✚ 207 D2 ✉ 79 rue de Varenne ☎ 01 44 18 61 10; www.musee-rodin.fr ⏰ Tue–Sun 10–5:45 (last entrance 5:15, park closes at 5:45); closed 1 May 💷 Moderate (garden inexpensive) 🍴 Café (Apr–Sep 9:30–6:30; Oct–Mar 9:30–4:30) 🚇 Varenne

The Église du Dôme at Les Invalides

⑩ Les Invalides

The Hôtel National des Invalides was built in the 17th century as a convalescent home for wounded soldiers. Still a home to war veterans, it is now a memorial to the endless battles and campaigns that have marked French history, all vividly portrayed in the Musée de l'Armée.

Admission to the museum also buys a visit to the Musée de l'Ordre de la Libération and the 17th-century Église du Dôme. The golden dome of this church symbolizes the glory of the Sun King, Louis XIV, who built the complex. Inside, the centrepiece is Napoleon's mausoleum: a circular crypt containing six coffins within a red porphyry sarcophagus. Adjoining

NAPOLEON BONAPARTE

Napoleon is strongly associated with **Les Invalides.** Her, he celebrated his military successes, staging grandiose parades on the Champ-de-Mars. He used the esplanade outside Les Invalides to show off his war spoils – guns captured in Vienna in 1803 and a lion statue plundered from St Mark's Square in Venice – and he honoured his victorious armies in Les Invalides and the nearby École Militaire, where he himself had trained as a young officer.

the Dôme, the Soldiers' Church is more tasteful, decorated only by a row of poignantly faded tricolore pennants.

🕇 207 D2 ✉ esplanade des Invalides
☎ 08 10 11 33 99; www.invalides.org
🕐 Oct–Mar daily 10–5; Apr–Sep 10–6.
Closed first Mon of the month 🎫 Moderate
🍴 Café 🚇 La Tour Maubourg, Varenne,
Invalides 🚉 RER Invalides

⑪ Place de la Concorde and Jardin des Tuileries

The vast, traffic-encircled square of place de la Concorde was laid out between 1755 and 1775, with a 3,300-year-old pink granite obelisk from the Temple of Rameses at Luxor

Relax and escape in the gardens on the west side of the Place de la Concorde

in Egypt at its centre and eight female statues representing France's largest cities at its four corners. In 1793 the square was the scene of the execution of Louis XVI, and in the next two years a further 1,343 "enemies of the Revolution" were guillotined here. At the end of this Reign of Terror, the square was renamed to evoke peace.

On the east side, bordering the Seine, the Tuileries is one of the oldest and most beautiful public gardens in Paris. It was created in the 16th century by Catherine de' Médicis, and transformed in the 17th century by André Le Nôtre (of Versailles fame, ➤ 66) into a formal and symmetrical garden, studded with statues and embellished with box-edged flower beds, topiarized trees and gravel walkways.

Place de la Concorde
🚇 207 E4 🚇 Concorde

Jardin des Tuileries
🚇 207 F3 ☎ 01 40 20 90 43 🕐 Apr–May daily 7am–9pm; Jun–Aug 7am–11pm; Sep–Mar 7:30am–7:30pm 🚇 Tuileries, Concorde

🔢 La Villette

La Villette was for many years a livestock market, but in 1984 its 55ha (135 acres) were turned into a spectacular urban park and science city. The chief crowd-puller is the Cité des Sciences et de l'Industrie – a vast science and technology museum. In the main part, Explora, you can experience optical illusions, chat to a robot and fly a flight simulator. On the ground floor, La Cité des Enfants introduces under-12s to basic scientific principles through games and dazzling hands-on displays. Don't miss La Géode, a giant, shiny steel marble with the world's largest hemispherical movie screen inside.

🚇 204, off C5 🚇 Parc de la Villette ☎ Musique: 01 44 84 45 00; www.cite-musique.fr; Sciences: 01 40 05 70 00; www.cite-sciences.fr 🕐 Tue–Sat 10–6, Sun 10–7 💰 Moderate 🍴 Several cafés 🚇 Porte de la Villette

🔢 Musée Picasso

Hidden in a unassuming back street in one of the finest 17th-century mansions in the Marais, this outstanding museum contains an unparalleled collection of works by the most acclaimed artist of modern times. Picasso kept the majority of his works himself, and on his death in 1973, his heirs donated to the State 3,500-plus paintings, drawings, sketch books, collages, reliefs, ceramics and sculptures, which form the basis of this museum. A second contribution, after his wife died in 1986, enhanced the museum further. Together with numerous key works by Picasso himself, treasures from his private collection include works by Cézanne, Matisse, Miró, Renoir, Degas and Braque. Closed until 2012.

🚇 207, off F5 🚇 Hôtel Salé, 5 rue de Thorigny ☎ 01 42 71 25 21; www.musee-picasso.fr 🕐 Wed–Mon 9:30–6 (until 5:30 Oct–Mar). Closed for renovations until 2012 💰 Moderate (free first Sun of month) 🚇 St-Paul, Chemin Vert, St-Sébastien-Froissart

🔢 Place des Vosges

The stately 17th-century town houses of the oldest and most gracious square in Paris, Place des Vosges, laid out by Henri IV, are arranged symmetrically around an

Relaxing by the fountain in the beautiful formal gardens of Place des Vosges

immaculately kept park, once a popular venue for duels. Novelist and poet Victor Hugo lived at No 6 from 1832 to 1848, and it is now a museum in his memory. Otherwise, the arcades house a variety of up-market galleries, antiques shops and elegant *salons de thé*.

After the Revolution, the Marais district sank into decay, but following a major face-lift in the 1960s it has become one of the most lively and fashionable quartiers of central Paris, a magnet for elegant shops, fine restaurants and bars.

Some of its restored mansions house museums, from the Musée Picasso (➤ opposite) to the Maison Européenne de la Photographie (5–7 rue de Fourcy).

🔁 209 F3 🚇 St-Paul, Bastille, Chemin Vert

🅖 Cimetière du Père-Lachaise

This must be the world's most fascinating cemetery – a silent village with countless occupants in higgledy-piggledy tombs, and the final resting place of Paris's most prestigious names: painters Corot, Delacroix, Pissaro and Ernst; composers Bizet and Chopin; writers Apollinaire, Daudet, Balzac, Molière and Proust; singers Maria Callas, Edith Piaf and former Doors lead vocalist, Jim Morrison, to name but a few. Oscar Wilde's grave is marked by a massive statue of a naked Egyptian flying skywards. Pick up a map at the entrance to see where the famous are buried.

🔁 209, off F5 ✉ boulevard de Ménilmontant
☎ 01 55 25 82 10; www.pere-lachaise.com
🕐 Mid-Mar–5 Nov Mon–Fri 8–6, Sat 8:30–6, Sun 9–6; 6 Nov–mid-Mar Mon–Fri 8–5:30, Sat 8:30–5:30, Sun 9–5:30 🚇 Père-Lachaise, Philippe Auguste, Gambetta

Statue in Cimetière du Père-Lachaise, an intriguing, and often moving, place to visit

Further Afield

16 Chantilly

Chantilly, 48km (30 miles) north of Paris, has always enjoyed a reputation for fine cuisine, and the name of the town is indelibly associated with fresh whipped and sweetened cream, ordered in the best restaurants worldwide as *crème chantilly*.

Visitors today come not only for the cream but also for the impressive (albeit heavily restored) Renaissance **château**, with its exceptional art collection (including works by Corot, Delacroix and Raphael), and its magnificent palatial 17th-century stables, which contain the superb **Musée Vivant du Cheval** (Living Horse Museum), known for dressage demonstrations and popular with horse-lovers and children.

🚩 223 E4 ☎ Château: 03 44 27 31 80; Musée Vivant du Cheval: 03 44 27 31 63 🕐 Château: Apr–4 Nov Wed–Mon 10–6; 5 Nov–Mar Wed–Mon 10:30–5. Musée Vivant du Cheval: closed until 2011 💰 Château: moderate; Horse Museum: expensive 🚃 Numerous trains from Paris's Gare du Nord to Chantilly-Gouvieux

17 Disneyland® Resort Paris

Despite a continued shaky financial state, this imported American theme park is now Europe's most popular tourist destination. The Resort offers such thrilling rides as Big Thunder Mountain, Indiana Jones and the Temple of Peril: Backwards! (including 360-degree loops backwards) and, scariest of all, Space Mountain: Mission 2. Peter Pan, 'it's a small world' and Dumbo the Flying Elephant are geared to toddlers, and a whole host of American-style eateries, shops and parades ensure non-stop entertainment. There is also the Walt Disney Studios® Park. While a visit to the Disneyland® Resort Paris is not an inexpensive option, for most children it has to be the ultimate treat. Avoid weekends and mornings, when the queues are at their worst.

🚩 223 E3 ✉ Marne-la-Vallée ☎ 09 09 03 03 03; www.disneylandparis.fr 🕐 Times vary according to season, check the website 💰 Expensive (2- or 3-day "multipass" is good value) 🚃 The RER (line A) takes 45

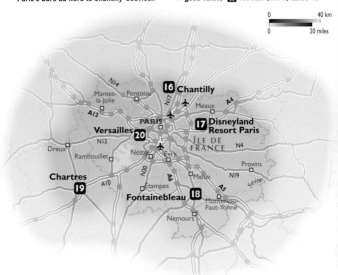

Inside one of France's largest and most opulent royal palaces – Fontainebleau

minutes–1 hour to Marne-la-Vallée or Chessy; the entrance to Disneyland is 100m (110 yards) from the station exit

18 Fontainebleau

If you can't face the crowds at Versailles (► 66), come to this château instead. It is equally grand and surprisingly overlooked. This splendid royal residence, 65km (40 miles) southeast of Paris, started out as a hunting pavilion and ornamental fountain (hence the name) at the heart of a dense royal hunting forest – the Forêt de Fontainebleau. François I converted the lodge into the beautiful Renaissance château it is today: one of France's largest erstwhile royal residences (1,900 rooms), celebrated for its splendid interior furnishings and immaculate grounds.

🚉 223 E3 ☎ 01 60 71 50 70; www.musee-chateau-fontainebleau.fr ⊙ Château: Jun–Sep Wed–Mon 9:30–6; Oct–May Wed–Mon 9:30–5. Gardens: May–Sep daily 9–7; Mar, Apr, Oct 9–6; Nov–Feb 9–5 🎫 Moderate 🚆 Trains leave Paris's Gare de Lyon approximately every hour for Fontainebleau-Avon. Then take Bus A to the château. Total journey time is about 1 hour

19 Chartres

The wonder of Chartres is its magnificent cathedral, dedicated to Notre-Dame and rebuilt in the 13th century with uneven spires. Yet it is not the superb Gothic architecture which is the most memorable feature of the cathedral, but rather the glowing, jewel-like colours of its medieval stained glass. There are 176 windows in all, richly illustrating biblical scenes and activities of daily life, including shoemaking and weaving. They were designed to be read from bottom to top, and from left to right, starting with Old Testament scenes in the north wall, and ending with the Last Judgement on the east wall. There are no less than three rose windows. If you are able to tear your eyes away from the rich glasswork, you'll also discover an unusual labyrinth laid out in the stone of the nave floor – a maze for devout pilgrims to crawl through on their knees.

A second church in the town centre, St-Pierre, also has fine medieval windows. More stained glass is on show in the Centre International du Vitrail, along with information about its preservation and restoration.

🚉 222 C3 🚆 Trains from Paris's Gare Montparnasse take one hour

Tourist Information Office
✉ place de la Cathédrale, BP289, 28005
☎ 02 37 18 26 26; www.chartres-tourism.com
⊙ Mon–Sat 10–6, Sun 9–5

🔟 Versailles

This monumental palace, 23km (14 miles) southwest of Paris, is on every visitor's must-see list. And it's all thanks to one person – Louis XIV, the Sun King – whose extravagant taste, passion for self-glorification and determination to project both at home and abroad the absolute power of the French monarchy created one of France's great treasures.

Louis planned a palace large enough to house 20,000 courtiers. He commissioned the greatest artists and craftsmen of the day: architects Louis Le Vau and Jules Hardouin-Mansart planned the buildings; Charles Le Brun designed the interior; and the landscaper André Le Nôtre started on the 100ha (247 acres) of gardens. The building took 50 years, and as no expense was spared, it wrought havoc on the kingdom's finances.

The palace became the centre of political power in France and was the seat of the royal court from 1682 until 1789, when Revolutionary mobs massacred the palace guard and seized the despised King Louis XVI and Marie-Antoinette, dragging them to Paris and the guillotine.

The vast palace complex is divided into four main parts – the palace

The magnificent exterior of Versailles, built to house the French royalty and 20,000 courtiers

itself with its innumerable wings, sumptuous halls and chambers (only certain parts are open to the public), the extensive gardens and two smaller châteaux in the grounds, used as royal guesthouses – the Grand Trianon and the Petit Trianon.

The highlight is the **Galerie des Glaces** (Hall of Mirrors), where 17 giant mirrors face tall windows. In 1919 it was the scene of the ratification of the Treaty of Versailles that marked the end of World War I. 🔷 223 D3 ✉ 78000 Versailles ☎ 01 30 83 78 00; www.chateauversailles.fr ⏰ Grands Appartements: Apr–Oct Tue–Sun 9–6:30 (Nov–Mar until 5:30). Grand Trianon and Petit Trianon: Apr–Oct daily 12–6:30; Nov–Mar 12–5:30; (last admission 30 mins before closing). Gardens: 9–dusk 💷 Palace: expensive; Grand Trianon and Petit Trianon (combined ticket): moderate (entrance to Versailles free Nov–Feb on first Sun of month); Gardens: inexpensive Mar–Oct, free rest of year 🚇 RER (Line C) to Versailles-Rive Gauche; main-line train from Gare Montparnasse to Gare des Chantiers; or train from Paris's Gare St-Lazare via La Défense to the Gare Rive Droite. All three stations are within walking distance of Versailles

Where to...
Stay

Prices
Expect to pay per night for a double room
€ under €120   €€ €120–€220   €€€ over €220

Hôtel Atlantis €€
There's a light, airy feel to this elegant two-star hotel, which features sleek furniture and quilted bedspreads. Most of the 27 well-appointed bedrooms overlook the bustling place St-Sulpice, with its fountains and cafés, and all have satellite TV
🚇 208 A2 ☒ 4 rue du Vieux-Colombier, 75006 St-Germain-des-Prés ☎ 01 45 48 31 81; www.hotelatlantis.com 🚇 St-Sulpice

Hôtel Cluny Sorbonne €–€€€
The French poet Rimbaud stayed here, before the building was turned into a family-run hotel. central. It occupies a renovated 17th-century building in which *jeu de paume* (an early form of tennis) was once played. The hotel has a music room, games room, library, billiards room with vaulted ceilings, and an attractive garden. The 30 bedrooms are all different and decorated with high-quality fabrics and furnishings.
🚇 209 E2 ☒ 54, rue Saint Louis en l'île, 75004 ☎ 01 43 26 14 18; www.jeudepaumehotel.com 🚇 Pont Marie

Hôtel Franklin Roosevelt €€–€€€
Top-class shopping is just steps away from this smart hotel, located off the Champs-Élysées. Inside, you'll find thick carpets and rich red fabrics for a feel of luxury, along with a reading room and winter garden if you're looking for peace and quiet. The hotel has air-conditioning throughout.
🚇 206 B4 ☒ 18 rue Clément Marot, 75008 Champs-Élysées ☎ 01 53 57 49 50; www.hroosevelt.com 🚇 Franklin D. Roosevelt, Alma Marceau

Hôtel St-Merry €€–€€€
A former Renaissance presbytery close to the Centre Georges Pompidou is the location for this intimate hotel. Gothic touches in the public rooms include wood carvings and sculptures, and some original beamed ceilings.
🚇 208 D3 ☒ 78 rue de la Verrerie, 75004 Le Marais ☎ 01 42 78 14 15; www.hotelmarais.com 🚇 Hôtel-de-Ville, Châtelet

L'Atelier Montparnasse €–€€
The artistic and cultured enclave of Montparnasse in the 1930s gives this comfortable and good value hotel its theme, with period furniture and paintings galore. Even the bathroom mosaics recall artwork of the age. Facilities are up-to-date, however, and the 17 bedrooms are comfortable and include cable TV and minibars.
🚇 208 A1 ☒ 49 rue Vavin, 75006 St-Germain-des-Prés ☎ 01 46 33 60 00; www.ateliermontparnasse.com 🚇 Notre-Dame-des-Champs, Montparnasse

Located on a quiet street facing the famous Sorbonne in the middle of the Quartier Latin, the hotel has many of the city sights on its doorstep. The 23 bedrooms are simply furnished but comfortable and good value if you want to stay in a central location.
🚇 208 C1 ☒ 8 rue Victor Cousin, 75005 ☎ 01 43 54 66 66; www.hotel-cluny.fr 🚇 Cluny Sorbonne

Hôtel du Jeu de Paume €€€
A charming hotel with a romantic atmosphere, which, located on the Île de Saint Louis within close reach of Notre-Dame, could not be more

Le Vert Galant €–€€

This small hotel facing an attractive park in the 13th *arrondissement*, near the place d'Italie and southeast of the Quartier Latin, has 15 pleasant and comfortable bedrooms, each decorated in warm colours. Some of the bedrooms have kitchenettes and they all have WiFi. There is a pleasant garden with a veranda where guests can eat breakfast in summer. Next door is a well-known restaurant, the Auberge Etchegorry (▶ 69), which specializes in the traditional cuisine of the Basque Country and southwest France.

✚ 209 off D1 ✉ 43 rue Croulebarbe, 75013
🕾 01 44 08 83 50; www.vertgalant.com
Ⓜ Place d'Italie

L'Hôtel €€€

Located on a quiet back street set back from the hustle and bustle of St-Germain-des-Prés, this discreet, luxurious hotel is full of character and history and will forever be associated with Oscar Wilde, who died here in 1900.

The 20 bedrooms are decorated in an opulent baroque style with rich colours and materials. Some of the rooms also feature canopied beds and plump armchairs, and the bedrooms lead off a spectacular stairwell. The restaurant has been awarded a Michelin star.

✚ 208 B3 ✉ 13 rue des Beaux-Arts, 75006
🕾 01 44 41 99 00; www.l-hotel.com
Ⓜ St-Germain-des-Prés

Pavillon de la Reine €€€

For serious luxury in a hotel fit for a queen, this former royal residence on the historic place des Vosges takes some beating. Louis XIII's queen, Anne of Austria, was responsible for the finest fittings, including the grand fireplace in the salon. Tapestries line the walls of the breakfast room. Style and a setting this good come at an appropriately breathtaking price.

✚ 209 F3 ✉ 28 place des Vosges, 75003 Le Marais 🕾 01 40 29 19 19; www.pavillon-de-la-reine.com Ⓜ Notre-Dame-des-Champs, Montparnasse

Relais-Hôtel du Vieux Paris €€€

This hotel, in an earlier incarnation, was the Paris address of the visiting American poets of the "Beat Generation" in the 1950s and 1960s. Entirely refurbished since then, it is now a comfortable place to stay and the hotel is ideally located for exploring St-Germain-des-Prés, Quartier Latin and Île de la Cité. It has 12 peaceful bedrooms, each decorated in a different style, with coordinated wall-fabrics and exposed beams. Ask for one of the three rooms which that has gorgeous views.

✚ 208 C2 ✉ 9 rue Gît-le-Coeur, 75006
🕾 01 44 32 15 90; www.vieuxparis.com
Ⓜ Saint Michel

Residence Foch €–€€

This charming small three-star 18-room hotel makes a comfortable base just outside the main tourist trail but surrounded by the lively residential 16th arondissement with ample restaurants within easy reach. There is a retro 1930s café bar/lounge but rooms have pretty chintz touches. Rooms vary in size. The breakfast is excellent for a hotel in this class.

✚ 206 off A5 ✉ 10 rue Marbeau, 75116 Porte Maillot 🕾 01 45 00 46 50;
www.foch-paris-hotel.com Ⓜ Porte Maillot

Sélect Hôtel-Rive Gauche €€

This sleek, modern hotel is supremely well located at the heart of the Quartier Latin, and built around an atrium on two levels with a glass roof, decorated in a Mediterranean style with small palm trees and cactus plants. The 67 bedrooms have attractive stone walls and are well appointed with modern bathrooms, contemporary furniture and fittings. Charming public spaces include a lounge with books and a 16th-century vaulted breakfast room. Ask for a room on the top floor if you want beautiful views over the city.

✚ 208 C1 ✉ 1 Place de la Sorbonne, 75005 🕾 01 46 34 14 80; www.selecthotel.fr Ⓜ Cluny Sorbonne, Saint Michel or Odeon

Where to...
Eat and Drink

Prices
Expect to pay per person for a meal, excluding drinks

€ under €30   €€ €30–€60   €€€ over €60

Auberge Etchegorry €€
The pretty red facade of this fantastic restaurant, decorated with potted plants, evokes buildings typical of the Basque Country, which gives a hint of what's on the menu. Here you'll find the best southwest regional cuisine, served here for more than 45 years. Inside, the restaurant is decorated in a cosy, rustic style with hanging hams, peppers and garlic. There is a terrace for outdoor eating in summer. Choice items to order include *pimientos del piquillo*, *haricots Tarbais*, *piperade*, *foie gras chaud*, and red peppers filled with cod. All the dishes are created using fresh seasonal produce, as you would expect. Le Vert Galant hotel (▶ 68) is next door.

🚹 209 off D1 🖂 541 rue Croulebarbe, 75013 ☎ 01 44 08 83 51 🕓 Tue–Sat 12–2, 7–9 🚇 Place d'Italie

Bofinger €€
This is a legendary brasserie, claiming to be Paris's oldest, is close to place de la Bastille, with an amazing turn-of-the-century belle-époque interior that should be a must-see on any visitor's list. The classic dishes on offer here include oysters and a wealth of other fresh shellfish, *choucroute* (sauerkraut), duck *foie gras*, steak *tartare* and grills, with a choice of delicious home-made desserts and ices to finish. The three-course fixed-price menu, which includes wine, is a popular choice and good value.

🚹 209 off F2 🖂 5–7 rue de la Bastille, 75004 ☎ 01 42 72 87 82; www.bofingerparis.com 🕓 Mon–Fri noon–3, 6:30–1am, Sat, Sun noon–1am 🚇 Bastille

Brasserie Flo €€
This famous brasserie has branches at the glamorous Au Printemps department store (▶ 70), Roissy airport and even in Barcelona and Amsterdam, but the original Flo still holds fort in this atmospheric location – along a narrow street off the colourful rue du Faubourg St-Denis. Banks of dripping shellfish outside and the bustling wooden-panelled interior tell you right away that you've come to a traditional Parisian brasserie and the food will be wonderful. Friendly, efficient service complements the succulent steaks and fresh fish dishes – sole *meunière* is just one of the classic offerings – while the prune and armagnac *vacherin* (meringue and ice-cream dessert) is a perfect finale to any meal. The wine list is faultless. Brasserie Flo is very busy at weekends until late.

🚹 209 off D5 🖂 7 cour des Petites-Écuries, 75010 ☎ 01 47 70 13 59 🕓 Daily 12–3, 7pm–1:30am 🚇 Château-d'Eau

La Rôtisserie d'En Face €€
Tucked away down a narrow street and across the road from his main restaurant at 14 rue des Grands-Augustins (tel: 01 43 26 49 39), this is Jacques Cagna's cheaper dining option and is usually very busy. The setting here is lively and informal with a good choice of dishes bearing the Cagna hallmark of care and quality. The suckling pig and spit-roast chicken from the rôtisserie are particularly delicious. Look for game in season, and for dessert opt for the delicious fruit tart of the day.

Where to... Shop

Shopping is part of the fun of Paris – and if the stylish haute couture for which the city is famous is beyond your budget, at least there's no charge for window shopping. At the other end of the scale, enjoy the markets – the floral displays of the Marché aux Fleurs near Notre-Dame (➤ 44); Montmartre's famous flea market, Marché aux Puces de St-Ouen, where you may find a bargain, after haggling; or the wonderful Sunday organic market (*marché biologique*) on boulevard Raspail, near Rennes Métro station.

DEPARTMENT STORES

No serious shopping trip would be complete without a visit to the great Paris department stores. **Bon Marché** (24 rue de Sèvres, tel: 01 44 39 80 00, Métro: Sèvres-Babylone) is the best department store on the Left Bank and houses the Grand Épicerie food hall.

The two glamorous grand dames of Paris shopping sit side by side on boulevard Haussmann, and typify the French attitude to style – both in their architecture and their range of goods, including perfumes, jewellery and ready-to-wear fashion. **Au Printemps** (64 boulevard Haussmann, tel: 01 42 82 57 87, www.printemps.fr, Métro: Havre-Caumartin) is the older of the two, opening the doors of its fabulous belle-époque façade in the 1870s, while the **Galeries Lafayette** (40 boulevard Haussmann, tel: 01 42 82 34 56, www.galerieslafayette.com, Métro:

Le Flauvert €€

Excellent regional cooking, especially that of Lyon, is the preserve of this, one of Michel Rostang's five successful and budget-conscious establishments, Les Bistrots d'à Côté, serving modern versions of traditional French dishes. Other branches are at 4 rue Boutard, 92200 Neuilly (tel: 01 47 45 34 55) and 24 place du Marché St-Honoré, 75001 (tel: 01 49 26 90 04). Specialities include a range of wonderful fish dishes, tempura of langoustines, chicken and *foie gras* tart, and calves' kidneys with red wine sauce. For dessert, try the warm melt-in-the-mouth chocolate soufflé. There is also an affordable wine list.

🕀 206 off A5 ⊠ 10 rue Gustave-Flaubert, 75017 ☎ 01 42 67 05 81; www.michelrostang.com ⓜ Tue–Fri noon–2, 7:30–11:30, Sat 7:30–11:30 Ⓜ Courcelles

Taillevent €€€

Named after Guillaume Tirel, the 14th-century chef, known as Taillevent, this is Paris's most enduring "grand" restaurant, whose panelled walls and discreet service help to create a civilized and refined ambiance favoured by the great and the good of the city's establishment. There is a wonderfully old-fashioned and classic basis to the cooking, with only a few modern trends. Specialities at Taillevent include *foie gras*, lobster and truffles. The delicious chocolate dessert served with an unusual thyme ice-cream will round off your meal in style. For food and surroundings of this quality, prices are not outrageous and there is a good-value set lunch menu.

🕀 206 B5 ⊠ 15 rue Lamennais, 75008 ☎ 01 44 95 15 01; www.taillevent.com ⓜ Mon–Fri 12:15–2, 7:15–9:30. Closed Sat, Sun, Aug Ⓜ George V

🕀 208 B2 ⊠ 2 rue Christine, 75006 ☎ 01 43 26 40 98; www.jacquescagna.com ⓜ Mon–Thu noon–2:30, 7–11; Fri 12–2:20, 7–11:30; Sat 7–11:30. Closed Sat lunch, Sun Ⓜ Odéon/St-Michel

Chaussée d'Antin, Opéra, Trinité) was completed in 1912 with a glass cupola topping the atrium.

FOOD

Place de la Madeleine is home to two of the greatest luxury gourmet emporia, **Fauchon** at 24–26, (tel: 01 70 39 38 00, closed Sun, Métro: Madeleine) and **Hédiard** at 21 (tel: 01 43 12 88 88, closed Sun). These are a must for all *épicures*.

Alléosse, off avenue des Ternes, is one of the finest cheese shops in the city, where Camembert, *Époisses*, *Reblochon* and goat's cheese are brought to the peak of maturity (13 rue Poncelet, tel: 01 46 22 50 45, closed Sun afternoon, all day Mon, Métro: Ternes). **La Ferme St-Aubin** (76 rue St-Louis-en-l'Île, tel: 01 43 54 74 54, closed Mon, Métro: Pont-Marie) has some 200 French and European cheeses on offer, all in peak condition. **Barthélemy (Sté)** is an old-fashioned cheese shop which supplies the homes of both

the president and prime minister of France, well-stocked with Brie, Mont d'Or, Roquefort and many other delights (51 rue de Grenelle, tel: 01 42 22 82 24, open Tue–Sat, Métro: rue du Bac).

For chocolate, try **Christian Constant** (37 rue d'Assas, tel: 01 53 63 15 15, Métro: Rennes) and **Debauve et Gallais** (30 rue des Sts-Pères, tel: 01 45 48 54 67, Métro: St-Germain-des-Prés).

Les Caves Augé (116 boulevard Haussmann, tel: 01 45 22 16 97, Métro: St-Augustin) is the oldest wine shop in Paris.

FASHION AND ACCESSORIES

Colette is the place to go for leading designs in both fashion and home furnishings – from Givenchy's Alexander McQueen to Tom Dixon and the latest from Sony (213 rue St-Honoré, tel: 01 55 35 33 90, www.colette.fr, Métro: Palais-Royal/Tuileries/Pyramides). The Water Bar, which has more than 100 brands of

bottled water, in the basement is a good place for a snack.

The *crème de la crème* of haute couture and one of the most exclusive shopping streets anywhere, is rue St-Honoré in the 1st *arrondissement*. A stroll westwards from Palais-Royal reveals a roll-call of famous designer names. Rue Cambon, crossing rue St-Honoré, is where **Chanel** is based – the place for chic clothing, though the accessories are a little more affordable (31 rue Cambon, tel: 01 42 86 26 00, www.chanel. com, Métro: Concorde/Madeleine).

It's easy to spot **Louis Vuitton**'s store outside (101 avenue des Champs-Élysées, tel: 0810 810 010, Métro: George). **Avenue Montaigne**, which crosses the Champs-Élysées, is a chic street lined by the likes of **Christian Dior, Dolce & Gabbana, Celine, Nina Ricci, Ungaro** and **Valentino**. **Armani**, (18 avenue Montaigne, tel: 01 42 61 55 09, Métro:

Concorde), has a state-of-the-art store not far from **Sonia Rykiel**'s ready-to-wear fashion house at No. 175 boulevard St-Germain, with its range of accessories and cosmetics (tel: 01 49 54 60 60). **Yves Saint Laurent** has a store for women (38 rue du Faubourg Saint Honoré, tel: 01 42 65 74 59, Métro: Concorde/ Madeleine; www.ysl.com). The YSL shop for men is at No.12 (tel: 01 43 25 84 40, Métro: Mabillon).

A small enclave of designer boutiques is located around **place de la Victoire**, which joins rue des Petits Champs and rue Étienne Marcel. A branch of innovative designer **Jean-Paul Gaultier**'s main store (44 avenue George V, tel: 01 44 43 00 44, Métro: George V) is located here in Galerie Vivienne.

Agnès B, northwest of the Forum des Halles, is an international chain of high repute, offering sharply-cut clothes with original details (2–19 rue du Jour, tel: 01 40 39 96 88, Métro: Réamur Sébastapol).

Where to...
Be Entertained

CINEMA

Mainstream and art-house cinemas are numerous across the city, generally showing films in their original languages. Check out the listings pages in *Pariscope*.

UGC Ciné Forum Les Halles (7 place de la Rotonde, tel: 08 92 70 00 00) is a 19-screen multiplex showing the latest releases. **La Pagode** (57 rue de Babylone, tel: 08 92 68 93 25, Métro: St-François Xavier) is probably the city's most charming cinema: shipped over in sections from Japan, it has velvet seats, painted screens and a Japanese garden. Cult classics and recent arty releases are shown in their original language on two screens. **La Géode** (26 avenue Corentin-Cariou, tel: 08 92 68 45 40, Métro: Porte de la Villette) has a vast hemispheric screen, and shows movies specially adapted to its unusual technology.

THEATRE AND CONCERTS

The capital's greatest diversity of entertainment venues is located between the Louvre and the Arc de Triomphe on the Right Bank. Look out for concerts held in some of the most spectacular churches around the city, which are often free.

The Orchestre Nationale de France is based at **Maison de Radio-France** (116 avenue du Président-Kennedy, tel: 01 56 40 12 12), which also offers numerous free classical concerts and operas throughout the year. The **Théâtre des Champs-Elysées** hosts opera,

ballet, classical and chamber music orchestras. The imposing **Opéra Palais Garnier** offers a repertoire of beautifully staged operas and ballets (place de l'Opéra, tel: 08 92 89 90 90; www.opera-paris.fr, closed Aug, Métro: Opéra).

The **Comédie Française** presents quality productions by masters such as Molière and Shakespeare (2 rue de Richelieu, tel: 01 44 58 15 15, closed Jul–Sep, Métro: Palais Royal).

NIGHTLIFE

You'll find infinite variety in the city. The **Caveau de la Huchette** nightclub (5 rue de la Huchette, tel: 01 43 26 65 05, closed Sun, Métro: St-Michel), in medieval cellars, is always busy at weekends, with a lively mix of swing, boogie and rock. **Aux Trois Maillets** (56 rue Galande, tel: 01 43 54 00 79, Métro: St-Michel) is a terrific jazz café. **Le Saint** (7 rue St-Séverin, tel: 01 40 20 43 23, open Tue–Sat,

Métro: St-Michel) is a small dance club playing music including techno and R&B.

If you speak some French, *Chansonniers* (singing cabarets) make a great night out with their mix of popular music and sharp-edged repartee. **Au Lapin Agile** (22 rue des Saules, tel: 01 46 06 85 87, closed Mon, Métro: Lamarck-Caulaincourt) is one of the best – book ahead. Montmartre is known for the rather *risqué* **Moulin Rouge** (82 boulevard de Clichy, tel: 01 53 09 82 82, Métro: Blanche). The **Lido de Paris** offers an excellent dinner and a spectacular show featuring the Bluebell Girls and special effects, twice nightly (116 bis avenue des Champs-Élysées, tel: 01 40 76 56 10).

Le Dépôt is a huge dance factory and a cult venue for the gay community in the heart of the Marais district (10 rue aux Ours, tel: 01 44 54 96 96, Métro: Étienne-Marcel). Expect techno, house, disco and cabaret theme nights.

Northwest France

Getting Your Bearings

A coastline riddled with little sandy bays and dotted with fishing ports marks out the northwest corner of France. To the west, around Brittany's rugged peninsulas, the landscape is rockier and rougher, with ancient stones set upright in endless rows at Carnac. Eastwards through Normandy and Picardy the sands sweep more generously, and the holiday resorts are correspondingly more chic.

Of the bigger cities, Rouen and Rennes hold considerable historic interest, but the major harbour ports such as Brest and Le Havre are more workaday places, rebuilt after World War II. Motorways make for quick access inland and along the coast from Calais and other main Channel ports, but the real pleasure of this area is to be found away from the main roads, in the little towns and villages of rural Normandy and Brittany.

Inland from the sheltered bays, picturesque harbours and fishing ports you'll discover an ancient landscape

Cap de
la Hague

Cherbourg ✈ ☐ Barfleur

**D-Day
Beaches** 10

Valognes ☐

Channel Islands/
Iles Normandes

Parc Naturel Régional
des Marais du Cotentin
et du Bessin 2

Bayeux

Coutances ☐ St-Lô

Golfe de St-Malo

BASS
NORMA

St-Pol-de-Léon   Lannion   ☐ Paimpol   Granville

Côte d'Émeraude

Île
d'Ouessant   ☐ Ploudalmézeau   Morlaix   **St-Malo** 4

Flers ☐

Guingamp   **Mont St-Michel** 3   Avranches

Brest   N12   St-Brieuc   N176   ☐ Do

Le Conquet   **St-Thégonnec** 12   **Dinan** 11   Fougères

Parc Nat. Rég.
d'Armorique   Carhaix-
Plouguer   **BRETAGNE**   A84

Douarnenez   N164   Loudéac   Montauban   Vitré

Le Faouët   N164

Quimper   Pontivy   Ploërmel   **Rennes** 5   N157

St-Guénolé   Quimperlé   N24   N24

Lorient ☐   Vannes   Redon

Carnac 13   N165

Belle-Île

in the west, where small communities such as St-Thégonnec take pride in their local tradition of carved stone calvaries and enclosed cemeteries. The rolling farmland of Normandy is a richer landscape, with timbered houses and great abbeys set amid orchards of cider apples and pears.

This land has been fought over for centuries, and you can follow trails of recent history – the battlefields of World War I around Amiens, and the D-Day beaches of World War II to the north of Caen.

★ **Don't Miss**

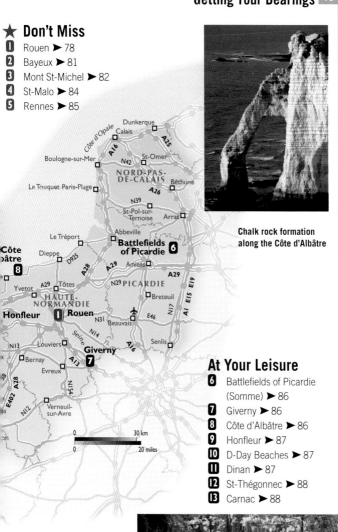

Chalk rock formation
along the Côte d'Albâtre

At Your Leisure

Page 73: Fishing boats in the
harbour at Honfleur
Right: Curved rustic footbridge
in the idyllic wooded gardens at
Giverny, Claude Monet's home

In Three Days

If you're not quite sure where to begin your travels, this itinerary
recommends a practical and enjoyable three days exploring
Northwest France, taking in some of the best places to see using
the Getting your Bearings map on the previous page. For more
information see the main entries.

Day 1

Morning
Plan to spend most of your day exploring ❶ **Rouen** (➤ 78–80). Start at
the **tourist office** on place de la Cathédrale (➤ 80), look into the **cathedral**
(➤ 78–79), and stroll around the **old quarter** to the northeast of here.

Afternoon
After lunch at **Dame Cakes** (➤ 90), visit the **Musée des Beaux-Arts** (➤ 79).

Evening
Take the D982 west towards Le Havre, then the N15 and turn south
on the D929 to spend the evening in one of the restaurants around the
picturesque harbour at ❾ **Honfleur** (➤ 87).

Day 2

Morning
Head west on the minor coastal roads, passing through Ouistreham
and the atmospheric ❿ **D-Day Beaches** (below; ➤ 87). Turn inland on
the D516 to reach ❷ **Bayeux** (➤ 81) and its famous tapestry. Dine at the
historic inn **Le Lion d'Or** (➤ 81).

Afternoon
Take the D572 to St-Lô, then head south towards Avranches via the coast roads, then the minor D43 to the unmissable island-bound abbey of **8 Mont St-Michel** (➤ 82–83).

Evening
Spend the evening, and enjoy the peace after the day-trippers have moved on, before taking the D797 and D155 to **St-Malo** (above) for the night.

Day 3

Morning
Explore the historic port of **4 St-Malo** (➤ 84), enjoying the views from the ramparts, and consider whether to take an extra day here and include the **Cap Fréhel Drive** (➤ 187–188) in your itinerary. Lunch on crêpes at **La Gallo** (➤ 84).

Afternoon
Head west along the coast, then south from Ploubalay on the D2 to visit the medieval town of **11 Dinan** (➤ 87–88). Continue south on the D68, joining the N137 into **5 Rennes** (right; ➤ 85), where the old masters in the **Musée des Beaux-Arts** and the timbered buildings of **rue de la Psalette** are must-see attractions.

RUE
DE LA PSALLETTE
MAISON DU XV.e SIECLE
C.on N.O.

❶ Rouen

Rouen, the capital of the Normandy region, is a thriving city with a compact historic heart. Despite severe bomb damage sustained during World War II, the centre of the old city has been restored with care and sensitivity, making it a fascinating place to explore. Rouen straddles the River Seine, and its two outstanding landmarks are the magnificent medieval Gothic cathedral, and the place du Vieux Marché, where Joan of Arc, the heroine who led the French army successfully against the occupying English, was burned at the stake on 30 May 1431 at the age of just 19.

A port at Rouen was established in **Roman times**, but the city's fortunes were made with the arrival of the Dukes of Normandy in the Middle Ages. The **magnificent medieval timbered buildings** bear witness to its later success as it served as France's fourth major port. The spectacular cathedral of **Notre-Dame** was built between the 12th and

The majestic and slow-moving Seine at Rouen

16th centuries, and is a highlight of any tour of the city. Its **distinctive spire** stands 151m (495ft) high.

Just along the pedestrianized rue du Gros Horloge is another famous landmark, a huge **one-handed clock**, which is mounted on a carved Renaissance arch above the street. The clock dates back to the 14th century, and was moved to this highly visible location in the 16th century.

West again from here is **place du Vieux Marché**, where a large cross marks the spot where Joan of Arc was martyred. In the northeast corner stands a remarkable modern church (1981) dedicated to the saint, which incorporates stained glass from a much older church that was destroyed during the bombing raids of World War II.

The famous one-handed clock dates from the 14th century

Two sites to the northeast of the cathedral are worth a closer look. One is the 14th-century church of **St-Ouen**, with its superb truncated, lacy Gothic spire. In the churchyard here, Joan of Arc recanted when first threatened with being burned to death, on 24 May. The other is a pretty courtyard

of timbered buildings called the **Aître St-Maclou**, on rue Martainville (open Apr–Oct 8–8, Nov–Mar 8–7, free).

It was built on the site of a charnel house, in use after the Great Plague of 1348 swept through the town, and is now occupied by the School of Fine Arts.

There's an impressive collection of paintings to see in the **Musée des Beaux-Arts**, including works by Renoir and Monet.

Gustave Flaubert (1821–80)

Flaubert is the **city's most famous son**. The great novelist and scourge of bourgeois society, notorious for keeping a parrot on his desk while writing *Un coeur simple* (*A Simple Heart,* 1877), was born at 51 rue de Lecat. His best-known novel was also his first, *Madame Bovary* (1857), about the adulterous love affair, downfall and eventual suicide of a provincial doctor's wife.

The tale was condemned and the author prosecuted, unsuccessfully, for immorality, causing a great scandal of the day.

Gustave Flaubert was the son of a noted surgeon in the town, and his birthplace doubles as an intriguing museum dedicated to the history of medicine.

TAKING A BREAK

Dame Cakes (➤ 90) is behind the cathedral and is perfect for lunch or afternoon tea.

The spires of
the Palais de
Justice

🗗 222 C4
Tourist Information Office
✉ 25 place de la Cathédrale, BP 666, 76008 ☎ 02 32 08 32 40;
www.rouen.fr; www.rouentourisme.com ⏰ May–Sep Mon–Sat 9–7, Sun
and public hols 9:30–12:30, 2–6; Oct–Apr Mon–Sat 9–6, Sun and public hols
10–1, 9:30–12:30, 1:30–6. Closed Sun

Musée des Beaux-Arts
✉ esplanade Marcel-Duchamp, 76000
☎ 02 35 71 28 40 ⏰ Wed–Mon 10–6 💶 Inexpensive

Musée Flaubert et d'Histoire de la Médicine
✉ 51 rue de Lecat, 76000
☎ 02 35 71 28 40 ⏰ Wed–Sat 10–noon 💶 Inexpensive; under 18s free

---

ROUEN: INSIDE INFO

Top tips The old centre of Rouen is compact enough to **explore easily on foot**,
so don't worry about métro maps and bus routes. The railway station is also
central and has good connections to Paris.

■ Start any visit by calling in to the tourist office, opposite the cathedral.
  Dating from 1509, it is Rouen's **oldest Renaissance building**, and the place
  where Monet sat to paint his famous *Cathédrales de Rouen* (1892–3).

■ The **Carte Rouen Vallée de Seine en Liberté** gives visitors to Rouen discounts on
  accommodation and museum entry.

■ Time your visit to coincide with the **annual Joan of Arc cultural festival**, in the
  last week of May. On the last Sunday of that month, children throw flowers
  from the Boïeldieu Bridge in memory of the saint, whose ashes were
  scattered from the same spot. Her feast day is celebrated on 30 May.

Hidden gem In local antiques shops you're likely to see the distinctive local
blue-and-white pottery or faïence known as Rouenware. It gets a museum all
to itself, the **Musée de la Céramique** (94 rue Jeanne d'Arc, tel: 02 35 07 31 74,
open Wed–Mon 10–1, 2–6, inexpensive).

One to miss Unless you're a particular fan of 17th-century dramatist Pierre
Corneille, skip the **Musée Corneille** at 4 rue de la Pie.

2 Bayeux

An extraordinary account of the invasion of England in 1066, Bayeux's famous tapestry reads like a medieval cartoon, as fresh today as when it was stitched in the 11th century. It's the highlight of this preserved small town: visit out of season or be prepared to wait in line for this top attraction.

TAPESTRY FACTS

Commissioned by Bishop Odo, half-brother of William the Conqueror
Length 70m/230ft
Width 50cm/20in
Stitched by nuns from 1070 to 1080
Made in England

See the **tapestry** around the walls of its own museum, well signed in the town centre. It's actually an embroidery, using wool on linen, and the **accompanying exhibition** gives an insight into its design and creation. The margins at the top and bottom of the tapestry repay closer study – while some of the designs are purely ornamental forms such as dragons and whimsical curls, other sections depict side-aspects to the main action, such as fallen warriors. **Multilingual audioguides** help to pick out notable events, including the arrival of Halley's Comet and the assassination of King Harold.

Elsewhere in the town, the 11th- to 15th-century **cathedral** is worth a look for its relief carving, which depicts the murder of English archbishop Thomas à Becket in Canterbury in 1170. The Normandy Landings of 1944 are commemorated in the **Musée Mémorial**.

TAKING A BREAK

For a top-notch lunch of regional specialities, try the 18th-century former coaching inn **Le Lion d'Or** (71 rue St-Jean, tel: 02 31 92 06 90, closed Jan).

Detail of the tapestry showing William steering the ship

🔢 221 F4
Tourist Information Office
✉ Pont St-Jean, 14400 ☎ 02 31 51 28 28; www.bayeux-tourism.com
🕐 Apr–Jun, Sep–Oct Mon–Sun 9:30–12:30, 2–6; Jul–Aug Mon–Sat 9:30–7; Sun 9:30–1, 2–6; Nov–Mar Mon–Sat 9:30–12:30, 2–5:30

Bayeux Tapestry
✉ Centre Guillaume Le Conquérant, rue de Nesmond ☎ 02 31 51 25 50;
www.tapisserie-bayeux.fr
🕐 Mid-Mar–mid-Nov daily 9–6:30 (7 in May–Aug); mid-Nov–mid-Mar 9:30–12:30, 2–6 🎫 Moderate

Musée Mémorial de la Bataille de Normandie
✉ boulevard Fabien Ware, 14400 ☎ 02 31 51 46 90 🕐 Jan–Apr daily 10–12:30, 2–6; May–Sep 9:30–6:30; Oct–Dec 10–12:30, 2–6 🎫 Moderate

❸ Mont St-Michel

Mont St-Michel is a must-see on every visitor's itinerary, an unmistakable vision rising from the shallow waters of its own bay on the north coast. The site, perched high on a rock, just off-shore, has been drawing pilgrims since the first century. Although the sheer number of visitors threatens to choke it at the height of summer, the fairytale appearance of the mount, with a village huddled below and the rock topped by the 157m (515ft) Gothic spire of the abbey church, cannot fail to delight the eye.

The first chapel was built here by St Aubert, Bishop of Avranches, in 708. Benedictine monks built a Romanesque church on the rock between the 11th and 17th centuries, transporting the granite blocks across the quicksands from the Îles Chausey to the north. A guided tour of the **abbey** reveals a treadmill, which operated a pulley system to haul the building materials up to the site. The **gold statue** of St Michel on the tip of the spire was added in 1897. There's still a monastic community here, which helps to counterbalance the touristy feel of the village below.

The Mount is linked to the mainland by **a causeway**, north of Pontorson, but an engineering project to dig out the silt and return the sea to this part of the bay means this will eventually be replaced by a bridge. The present car park by the causeway is to be replaced with a bigger one, 1km (0.5 mile), on the mainland. The parking charge will include a free shuttle bus service to the Mount. The work is due to be finished by 2012. Buses go to the mount from Rennes and St-Malo, the former connecting in the morning with the TGV rail link at Rennes. The nearest railway station, Pontorson, is 9km (5.5 miles) away.

The peaceful cloisters and gardens of the abbey

READY-SEASONED LAMB
You may see *Mouton pré-salé* on the menu in restaurants, this is a naturally pre-salted lamb that is considered a great delicacy throughout France. It comes from the sheep that graze the salty pastures and samphire at the margins of the Baie du Mont St-Michel. It is a seasonal dish and usually served lightly grilled and doesn't require any additional seasoning.

Pilgrims have visited Mont St-Michel since the first century

TAKING A BREAK

Enjoy the seafood and the views over the bay from **Du Guesclin**, on Grande Rue. There's even a kids' menu (tel: 02 33 60 14 10, closed Nov–Mar).

✚ 221 E3
Tourist Information Office
✉ BP4, Mont St-Michel 50170 ☎ 02 33 60 14 30; www.ot-montsaintmichel.com ⏰ Mar Mon–Sat 9:30–2:30, 2–6, Sun 9:30–12, 2–5; Apr–Jun, Sep Mon–Sat 9–6:30, Sun 9–10:30, 2–6; Jul–Aug daily 9–7; Oct Mon–Sat 9:30–12:30, 2–5:30, Sun 9:30–12, 2–5; Nov–Feb daily 10–12:30, 2–5

The Abbey
☎ 02 33 89 80 00; www.monum.fr ⏰ May–Aug daily 9–7; Sep–Apr 9:30–6 💶 Moderate; audioguide available 💶 Moderate (free during midday mass)

MONT ST-MICHEL: INSIDE INFO

Top tips If the Grand Rue is choked with visitors, make your way straight up to the **abbey ramparts**, from where the views are superb.
- The swift, incoming tides make the bay dangerous. The tourist office can provide information about safe guided walks around the bay.
- In July and August there are night visits to the abbey (Mon–Sat 7–10:30).

④ St-Malo

The most magnificent and appealing of the Channel ports, St-Malo has a rich history of adventurers and pirates to discover, along with 1.6km (1 mile) of walls around the restored old town centre. This area, known as the Intra Muros (within the walls), includes outdoor cafés and stylish shops.

The heart of St-Malo was bombed out during World War II, and what you see today is a careful reconstruction, including the **Cathédrale St-Vincent** with its medieval stained glass. A mosaic here recalls the navigator Jacques Cartier (1491–1557), who discovered and first explored Newfoundland in Canada. The massive grey Fort National holds a **museum of local history**, including information about nautical heroes and villains such as privateers René Dugay-Trouin and Robert Surcouf, who brought such wealth to the town.

The small golden sand beach at St-Malo

Climb the steps on to the 14th-century **ramparts** for the best views, with the old town on one side, the sea on the other, and Dinard on the opposite bank of the Rance estuary. You can also follow the causeway out to the rocky tidal island of **Grand Bé**, where the romantic writer Châteaubriand (1768–1848) is buried.

TAKING A BREAK

Tuck into the local speciality – freshly made *crêpes*, with savoury or sweet fillings, at **Le Gallo**, a venerable *crêperie* in the old part of town (21 rue de Dinan, tel: 02 99 40 84 17).

✚ 221 E3
Tourist Information Office
✉ esplanade St-Vincent, 35400 ☎ 08 25 13 52 00;
www.saint-malo-tourisme.com 🕐 Apr–Jun, Sep Mon–Sat 9–12:30, 1:30–6:30, Sun 10–12, 2–6; Oct–Mar Mon–Sat 9–12:30, 1:30–6. Closed Sun

Cathédrale St-Vincent
✉ place Jean de Châtillon ☎ 02 99 40 82 31 🕐 Daily 9:45–6

Fort National
✉ Château de St-Malo 🕐 Closed Mon, Sep–Jun 🎟 Inexpensive

5 Rennes

The Breton capital is a fine old mixture of 15th-century timbered houses and grand 18th-century architecture in the classical style, imposed after a devastating fire all but destroyed the city in 1720. Today it's a bustling, sprawling place with its own (single) métro line and a wide industrial hinterland, but the centre has some notable features that make it well worth exploring.

The Tourist Information Office is a good place from which to start exploring the old town, the area bounded by the place des Lices market square and the Ille and Vilaine rivers, which largely escaped destruction by the fire.

Top of the attractions is the **Musée des Beaux-Arts**, with a host of paintings by the old masters, including Rubens and da Vinci, as well as more modern works by the likes of Gauguin and Picasso. Look out for the 16th-century carved wooden altar panels in the **Cathédrale St-Pierre**, and admire the restored timber-framed roof of the **Palais du Parlement de Bretagne**. When you've looked in the cathedral, stroll along the **rue de la Psallette** just behind it for some of the best medieval houses in Rennes. Saturday is market day in the place des Lices, with fresh vegetables galore (ends 1pm). This is a great place to purchase provisions for a picnic, which you can take to the hilltop **Parc du Thabor**, a public park.

The attractive half-timbered houses and shop frontages date from the 17th century

TAKING A BREAK

Treat yourself to traditional roast sausage with apple *compote* at **Le Bocal-P'ty Resto** (6 rue d'Argentré, tel: 02 99 78 34 10, Métro: République).

✚ 221 E2
Tourist Information Office
✉ 11 rue St-Yves, 35000
☎ 02 99 67 11 11;
www.tourisme-rennes.com
🕐 Sep–Jun Mon–Sat 10–6, Sun 11–1, 2–6; Jul–Aug 9–7, Sun 11–1, 2–6

Musée des Beaux-Arts
✉ 20 quai Émile Zola, 35000
☎ 02 23 62 17 45;
www.mbar.org 🕐 Wed–Sun 10–12, 2–6, Tue 10–6
💶 Inexpensive

At Your Leisure

6 Battlefields of Picardie (Somme)

The gentle farmland around the River Somme today seems a world away from the muddy trenches of World War I, but the vast, neatly tended graveyards are a poignant reminder that more than one million young men died in the appalling fighting here. The 60km (37-mile) **Circuit de Souvenir**, starting from the town of Albert and signed with a poppy, takes in the key battlefields, cemeteries and museums. Sites include the dramatic **Mémorial Franco-Britannique** at Thiepval, which recalls 73,367 French and British soldiers whose bodies were never found, and the Canadian **Vimy Parc Memorial** at Vimy Ridge.

➕ 226 C1

Tourist Information Office

✉ 9 rue Léon Gambetta, Albert, BP 82, 80300
☎ 03 22 75 16 42; www.ville-albert.fr 🕐 Apr–Sep Mon–Fri 9–12:30, 1:30–6:30, Sat 9–noon, 2–6:30, Sun 10–12:30; Oct–Mar Mon–Fri 10–12:30, 1:30–5, Sat 9–noon, 3–5

7 Giverny

Claude Monet's home and the garden that inspired his series of water lily paintings are well worth a detour, especially in early summer when the gardens look their best. Monet, born in Paris in 1840, was a founder of the Impressionist school of painting, capturing light and colour in his landscapes. He lived here from 1895 until his death in 1926, by which time he was a recluse. The gardens, willow-fringed ponds and wooden bridge will be familiar to anyone who has admired his paintings, and the interior of the house reflects the artist's delight in colour and pattern.

➕ 224 C4

Tourist Information Office

✉ 36 rue Carnot, 27201 Vernon
☎ 02 32 51 39 60; www.cape-tourisme.fr
🕐 May–Sep Tue–Sat 9:30–12:30, 2–6, Sun 10–12; Oct–Apr 9–12:30, 2–5:30; closed Sun

Memorial to the fallen at Thiepval

Fondation Claude Monet

✉ 84 rue Claude Monet, 27620 ☎ 02 32 51 28 21; www.fondation-monet.com 🕐 Apr–Nov daily 9:30–6 💶 Moderate

8 Côte d'Albâtre

Tall white cliffs along the seaboard from Le Havre to Le Tréport have earned the epithet the "Alabaster Coast". The scenery is most magnificent at **Étretat**, which has long been a place of inspiration for writers and painters. There is an easy walk from the town centre to see the enormous **rock arch of the Falaise d'Aval**. Dieppe is a working Channel port with some lively streets and a château transformed into an art gallery. **Fécamp**, meanwhile, is renowned as the place that produces Benedictine liqueur. The distillery is housed in an extraordinary building and can be visited.

➕ 222 B5

Tourist Information Office

✉ Pont d'Ango, 76204 Dieppe
☎ 02 32 14 40 60; www.dieppetourisme.com; www.seine-maritime-tourisme.com 🕐 May, Jun, Sep Mon–Sat 9–1, 2–6, Sun 10–1, 2–6; Jul–Aug Mon–Thu 9–1, 2–6, Fri–Sat 9–1, 2–7, Sun 10–1, 2–5; Oct–Apr Mon–Sat 9–12, 2–6

9 Honfleur

Honfleur is an old harbour town with tall slate-fronted and timbered buildings, fishing craft and romantic corners, and it's easy to see why. Eugène Boudin (1824–98) was born here and became one of the first artists to paint outdoors. You can catch his work, including local views, in the **Musée Eugène Boudin**, in place Erik Satie. The square is named after the composer and Honfleur's second famous son, who is celebrated in the **Maison Satie** on boulevard Charles V. There are lots of good fish restaurants to explore at leisure, too.

222 B4

Tourist Information Office

quai Lepaulmier, 14600 02 31 89 23 30 Easter–Jun Mon–Sat 9:30–12:30, 2–6:30, Sun 9:30–12:30, 2–5; Jul–Aug daily 9:30–7; Sep 10–12:30, 2–6:30; Oct–Easter Mon–Sat 9:30–12:30, 2–6

Musée Eugène Boudin

place Erik Satie 02 31 89 54 00 Wed–Mon 9:30–12:30, 2–6 (until 6:30 Easter–Jun, 7 Jul–Aug) Moderate

Maison Satie

boulevard Charles V 02 31 89 11 11 May–Sep Wed–Mon 10–7; mid-Feb to May and Oct–Dec Wed–Mon 11–6; closed Jan Moderate

10 D-Day Beaches

The beaches of the Normandy coast along the **Baie de la Seine** became the focus of the war in Europe on the night of 5 June 1944, when Allied troops began a massive invasion from England to kick-start the liberation of France. Parachute and glider forces of the American 88th and 101st Airborne Division led the way, followed by 4,000 landing craft, which arrived on the five key beaches at dawn, code-named Sword, Juno, Gold, Omaha and Utah. A **free booklet** from local tourist offices, *The D-Day Landings and The Battle of Normandy*, outlines events and locations, including **Arromanches, the American cemetery** at Colleville-sur-Mer, and the **Mémorial Pegasus museum** in Ranville.

222 A4

Tourist Information Office

place St-Pierre, 14000 Caen 02 31 27 14 13; www.caen.fr/tourisme Apr–Jun, Sep Mon–Sat 9:30–6:30, Sun 10–1; Jul–Aug Mon–Sat 9–6, Sun 10–1, 2–5; Oct–Mar Mon–Sat 9:30–1, 2–6

11 Dinan

The cobbled **rue de Jerzual**, at the heart of this medieval town, is one of the most photographed streets in all Brittany. Explore the narrow lanes of the old quarter on foot, past timbered merchants' houses (the best are on **place Merciers**) and the Gothic **Église St-Malo**, and the

The picturesque harbour at Honfleur, famously depicted by Eugène Boudin

The cobbled reu de Jerzual in the centre
of the medieval town of Dinan

Basilique St-Sauveur, where the
remains of a 14th-century soldier
and local hero, Bertrand du Guesclin,
lie entombed. Sections of the town's
ramparts can still be followed,
and you can climb the 16th-century
clock tower, presented to the town
by Duchesse Anne in gratitude for
refuge, for great views over and
beyond the town.

⊞ 221 D3
Tourist Information Office
✉ 9 rue du Château, 22105 ☎ 02 96 87 69
76; www.dinan-tourisme.com 🕐 Jul–Aug
Mon–Sat 9–7, Sun 10–12:30, 2:30–6; Sep–Jun
Mon–Sat 9–12:30, 2–6

🔟 St-Thégonnec

If you see only one traditional Breton
parish close, then this is the one
to go for – St-Thégonnec has one of
the finest, most exuberantly carved
examples in the country. The calvary
dates from 1610, and its many stone
figures are in medieval dress. They
portray the events of Christ's Passion,
but slightly out of order – the cross
was dismantled and hidden for safety
during the Revolution, and may
have been wrongly reassembled.

The interior of the church is an
ostentatious revelation of the wealth
of this parish in the 17th and
18th centuries, with statues and
altarpieces, and a magnificent carved
wooden pulpit.

⊞ 220 B3 🕐 Daily 9–6; Jul–Aug 9–7 (no visits
during Sunday mass at 10:30)

🔟 Carnac

More than 3,000 standing stones
and other prehistoric monuments
are found in and around Carnac,
dating to between 5000 and 2000BC.
Three of the biggest groups of stones
(*menhirs*) are carefully set in long
parallel lines (*alignements*) to the
north of the town, and their purpose
– religious, astrological or ritual – is
a total mystery. Wander among the
stones at **Kermario** and discover the
extent of this extraordinary site from
the scale model in the information
centre there, open daily.

The nearby resort of **Carnac-Plage**
has six beaches, with plenty of bars,
restaurants and luxurious villas.

⊞ 220 C1
Tourist Information Office
✉ 74 avenue des Druides, Carnac ☎ 02 97 52
13 52 (Carnac-Plage); www.carnac.fr 🕐 Apr–
Sep Mon–Sat 9–12:30, 2–7, Sun 9–12:30

FOR KIDS

- **Carnac:** When they tire of gazing
  at standing stones, buy them a
  niniche, or long, thin lollypop,
  which is a speciality of the
  Quiberon region of Brittany, and
  available in local sweet shops.
- **Dinan:** Discover the zoo and
  playground in the grounds of the
  Château de Bourbansais, east of
  town at Pleugueneuc (tel: 02 99
  69 40 07; open Apr–Sep daily
  10–7; Oct–Mar 2–6; expensive).
- **Plailly:** Cartoon heroes Astérix
  and Obélix star at Parc Astérix,
  with all the rides, shows and
  attractions you could hope for.
  The park is signed off the A1
  between Paris and Lille (tel: 08
  26 30 10 40, www.parcasterix.fr,
  open Apr–Oct; expensive).

Where to...
Stay

Prices
Expect to pay per night for a double room
€ under €120   €€ €120–€220   €€€ over €220

Hôtel de la Digue €
La Digue, a hotel since 1922, looks over the bay of Mont St-Michel. Its 35 spacious bedrooms have views of the bay and the abbey, and by night are peaceful, once the day-trippers have gone home. The restaurant shares the same magnificent view. WiFi and parking are also included.
➕ 221 E3 ⊠ 24 Grande Rue, 50116 Le Mont St-Michel ☎ 02 33 60 14 02; www.ladigue.eu

Hôtel des Abers €–€€
This friendly hotel lies within the walls of the old city, behind a gorgeous 16th-century façade. There are 14 well-appointed and comfortable rooms. Coffee and tea is on tap in the reception area, and for a change of menu, try the Indonesian restaurant next door, also part of the hotel.
➕ 221 E3 ⊠ 10 rue de la Corne-du-Cerf, 35400 St-Malo ☎ 02 99 40 85 60; www.abershotel.com

L'Absinthe €€
For a small hotel with character, try this former presbytery, which offers just 11 rooms and one suite. There's lots of wooden panelling, stained glass in the reception area, beamed ceilings and luxuriously draped curtains. The facilities are up to date and each room has its own Jacuzzi. Breakfast is an extra €12.
➕ 222 B4 ⊠ 1 rue de la Ville, 14600 Honfleur ☎ 02 31 89 23 23; www.absinthe.fr

La Butte de St-Laurent €
Josselin is a pretty village to the southwest of Dinan, and this cosy bed-and-breakfast stands on top of the *butte*, or small hill, which gives it its name. It also gives it superb views over the village and the nearby château. There are just four bedrooms, and the large garden makes it a delight for children as well as adults. Rooms are located under the eaves (no smoking). Credit cards are not accepted here.
➕ 221 D2 ⊠ 56120 Josselin ☎ 02 97 22 22 09; www.chambres-bretagne.com
🕒 Closed mid-Sep to Jun

Le Relais de Fréhel €
Cap Fréhel is a rugged point on the Emerald Coast (▶187), and this restored farmhouse is a great place from which to explore this northern shore. The building is a *longère* – a long, narrow farmhouse typical of this part of Brittany, with an extensive garden and even a tennis court. There are five bedrooms.
➕ 221 D3 Broute du Cap. Plévenon, 22240 Fréhel ☎ 02 96 41 43 02; www.relaiscapfrehel.fr 🕒 Closed mid-Nov to Apr

Manoir de Lan Kerellec €€–€€€
Beautiful renovated 19th-century manor house with breathtaking views over Brittany's Côte de Granit Rose. The 19 rooms are all individually decorated and those at the front of the house overlook the rocky bay. The gastronomic restaurant sits under an unusual towering wooden vaulted ceiling, and has picture windows also making the best of the views (closed for lunch Mon–Thu). The gardens are wonderful on a warm evening.
➕ 221 E3 Ballée centrale de Lan-Kerellec, 22560 Trébeurden ☎ 02 96 15 00 00; www.lankerellec.com

Where to…
Eat and Drink

Prices
Expect to pay per person for a meal, excluding drinks

€ under €30   €€ €30–€60   €€€ over €60

Dame Cakes €
This English-style tea room, restaurant and shop close to the cathedral is a useful place for snacks and lunch (the menu changes every month). There is an enclosed terrace to sit out in good weather.
☗ 222 C4 ⊠ 70 rue Saint Romain, 76000 Rouen ☎ 02 35 07 49 31 ⓘ tea rooms and shop 10:30–7; restaurant 12 –3

La Ferme St-Siméon €€€
For a gourmet treat, book a meal at this classy restaurant overlooking the sea. It is housed in a 19th-century mansion which is also a hotel and beauty spa – and it is said

that Claude Monet and fellow artists stayed here. The menu is pricey but the quality makes it worthwhile, with dishes such as mouth-watering lobster risotto, oysters, and langoustines with caviar.
☗ 222 B4 ⊠ 4 Rue Adolphe Marais, 14600 Honfleur ☎ 02 31 81 78 00; www.fermesaintsimeon.fr ⓘ Wed–Sun 12:30–2, 7:30–9:30, Tue 7:30–9:30

La Marine €–€€
Enjoy views over the river and the château from the terrace of this modern, airy restaurant, while you tuck into the local crêpe "La Josselinoise". It's filled

with a fragrant concoction of black pudding and fried apples. If you prefer, "L'Automne" has a combination of sweet chestnut purée and apple and pear jam, and if this all sounds too much, then there are plenty of crêpe-free and vegetarian choices on the menu, too. Children have their own menu. Book ahead in summer.
☗ 221 D2 ⊠ 8 rue du Canal, 56120 Josselin ☎ 02 97 22 21 98 ⓘ Jul–Aug daily noon–1:45, 7–9; Sep–Jun Mon–Tue 12–1:45, Wed–Sun 12–1:45, 7–9

Le Catelier €€
This restaurant, close to the botanic garden in Rouen, has a stylishly designed interior. Daniel Atinhault acts as sommelier and front-of-house, while his wife Marie-France is the chef. Take your pick from the good value prix-fixe menus, but seafood is at the top of the bill, with fresh lobster served in a salad with cider-butter and fried apples, or perhaps turbot in a mouth-watering white wine sauce.

☗ 222 C4 ⊠ 134 bis avenue des Martyrs de la Résistance, 76100 Rouen ☎ 02 35 72 59 90 ⓘ Tue–Sat noon–2, 7–9. Closed 3 weeks in Aug

Les Embruns €€
Look for this restaurant among the hotels close to the beach in St-Malo doubles as an art gallery – the paintings on the walls are for sale. You can choose your own lobster from the display tank, or sample scampi with mayonnaise, or salmon with asparagus. It's not all fish and seafood – lamb's kidneys served with purple Brive mustard are another highlight of the menu.
☗ 221 E3 ⊠ 120 chaussée du Sillon, 35400 St-Malo ☎ 02 99 56 33 57; www.restaurant-les-embruns.com ⓘ Tue–Sat 12–2, 7–10, Sun 12–2; closed Jan

Les Marissons €€–€€€
An ancient shipyard on the banks of the River Somme is an unusual location for a restaurant, but Les Marissons is worth seeking out. There's a lovely garden, and the

and apple juice) from local orchards on sale at the organic market in Honfleur, **Le Marché Bio** (Place Sainte-Catherine, open Wed 8:30–1).

Striped nautical sweaters are a Breton classic, and you'll find them in lots of places. One of the best is **Armor Lux** in Quimper (Centre Commercial Géant, tel: 02 98 53 20 18, open Mon–Sat 9–7). You can also book ahead for a tour of the factory where they've been making the garments for more than 60 years (tel: 02 98 90 05 29).

Nautical clothing is also sold at **Galeries de Ker Iliz** (8 rue du Général de Gaulle, Perros-Guirec, tel: 02 96 91 00 96, open Apr–Sep daily 10–noon, 2-30–7; Oct–Mar closed Sun pm and Mon am). It is an extensive mall that specializes in Breton crafts, and you'll also find locally made porcelain, Celtic jewellery and wood carving here.

Where to... Shop

Beyond the cities in this part of France, you'll discover local suppliers of regional delicacies, including cheeses and apple products, such as Calvados.

Saturday markets are a feature across France, and always good places to source local cheeses and other distinctive produce. For a great setting amid the historic, timbered houses of Honfleur, try its **Marché Traditionnel** (place Sainte-Catherine, Sat 9:30–12:30, where locally caught fresh fish is sold alongside the more usual array of fruit and vegetables.

There's also a **Farmer's Market** on Friday mornings at Dury, in Picardie, where you can buy home-made *foie gras* and preserves, as well as local honey, flowers and organic vegetables (facing IME, route de Paris, Fri 8:30–1:30).

Apples are a regional speciality, and at Villerville, just west of Honfleur, you'll find cider, Calvados and *pommeau* (a blend of Calvados

FOOD AND DRINK

Take the drive to Cap Fréhel (▶ 187) and you'll discover one of the best *pâtisseries* in Brittany. **Patissier-Chocolatier R. Jouault** is located in a modest building in Fréhel, but has been awarded the European Lauriers d'Or for its *kouignamann*, an almond cake. *Palet de Fréhel* – a nougat made with almond and chocolate depicting the Cap – is another speciality (place de Chamblis, tel: 02 96 41 41 31, open daily 8–8, Easter to mid-Sep; mid-Sep–Easter Fri–Sun 8–7).

15th-century buildings have an attractive blue and yellow décor. The menu varies according to season, but you might find locally caught eels (smoked, or perhaps stewed in a fragrant sauce of herbs), duck pie and *gâteau battu* – a sugared brioche. On fine days, you can dine outside on the terrace.
➕ **223 D5** 🗺 **Pont de la Dodane, Quartier St-Leu, 8000 Amiens** ☎ **03 22 92 96 66** 🕐 **Mon–Fri 12–2, 7–10, Sat 7–10**

Le Relais Saint Aubin €€

This restaurant, housed in a restored 17th-century country priory close to the Cap Fréhel coast has an elegant yet cosy dining room and a terrace to eat in summer. The chef's specialities are roasts but the fresh fish, seafood and regional dishes are also excellent. Try the oysters, *coquilles de St Jacques*, lobster or duck and pork terrines.
➕ **221 D3** 🗺 **Lieu dit Saint Aubin, 22430** ☎ **02 96 72 13 22; www.relais-saint-aubin.fr** 🕐 **Jul–Aug Tue–Sun 12–1:30, 7–9; Sep–Jun Wed–Sun 12–1:30, 7–9**

Where to...
Be Entertained

While families may prefer the traditional and simple pleasures of resorts such as St-Malo, younger visitors head for the bright lights of the bars and clubs in Rennes. With its racecourse, blackjack tables and film festival, Deauville is the place for gambling with the jet set.

CASINOS

If gambling is your thing, then try the Casino Barrière at Dinard (4 boulevard Wilson, tel: 02 99 16 30 30, www.lucienbarriere.com, open Sun–Thu 10am–3am, Fri-Sat 10am–4am, over-18s only), where you can play roulette, blackjack and stud poker, hit the one-armed bandits and enjoy the beach views from the cocktail bar.

Big shots will want to head for Deauville's famous seafront Casino (rue Edmond Blanc, BP 32400, tel: 02 31 14 31 14, www. lucienbarriere.com, open Mon–Thu 10am–2am, Fri 11am–3am, Sat 11am–4am, Sun 10am–3am), where the building is belle époque, the dress code formal, and you can divide your time between the intensity of the gaming tables, the gourmet delights of three restaurants and the nightclub.

THEATRE AND CINEMA

St-Malo has one of the biggest theatres in the area, with big touring productions, concerts and opera (6 place Bouvet, tel: 02 99 81 62 61; www.theatresaintmalo.com, open Tue–Sat).

Rennes has the Théâtre Nationale de Bretagne (TNB) which includes concert halls and a cinema in its complex (1 rue St-Hélier, tel: 02 99 31 12 31, www.t-n-b.fr, open Tue–Sat), and the Péniche Spectacle. This rather unusual venue occupies two barges, L'Arbre d'Eau and La Dame Blanche that have been converted to host a wide range of live music, jazz and cabaret performances, and a variety of interesting exhibitions (quai St-Cyr; tel: 02 99 59 35 38; www.penichespectacle.com).

Le Théâtre du Pays de Morlaix is a great venue for local and world music events as well as plays, movies and dance, while its Wednesday evening street performances in the height of summer, are also a popular tourist attraction (20 rue Gambetta, Morlaix; tel: 02 98 15 22 77, performances daily 8pm).

The four-screen cinema at St-Lô, Le Drakkar, shows all the usual mainstream blockbusters and some independent films in their original language (29 rue Alsace-Lorraine, tel: 08 92 68 01 31, open daily).

CLUBS

If you want to boogie the night away in Paimpol, try the piano-bar Le Pub, which has a bar on the ground floor, dancing upstairs and music for all ages (3 rue des Islandais, tel: 02 96 20 82 31, open May–Sep Tue–Sun 9pm–5am; Oct–Apr 9pm–4am).

Quiberon has its own rum bar, Bar le Nelson, where you can taste up to 54 different sorts of rum to the retro-pop beat (20 place Hoche, tel: 02 97 50 31 37, telephone for opening times).

At Blonville-sur-Mer, near Deauville, Les Planches is a lively nightclub with one dance floor (of two) dedicated to music from the 1960s to the 1990s (Domaine du bois Lauret, tel: 02 31 87 58 09, closed Sun Sep–Jun).

Northeast France

Getting Your Bearings

The northeast is France's richest and most varied border country, sharing boundaries and influences with Belgium, Luxembourg, Germany and Switzerland. There is much to see, and many gastronomic treats to enjoy along the way.

Above: Superb Reims Cathedral
Right: Outdoor café in Strasbourg

The vibrant city of Lille, close to the seaport of Dunkerque, is the capital of the plains to the north of the region, while Strasbourg, home of the European Parliament, is queen of the south. In the middle come the chalky hills of the Champagne-Ardenne country, which spreads out to the south of the great cathedral city of Reims. Some of France's greatest waterways are found to the south of here, including the rivers Seine and Marne and canals such as the Canal de Bourgogne.

To the east, the lively cities of Metz and Nancy are, respectively, current and one-time capitals of the formerly independent Lorraine. In the southeast the verdant mountains of the Vosges form a natural barrier, with the River Rhine on the far side marking the German border. Dijon, with a medieval heart overlaying Roman foundations, is the focus for the southwest corner, while nearby Beaune is a must-see historic highlight.

A good network of motorways ensures easy access to all the major cities in this area, as well as west to Paris, south to Lyon and across international frontiers. The Route des Vins d'Alsace is a 170km (105-mile) driving route celebrating local wine production that goes from Marlenheim, just west of Strasbourg, south to Thann, which lies just west of Mulhouse.

Page 93: The shuttered, half-timbered houses of Riquewihr

In Four Days

If you're not quite sure where to begin your travels, this itinerary recommends a practical and enjoyable four days exploring Northeast France, taking in some of the best places to see using the Getting your Bearings map on the previous page. For more information see the main entries.

Day 1

Morning
Start at ❶ Lille (➤ 98–99), with a morning dedicated to exploring the landmarks of the city and shopping at the **Centre Euralille** (➤ 99). Have lunch at La Chicorée (➤ 99).

Afternoon
Wander through the collection of old masters at the **Palais des Beaux-Arts** (➤ 98–99). Then head south out of town, picking up the A26/E17 autoroute or the slower N43/N44, to spend the night near Reims.

Day 2

Morning
Make an early start and explore the heart of the historic city of ❷ Reims (➤ 100), with a tour of its World Heritage sites and a quick visit to a Champagne cave. Lunch at **Le Grand Café** (➤ 100).

Afternoon
Head southeast on the A4 autoroute towards Metz, stopping off to visit the World War I sites at ❻ Verdun (➤ 108). Reach the attractive old city of ❼ Metz (➤ 108), and either plan to stay here and perhaps catch a concert of classical music in the evening, or continue south on the A31 to ❽ Nancy (left; ➤ 109).

Day 3

Morning
Continue southeast to reach **3 Strasbourg** (above; ➤ 101–103), a lively city at the heart of the European community. Visit the tourist office by the **cathedral** (➤ 103), and hire bicycles to travel around and get your bearings. Dine on local fare by the riverside (➤ 103).

Afternoon
Treat yourself to modern art and folk art in the city's top museums (➤ 102), and perhaps a one-hour river cruise by **bateau-mouche** (➤ 103).

Evening
Try out the city's nightlife at a themed bar (➤ 116).

Day 4

Morning
Head southwest on the N83/E25, passing through **11 Colmar** (➤ 110), pausing to see the Issenheim altarpiece in the Musée d'Unterlinden. Continue west on the A36/E60 via **12 Besançon** (➤ 111) to reach **4 Dijon** (➤ 104–105) in time for a late lunch washed down with a glass of *kir*.

Afternoon
Explore Dijon at leisure, before finally driving southwest to historic **5 Beaune** (➤ 106–107), with its magnificent Hôtel-Dieu.

ⓞ Lille

Lille is a major city, with one of the country's most prestigious art museums, and plenty of historical interest that makes for enjoyable exploring. Add to that one of the best shopping centres at Euralille, a fun Sunday market at Wazemmes and a sprinkling of historic gems, and you've got the makings of a perfect short-break destination.

Lille has always been a prosperous and vibrant trading town, and its prime location at a hub of main waterways and major land routes made it a valuable prize as it passed between French, Spanish, Burgundian, Flemish, Dutch and – during the two world wars – German hands. Its excellent transport links today make it a highly accessible to visitors from all over Europe, including Britain.

The elaborate frontage of one of Lille's top shopping malls

At its heart is the handsome, broad square known as **Grand' Place**, surrounded by tall, 17th-century buildings in brick and white Lezennes stone, and little side-streets with cafés and bars. The square is officially named after the city's most famous son, Général Charles de Gaulle (1890–1970). His **birthplace** north of here is now a dedicated museum, celebrating the life of the wartime hero who led the country in the vital post-war period and rose to be the first president of the Fifth Republic in 1958.

Markets take place in different quarters on different days (► 115), and modern shopping is based around **Euralille**, between the two railway stations east of Grand' Place.

Palais des Beaux-Arts

It's well worth setting aside an hour or two of your visit to explore this world-class collection of fine art, amassed in a former palace to the south of the Grand' Place. The Flemish

The elegantly stark exterior of the cathedral

and Dutch masters are well represented, as you might expect so close to the Belgian border, and 40 Raphael cartoons are a highlight of the displays. There are many works by French artists, too, including Impressionists Monet and Renoir. For local interest, there are the great military engineer Vauban's models for the **Citadelle**, a star-shaped fortress of 1670 that lies west of Grand' Place.

Retail Therapy

Centre Euralille is a massive temple to the modern goddess of shopping, in the east of the Old Town and next door to the bizarrely ski-boot-shaped Gare de Lille Europe train station. There are around 140 retail outlets in the mall, which opened in 1994 as part of a futuristic 70ha (173-acre) development designed by Dutchman Rem Koolhaas. There is also a massive concert hall, a hypermarket and plenty of restaurants to collapse in when you've shopped 'til you've dropped.

TAKING A BREAK

Sample the onion soup or perhaps the rabbit at **La Chicorée**, an appealing brasserie in the town centre (15 place Rihour, 59000, tel: 03 20 54 81 52).

✚ 226 C2
Tourist Information Office
✉ Palais Rihour, place Rihour, BP 205, 59002 ☎ 08 91 56 20 04; www.lilletourism.com ◷ Mon–Sat 9:30–6:30, Sun 10–12, 2–5

Maison Natale Général de Gaulle
✉ 9 rue Princesse ☎ 03 28 38 12 05 ◷ Wed–Sat 10–12, 2–5, Sun 1:30–5:30 ▯ Inexpensive

Palais des Beaux-Arts
✉ place de la République ☎ 03 20 06 78 00 ◷ Mon 2–6, Wed–Sun 10–6, Fri 10–7. Closed first weekend in Sep ▯ Inexpensive

LILLE: INSIDE INFO

Top tips Lille is particularly **well connected**: just 40 minutes by train from Brussels, an hour by TGV from Paris, and only two hours from London on the Eurostar.
- A City Pass from the tourist office allows unlimited travel on buses, trams and the Métro within the city, and even free entry to some museums. Passes cost €18 for one day, €30 for two days and €45 for three.
- If you're not sure where you are, look out for the **town stewards** in their yellow jackets – they're there to help visitors with directions and advice.

One to miss Don't bother with the **guided tour inside the Citadelle** unless you're seriously into military history – you can admire Vauban's five-point design from the encircling Bois de Boulogne park for free.

② Reims

A busy industrial city in the heart of France's Champagne-producing country, Reims has witnessed great events in history including the crowning of 25 sovereigns and the surrender of the Nazis at the end of World War II, in 1945.

The city centre is dominated by the **Gothic Cathédrale Notre-Dame**, which dates back to 1211 and is the result of meticulous restoration. The cathedral is adorned with 2,300 statues, including many angels. Don't miss the inner portal or the stained glass windows.

Adjoining the cathedral is formerly the residence of the archbishops, the **Palais de Tau**, now a museum containing sculptures from the cathedral and displays on the royal coronations in Reims.

Reims' other important historical sight is a short bus ride from the city centre, the essentially 11th-century **Romanesque Basilique St-Rémi**, which, the cathedral, is a listed UNESCO World Heritage Site.

Book a tour and tasting (*dégustation*) at one of the top **Champagne houses** (*maisons de Champagne*) via the tourist office. You can visit the chalk storage caverns of familiar names such as Mumm & Cie, Taittinger and Piper-Heidsieck without prior appointment. Most champagne houses are open daily, though they may close at weekends out of season.

St-Remi's tomb is surrounded by ornately carved statues

TAKING A BREAK

Le Grand Café, at 92 place Drouet d'Erlon, has a large terrace opening on to the square where you can try 13 different varieties of mussels, or tuck into pasta, salads and gâteaux (tel: 03 26 47 61 50).

✚ 224 A4
Tourist Information Office
✉ 2 rue Guillaume de Machault ☎ 08 92 70 13 51; www.reims-tourisme.com
🕐 Apr Mon–Sat 9–6, Sun 10–6; May–Sep Mon–Sat 9–7, Sun 10–6; Oct–Mar Mon–Sat 2–6, Sun 10–1

Basilique St-Rémi
✉ place St-Rémi 🕐 Daily 8–7 or dusk if earlier. Closed during services

Cathédrale Notre-Dame
✉ place du Cardinal-Luçon 🕐 Daily 7:30–7:30. Closed during services

3 Strasbourg

Strasbourg is a city of brilliance, with a picturesque medieval quarter – La Petite France – a remarkable Gothic cathedral and a vibrant attitude to life and culture that comes from its historically tenuous location on the border with Germany. It's a university city, the place where the talents of Gutenberg and Goethe were nurtured, and is now home to the Council of Europe and the ultra-modern architecture of the Palais des Droits de l'Homme (1995), where the European Court of Human Rights sits. Its ancient heart of timbered buildings lies on an island, Grand Île, and the city's blend of ancient and modern is bewitching.

Cathédrale de Notre-Dame de Strasbourg

The single spire of this red sandstone edifice towers above the roofs of the city, offering a great view from its platform, 332 steps and 142m (465ft) up. Added in 1439, it was the crowning glory to a cathedral started in 1015, and paid for by the people of the town. Look out for a stork, symbol of Strasbourg, carved on the western facade. Lacy stonework on the exterior is reflected in the elaborate design of the organ inside. In the south transept, behind the carved, three-sided Pillar of Angels, stands an elaborate astronomical clock – at 12:30 it comes to life as the Apostles parade before Christ, the rooster crows and flaps its wings, and Death strikes the hour.

The elegant Ponts-Couverts on the edge of La Petite France

Museum Choices

There are several excellent museums in the city, and three
of the best are located under one roof in the 18th-century
bishops' palace, **Palais Rohan**. Exhibits cover all periods from
prehistory up to the 19th century, including art by Giotto,
Boticelli, El Greco and Corot, and you'll find archaeology in
the basement, decorative arts on the ground floor and fine art
upstairs. The story is brought up to date with photography
and graphic art, as well as paintings by Monet, Picasso,
Gustave Doré and others, in the **Musée d'Art Moderne et
Contemporain**, west of Petite France. For a less sophisticated
but thoroughly engaging view of Alsatian culture, cross the
River Ill and walk south to the **Musée Alsacien**, dedicated to
humbler folk art and crafts of the region.

City of Bridges

The bridges which criss-cross the river and canals are a
distinctive feature of the city. The most famous are the three
Ponts Couverts (Covered Bridges) on the western tip of
Grand Île, on the edge of the Petite France district, though
they lost their wooden roofs in the 19th century. They are
strung in a line, punctuated by four tall, severe square towers,
which were intended for defence and later served as prisons.

Another bridge with a grim reputation is the **Pont de
Corbeau** (Raven Bridge), on the south side near the 14th-
century Customs House. In days gone by, unlucky criminals
were locked in cages and thrown from its stonework to drown
in the river below.

**The Ponts
Couverts were
originally built
to reinforce
the town's
defences**

TAKING A BREAK

For a taste of local Alsatian cuisine, call in at **À l'Ancienne Douane**, by the river, and sample the delicious *flameküche* (thin-crust pizza) and *sauerkraut* (6 rue de la Douane, tel: 03 88 15 78 78).

➕ 222 E3
Tourist Information Office
✉ 17 place de la Cathédrale, 67082 (also an office at place de la Gare
☎ 03 88 52 28 28; www.ot-strasbourg.fr ⏰ Mon–Sat 9–7

Cathédrale de Notre-Dame de Strasbourg
✉ place de la Cathédrale ☎ 03 88 43 60 32 ⏰ Mon–Sat 7–11:20, 12:35–7, Sun 12:40–7. Viewing platform: Apr–Jun and Sep 9–7:30; Jul–Aug daily 9–10; Oct–Mar 10–5:30 💰 Inexpensive

Palais Rohan (Musée Archaeologique, Musée des Arts Décoratifs, Musée des Beaux-Arts)
✉ 2 place du Château ☎ 03 88 52 50 00 ⏰ Mon, Wed–Fri 12–6, Sat–Sun 10–6 💰 Inexpensive

Musée d'Art Moderne et Contemporain
✉ 1 place Hans-Jean Arp ⏰ Tue–Wed, Fri 12–7, Thu 12–9; Sat–Sun 10–6 💰 Inexpensive

Musée Alsacien
✉ 23–25 quai St-Nicolas ☎ 03 88 52 50 01 ⏰ Wed–Mon 10–6 💰 Inexpensive, under-18s free

STRASBOURG: INSIDE INFO

Top tips The three-day **Strasbourg-Pass**, available from the tourist office (€11), gives visitors free admission to one museum and reductions at other attractions, plus a free *bateau-mouche* river tour, access to the cathedral tower and a day's cycle rental.
■ You can visit the **European Parliament** during the week but only on a guided tour as part of a group and by prior reservation, tel: 03 88 17 20 07. The building is 2km (1.2 miles) east of the centre, and tours last one hour.
■ **Christmas street markets** bring the city to life in winter. Catch them from late November through December at place Broglie, by the railway station and in front of the cathedral.
■ **Boat trips on the River Ill** offer a different perspective of the city. *Bateaux-mouche* leave from near the Palais Rohan, and tours last around an hour.

Hidden Gem Seek out weekday tranquillity in the 3.5ha (8.5-acre) **botanic garden** on rue Goethe, part of the university, where more than 6,000 different plant species flourish. Access is free, and the site is open Mar–Apr and Sep–Oct Mon–Fri 8–6, Sat–Sun 10–6; May–Aug Mon–Fri 8–7:30, Sat–Sun 10–7:30; Nov–Mar Mon–Sat 8–12, 2–4, Sun 2–4.

One to miss Unless your time is unlimited, bypass the **Musée de l'Oeuvre Notre-Dame** on place du Château, which tells of the building of the cathedral and acts as an overspill for replaced statues and other relics.

❹ Dijon

The city of Dijon is famed for its gastronomical delights, with a pleasantly walkable centre bursting with boutiques, bars, green parks, historic buildings and interesting galleries and museums. It's also the home of *kir*, a refreshing aperitif made from a blend of the local white wine and *crème de cassis* (blackcurrant liqueur).

Originally a Roman settlement, Dijon rose to prominence in the 14th century as the seat of the powerful dukes of Burgundy, and its medieval wealth can still be seen in the buildings at its heart. Seek out the little streets behind the Palais des Ducs, such as **rue Verrerie** and **rue des Forges**, which recall the trades – glass and ironworks – that once flourished there. **Rue de la Chouette** is named after the owl, a symbol of the town that you will also see carved on a side-wall of the Gothic **Église Notre-Dame**.

Rue de la Liberté is filled with stylish boutiques and restaurants

For contrast, the **place de la Libération** is an elegant crescent of houses dating from the 17th century. The arcades beneath are occupied by appealing little boutiques and restaurants. **Rue de la Liberté** is the main shopping street, its arteries filled with cafés and interesting food shops, and markets are held in and around the 19th-century covered market, **Les Halles**.

Musée des Beaux-Arts

This outstanding museum shares a roof with the town hall, in the 18th-century ducal palace. There's a great collection of paintings and sculptures, including some modern and

CUTTING THE MUSTARD

Strong and flavoursome, **Dijon mustard** is known across the world, and a pot or two makes a great souvenir. Brown or black mustard seeds are crushed before being emulsified in verjuice – a wine made from unripe grapes. It's still produced to a standard set down by the Dijon Academy in the 19th century, but the name is not fiercely protected by a patent in the way that Champagne is, so make sure you're buying the local stuff. **Fallot** is a trustworthy and renowned company.

Timbered house at the corner of Vauban and rue Amiral Roussin

contemporary art. Don't miss the carved 14th- and 15th-century tombs of Philip the Bold, first Duke of Burgundy, and his quarrelsome son John the Fearless, murdered in 1419.

TAKING A BREAK

Maison Millière, at 10 rue de la Chouette, sells regional products and gifts, and has a restaurant and tea room serving 20 tea varieties to accompany its pastries (tel: 03 80 30 99 99). To find it, look for the animal figures on the roof.

⊞ 224 B1
Tourist Information Office
✉ place Darcy, 21000 (also a smaller office at 11 rue des Forges)
☎ 08 92 70 05 58; www.dijon-tourism.com ⏱ Apr–Sep Mon–Sat 9:30–6:30, Sun 10–6; Oct–Mar Mon–Sat 9:30–1, 2–6, Sun 10–4

Musée des Beaux-Arts
✉ Palais des Ducs et des États de Bourgogne ☎ 03 80 74 52 70 ⏱ May–Oct Wed–Mon 9:30–6; Nov–Apr 10–5 💷 Inexpensive, under-18s free, free on Sun

---

DIJON: INSIDE INFO

Top tips The **Dijon-Côte de Nuit Pass** (visitor pass) available from the tourist office, offers excellent value for money (€18 for one day, €32 for two days, €45 for three days). It includes a guided walking tour, free entry to most of the museums and unlimited bus travel.

■ **Take your own tour** around the town's historic buildings for free by following the red arrows on the ground and reading the multilingual information boards at each site. The *Owl's Trail* guidebook, available from the tourist office (€2.50), gives more details.

5 Beaune

The irresistible wine capital of Burgundy, the lovely old town of Beaune has one of the most remarkable medieval buildings in France, with a tiled roof that is an icon of the area.

The arcaded penthouse of the Hôtel-Dieu

Beaune's prosperity was built on a foundation of trade in cloth, iron and wine, and today its ancient centre of narrow cobbled streets and pretty squares is a delightful distraction as you while away the time and perhaps plan a visit to one of the famous wine cellars or a stroll around the ramparts. The **Musée du Vin**, in a former palace of the dukes of Burgundy, is worth a look.

Hôtel-Dieu

If a charitable hospital for the poor founded in 1443 by Nicolas Rolin and his wife Guigone de Salins, sounds a dispiriting and worthy sort of place, don't be put off: this is Beaune's must-see attraction.

Rolin was the wealthy chancellor of Philip the Bold, and at the age of 67, felt the need to make an ostentatious gesture of bounty in this world in order to bag his place in the next. Inspired by hospitals he had seen in Flanders, he commissioned this superb structure, sparing no expense.

Painting showing the annual grape harvest

The most notable feature is the steep roof around three sides of the interior coutyard, covered with coloured, glazed tiles in rich geometric patterns. An open gallery runs below, supported on slender pillars. Inside there are the vaulted wards, the great hall and the old kitchens. Among the tapestries, fine furniture and medical exhibits here, look out for the superb painted polyptych of the Last Judgement, by Flemish painter Rogier van der Weyden, which Rolin commissioned to hang in the chapel.

TAKING A BREAK

La Grilladine is a friendly restaurant between boulevard Bretonnière and rue Gardin, serving Burgundian fare such as *boeuf bourguignon*, *oeufs en meurette* (poached eggs in red wine sauce) and snails (17 rue Maufoux, tel: 03 80 22 22 36).

➕ 218 C5
Tourist Information Office
✉ 6 boulevard Perpreuil, 21203 ☎ 03 80 26 21 30; www.ot-beaune.fr
🕐 Jan–Mar, Nov–Dec Mon–Sat 9–6, Sun 10–12:30, 1:30–6; Apr–May, Oct Mon–Sat 9–6:30, Sun 9–6; Jun–Sep Mon–Sat 9–7, Sun 9–6

Musée du Vin
✉ rue d'Enfer, Hôtel des Ducs de Bourgogne ☎ 03 80 22 08 19 🕐 Apr–Nov daily 9:30–6; Dec–Mar Wed–Mon 9:30–5. Closed Tue Dec–Mar 💶 Moderate. The ticket also gives access to the Museé des Beaux Arts

Hôtel-Dieu
✉ 2 rue de l'Hôtel-Dieu ☎ 03 80 24 45 00 🕐 21 Mar–15 Nov daily 9–6:30; 16 Nov–20 Mar 9–11:30, 2–5:30 💶 Moderate

---

BEAUNE: INSIDE INFO

Top tips There are 15 different **wine cellars**, or *caves*, to visit in the locale, each offering tastings. The tourist office can advise you where to start.

■ The town fills up quickly for the annual grape harvest in September and October, so **book ahead** for a visit at this time.

■ The **Beaune Pass**, available from the tourist office, gives reduced rates for all sorts of activities, from wine cellar tours and tastings to helicopter flights and rides on the *petit train*, which transports visitors around the key sites.

■ The Hôtel-Dieu owns 60ha (148 acres) of prime vineyards around the town, and on the third Sunday in November its **wines are auctioned** to raise funds. It's an event that attracts buyers from around the world.

One to miss Unless you're a dedicated gallery-bagger, skip the **Musée des Beaux-Arts** in the Porte Marie de Bourgogne and make the most of the viticulture instead.

At Your Leisure

6 Verdun

It's estimated that three quarters of a million soldiers died in the terrible fighting that took place along the banks of the River Meuse and around this peaceful little town in the middle of World War I. Today, many of the battle sites are hidden under a blanket of picturesque woodland, but you can get a feel for the time by visiting the restored **Citadelle Souterraine** on avenue du 5ème RAP, an underground French command post (open daily). The village of **Fleury**, 6km (4 miles) northeast, was wiped out during the battle and now has a museum that explains and commemorates events (closed mid-Dec to Feb). Tour buses visit the main wartime sites daily between May and September – contact the tourist office for details.

🔁 224 B4
Tourist Information Office
✉ Maison du Tourisme, place de la Nation, BP 232 55106 ☎ 03 29 86 14 18;
www.verdun-tourisme.com 🕐 Jan Mon–Fri 9–12, 1:30–5; Feb–Mar Mon–Sat 9–12, 1:30–5:30; Apr–Sat 9–12, 1:30–6; May–Sep Mon–Sat 8:30–6:30, Sun 9–4; Oct–Nov Mon–Sat 9–12, 1:30–5; Dec Mon–Sat 9–12, 1:30–5

The magnificent stained glass windows in the Cathedral St-Etienne

7 Metz

Metz (pronounced Mess) is an attractive old city on the Moselle river near the German border, and has changed hands between the two nations a few times in its history. It was most recently restored to France in 1918, after 47 years of German control – influence which can be seen in buildings such as the railway station. Graceful bridges across the River Seille are built of the local dark yellow stone, *pierre de jaumont*. Look out for stained glass by Surrealist Marc Chagall (1887–1985) in the north transept and ambulatory of the 12th-century Gothic **Cathédrale St-Étienne**. The building, on place d'Armes, is nicknamed the *Lanterne du Bon Dieu* (God's lantern) for its lofty interior and 6,500sq m (70,000 sq ft) of windows. You'll find the main shopping area south of here, around place St-Louis. Metz is also known as a centre for classical music, with a summer festival and regular concerts. A branch of the Pompidou Centre is due to open here in 2010.

🔁 225 D4
Tourist Information Office
✉ 2 place d'Armes, BP 80367, 57007
☎ 03 87 55 53 76; www.tourisme.metz.fr
🕐 Apr–Sep Mon–Sat 9–7, Sun 10–5; Oct–Mar Mon–Sat 9–7, Sun 10–3

Enjoy the beautiful woodland views from the Château de Haut Kœnigsbourg

8 Nancy

Eighteenth-century urban planning on a grand scale by a deposed king of Poland made Nancy the attraction it is today. The man responsible was Stanislas Leszczyński, Duke of Lorraine, and the splendid buildings, fountain and gilded gateway of the long central square that now bears his name are his greatest monument. Nancy was also prominent in the art nouveau movement, thanks largely to the efforts of locally born designer Émile Gallé, who founded a glass workshop here in 1874. You can admire his sumptuous works, including furniture, in the fabulous **Musée de l'École de Nancy**, housed in a delightful mansion. The Majorelle Villa and other buildings across the city also reveal the exuberant, organic influence of art nouveau, most notably in window surrounds and doorways throughout the town.

🛑 225 D3

Tourist Information Office

✉ place Stanislas, BP 810, 54011

☎ 03 83 35 22 41; www.ot-nancy.fr

🕐 Apr–Oct Mon–Sat 9–7, Sun 10–5; Nov–Mar Mon–Sat 9–6, Sun 10–1

Musée de l'École de Nancy

✉ 36 rue du Sergent Blandan

☎ 03 83 40 14 86 🕐 Wed–Sun 10–6

9 Château de Haut Kœnigsbourg

This much-visited castle, looming above the woodland west of Sélestat on a crag 757m (2,483ft) high, has attracted controversy since its re-construction in the early 20th century.

It's a debate fed by the ambiguity of the comment inscribed on a fire screen in the great hall by its restorer, Kaiser Willhelm II, on his last visit in 1918: "*Ich habe es nicht gewollt*" ("I didn't want this"). Did he mean World War I, which would see the château returned to French control, along with the region of Alsace, or the neatly executed but dubiously neo-Gothic reconstruction of his medieval castle? You'll have to make your own mind up when you see it.

🛑 225 E3 ✉ 67600 Orschwiller

☎ 03 88 82 50 60; www.haut-koenigsbourg. fr 🕐 Mar, Oct daily 9:30–5; Apr–May, Sep 9:15–5:15; Jun–Aug 9:15–6; Nov–Feb 9:45–12, 1–4:30 🎟 Moderate

⑩ Riquewihr

Riquewihr, in the foothills of the Vosges mountains, surrounded by vineyards, is an essential stop on the 170km (105 mile) Route des Vins d'Alsace, which runs from Marlenheim south to Thann.

Traffic is banned from the cobbled streets, which throng with visitors in summer, eager to sample the local wines in a beautiful setting of mellow stone and timbered buildings decked with scarlet geraniums. Medieval citizens threw up a wall to protect Riquewihr, and parts of this survive, along with two of the gate towers. One of these, the **Tour des Voleurs**, became a prison and you can now visit the a grisly reconstruction of a torture chamber (daily 10:30–1, 2–5).

✚ 225 E2
Tourist Information Office
✉ 2 rue de la 1ière Armée, 68340
☎ 03 89 73 23 23; www.ribeauville-riquewihr. com ◷ Jan–mid-Apr, Oct–Nov Mon–Sat 10–12, 2–5;mid-Apr–Sep, Dec Mon–Sat 9:30–12, 2–6, Sun 10–1

⑪ Colmar

Most visitors finding their way to Colmar do so to visit the **Musée d'Unterlinden** (in the street of the same name), one of the most popular attractions in France. The reason is the dramatic Issenheim altarpiece, the masterwork of Matthias Grünewald, which he painted for a nearby monastery between 1512 and 1516. Eight panels conceal vivid depictions of religious scenes, most famously the agony of Christ on the cross. The museum, in a former Dominican convent, has other treasures, including popular art from the local area.

The town itself, a key location on the Route des Vins d'Alsace, has a charming centre of narrow cobbled streets, timbered houses painted in warm colours and cafés spilling on to pretty squares. The Krutenau district, with its small houses and pretty gardens set around the channels of the River Lauch, is known as **Petite Venise**.

Colmar's most famous son was the sculptor Frédéric Auguste Bartholdi, who created the Statue of Liberty for New York in 1886, and there's a small **museum** in his birthplace on rue des Marchands (Mar–Dec Wed–Mon 10–12, 2–6).

✚ 225 E2
Tourist Information Office
✉ 4 rue d'Unterlinden, 68000
☎ 03 89 20 68 92; www.ot-colmar.fr

The canals of Colmar have earned the town the name of Little Venice

🕐 Apr–Jun, Sep–Oct Mon–Sat 9–6, Sun 10–1; Jul–Aug Mon–Sat 9–7, Sun 10–1; Nov–Mar Mon–Sat 9–12, 2–6, Sun 10–1

Musée d'Unterlinden

✉ 1 rue d'Unterlinden, 68000 ☎ 03 89 20 15 50 🕐 May–Oct daily 9–6; Nov–Apr Wed–Mon 9–12, 2–5 💶 Moderate

🅱 Besançon

This majestic city, capital of Franche-Comté, grew up in a loop of the River Doubs, overlooked by the superb 17th-century Citadelle. Poet Victor Hugo was born here in 1802.

It was a major centre of clock- and watchmaking, and this is celebrated in the fascinating 19th-century **astronomical clock** below the bell tower inside the cathedral, which has 30,000 parts, 57 faces and various automata that come and go on the hour. Learn more at the **Musée du Temps**, which is in the splendid Renaissance Palais Granvelle on Grand Rue, designed for Charles V's chancellor, Nicolas Perrenot (open Wed–Sun from 1pm).

The views from the **Citadelle** are spectacular. The fortress was designed by the great military engineer Sébastien le Prestre de Vauban, and begun in 1668. There are several attractions within its walls, including a zoo and a museum dedicated to the Resistance (open daily).

➕ 219 E5
Tourist Information Office
✉ 2 place de la 1ère Armée Française,25000 ☎ 03 81 80 92 55; www.besancon-tourisme.com
🕐 Mon–Sat 10–6

🅱 Vézelay

Burgundy was the fulcrum of the great monastic movements of medieval western Europe, and the region's most interesting surviving abbey church is the hilltop shrine of Vézelay, a rallying point for pilgrims setting out on the long road to Santiago de Compostela in Spain. Although much restored in the 19th century, the church is still considered to be an undisputed masterpiece of Romanesque art for its wealth of

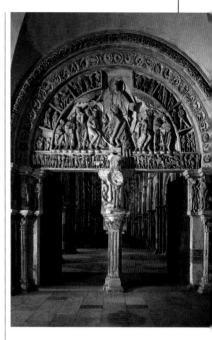

The beautiful romanesque basilica of Sainte Marie-Madeleine in Vézelay

carving on the facade, on the capitals in the aisle and, above all, on the portal in the narthex, the "porch" of the church.

➕ 223 F1
Tourist Information Office
✉ 12 rue Saint-Etienne
www.vezelaytourisme.com ☎ 03 86 33 23 69
🕐 Jun–Sep daily; Oct–May Mon–Wed, Fri–Sat 10–1, 2–6

🅳 Troyes

Troyes was a wealthy city in medieval times – a major centre for the manufacture of stained glass, and a Champagne capital to which merchants came from all over Europe for the great fairs. At the Council of Troyes in 1129 the Catholic Church officially recognized the Order of Knights Templar. Chrétien de Troyes, poet of the great Arthurian romances, was born in the town around 1135.

Today, its medieval heart is still largely intact, with narrow streets and

Statue of the monk Dom Perignon, the inventor of Champagne, in Épernay

rambling timbered buildings housing intriguing small museums, and nine churches with stained-glass windows.

The most interesting of the churches in the centre are the **Cathédrale St Pierre St Paul**, the **Église Saint-Urbain** and the **Église Sainte-Madeleine**, which has an ornate stone rood screen. The **Museum of Modern Art** in the episcopal palace next to the cathedral focuses on the Fauve and Expressionist movements but also has superb works of arts by Picasso and Cézanne.

➕ 224 A2
Tourist Information Office
✉ 16 boulevard Carnot, BP 4082 10018
☎ 03 25 82 62 00; www.tourisme-troyes.com
🕐 Mon–Sat 9–12:30, 2–6:30

🔟 Épernay

They've been making Champagne in Épernay since 1743, and today it's home to some of the greatest labels in the history of bubbly. Vineyards surround the town, and the names of the *maisons de Champagne* read like a top-quality restaurant listing, including De Castellane and Mercier. Moët et Chandon operate **guided tours** of their vast cellars, and you can sample it at their *dégustation* at 18 avenue de Champagne (tel: 03 26 51 20 20, open Apr–Nov daily 9:30–11:30, 2–4:30; Dec–Mar Mon–Fri).

➕ 223 F4
Tourist Information Office
✉ 7 avenue de Champagne, 51201
☎ 03 26 53 33 00; www.ot-epernay.fr
🕐 Mid-Apr to mid-Oct Mon–Sat 9:30–12:30, 1:30–7, Sun 11–4; mid-Oct to mid-Apr Mon–Sat 9:30–12:30, 1:30–5:30

FOR KIDS

- **Beaune**: Take a one-hour interactive tour of the historic Fallot mustard mill, complete with infrared lighting and 3-D animation (La Moutarderie Fallot, 31 Faubourg Bretonnière; tours Mar to mid-Nov Mon–Sat 10am and 11:30am; moderate).

- **Besançon**: The cathedral has one of the best moving clocks of the region, with automata that take off on the hour (➤ 111).

- **Strasbourg**: Treat them to a Christmas market in December, when the city is transformed into a storybook wonderland of wooden chalets selling toys and gingerbread (tourist office, tel: 03 88 52 28 28).

Where to... Stay

Prices

Expect to pay per night for a double room

€ under €120   €€ €120–€220   €€€ over €220

Hostellerie le Maréchal €–€€€

This half-timbered, waterfront hotel, with its floral window boxes, is a charming place to stay. It's in Colmar's "Little Venice" district, and has its own restaurant. The interior has beamed ceilings, period furnishings and canopied beds in most rooms. All 30 bedrooms have power-showers and satellite TV.

🚏 225 E2 ⊠ place des Six Montagnes Noires, 68000 Colmar ☎ 03 89 41 60 32; www.hotel-le-marechal.com

Hôtel Brueghel €

This hotel is conveniently close to the railway station in Lille, on a traffic-free street. It overlooks an attractive Gothic church, and is named after the 16th-century Flemish artist Pieter Breughel. The 65 bedrooms are light and airy, with a decorative style influenced by Breughel.

🚏 226 C2 ⊠ 5 parvis St-Maurice, 59000 Lille ☎ 03 20 06 06 69; www.hotel-brueghel.com

Hôtel de la Cathédrale €

You can't exactly miss this attractive old hotel in the middle of Metz, right by the famous cathedral. It's in a historic town house that dates back to 1627, with interesting period furniture, paintings and objets d'art in the public areas. Some of the 30 bedrooms have wrought-iron bedsteads and beamed ceilings. There is no restaurant but there are plenty of places to eat nearby.

🚏 225 D4 ⊠ 25 place de Chambre, 57000 Metz ☎ 03 87 75 00 02; www.hotelcathedrale-metz.fr

Hôtel du Dragon €–€€

For a special place to stay in the heart of Strasbourg, try this 32-bedroom hotel, which is a pleasing blend of ancient and modern. It is housed in a 17th-century building, but inside you'll find the style is cool and contemporary, with grey-on-grey colour schemes and furniture designed by modern masters such as Mallet Stevens, Philippe Starck and Gaetano Pesce. Ask for a room with a king-size bed.

🚏 225 F3 ⊠ 12 rue du Dragon, 67000 Strasbourg ☎ 03 88 35 79 80; www.dragon.fr

La Gremelle €

This small hotel is perfect if you're touring the Côte d'Or. Rooms are new, well equipped and bright, and with comfortable beds, though bathrooms are small, and there's a pool and sun terrace for relaxing. But what really makes the Gremelle so welcoming is the restaurant. The food is tremendous, with some excellent traditional Burgundian dishes on the menu.

🚏 218 C5 ⊠ RN74, 21550 Ladoix Serrigny ☎ 03 80 26 40 56; www.lagremelle.com

Le Clos Raymi €€

Tuscany, Provence and Champagne are not the views from the rooms, but the names of some of the bedrooms in this comfortable, small hotel in Épernay. It's set in a 19th-century mansion, with a 1930s interior. There are seven bedrooms, and on sunny mornings breakfast is served on the terrace.

🚏 223 F4 ⊠ 3 rue Joseph de Venoge, 51200 Épernay ☎ 03 26 51 00 58; www.closraymi-hotel.com

Where to...
Eat and Drink

Prices

Expect to pay per person for a meal, excluding drinks

€ under €30   €€ €30–€60   €€€ over €60

Alcide €€–€€€

Dine on *moules frites* (mussels and chips) and *potjevleesch* (cold cuts of meat in aspic) at this classic, timber-fronted brasserie near the centre of Lille. Inside, beneath a glass ceiling, the style is 1930s-retro, with comfortable bench seats.

+ 226 C2 ⊠ 5 rue des Débris St-Etienne, 59800 Lille ☎ 03 20 12 06 95; www.restaurantalcide.fr ⓦ Mon–Fri noon–2:30, 7:30–10, Sat 7:30–10, Sun noon–2:30

À l'Huîtrière €–€€

If you're looking for a very special dining experience in Lille, try this top-notch restaurant, set in a venerable house with an art deco frontage. The menu is classic seafood, and the wine list extensive. Inside it's all pale oak panelling and grand Aubusson tapestries.

+ 226 C2 ⊠ 3 rue des Chats Bossus, 59800 Lille ☎ 03 20 55 43 41; www.huitriere.fr ⓦ Mon–Sat 12–2:30, 7:30–10, Sun noon–2:30

Au Crocodile €€€

This gourmet restaurant in Strasbourg owes its reputation to the inventive cooking of chef Émile Jung. The menu, which includes dishes such as lobster served with vermicelli and pink peppercorns with a citrus sauce, gives an idea of the richness of the flavour combinations. The setting is traditional with antique furniture, heavy drapes and wood panelling.

+ 225 F3 ⊠ 10 rue de l'Outre-France, 67060 Strasbourg ☎ 03 88 32 13 02; www.au-crocodile.com ⓦ Tue–Sat 12–1:30, 7:30–9:30. Open some Sun. Closed mid-Jun–mid-Aug

Château Les Crayères €€€

Dine in luxury in this magnificent restaurant, Le Parc, housed in an château standing in its own park. It serves haute cuisine accompanied by the best Champagnes. There is a large terrace out onto the garden. For a slightly cheaper and less formal option try La Brasserie Le Jardin (tel: 03 26 24 90 90), in the château's garden, which specializes in regional cuisine.

+ 224 A4 ⊠ boulevard Henry Vasnier, 51454 Reims ☎ 03 26 24 90 10; www.lescrayeres.com ⓦ Restaurant: Wed–Sun 12–2, 7:15–9:30; Brasserie: daily 12:15–2:30, 7:15–10.30 (until 11 Sat–Sun)

Le Grenier à Sel €€€

Housed in a building dating from 1714, Le Grenier à Sel is overseen by Patrick Fréchin, who has built a reputation in the city for the quality of his classical dishes served in very modern style. Desserts are his speciality with mouth-watering apple tarts a favourite.

+ 225 D3 ⊠ rue GustaveSimon, 54000 Nancy ☎ 03 83 32 31 98; www.legrenierasel.eu ⓦ Tue–Sat 7:30–9.30. Closed 1–15 Aug

Restaurant Stéphane Derbord €€€

This graceful modern restaurant in Dijon serves Burgundian specialities, from crayfish roasted with ginger, pineapple and red pepper compote to black pudding in spicy breadcrumbs. Save space for a dessert such as caramelised pear with ice-cream.

+ 224 B1 ⊠ 10 place Wilson, 21000 Dijon ☎ 03 80 67 74 64; www.restaurantstephanederbord.fr ⓦ Tue–Sat noon–1:15, 7:30–9.15. Closed 1 week late May and 3 weeks Aug

Where to... Shop

There's lots of shopping choice for bargain hunters in this varied area of France – quite apart from all the local food delicacies you might expect to find spread across the region, this is the centre of the country's mail-order retail industry, and huge outlet stores sell designer clothes at discount prices.

Lille is famous for its shopping, and also has a number of markets. **Artisans du Monde** is a French chain dedicated to Fair Trade products. It sells crafts made locally (6 rue du Palais Rihour, tel: 03 20 06 03 12, www.lille. artisansdumonde.org, open Mon 2–7, Tue–Sat 11–7).

To buy original fashion in Lille, try **Le Faubourg des Modes**, which groups together 18 workshop-cum-shops where young designers make and sell their collections (Maison de Mode, 58–60 rue du Faubourg des Postes, tel: 03 20 99 91 20, www. maisonsdemode.com, open Wed–Fri 2–7, Sat 10–7), while **Charles et Charlus** has excellent leather goods (4 rue Basse, tel: 03 20 51 01 01, open Mon 2.30–7, Tue–Fri 10:30–1, 2–7, Sat 10:30–7).

The **Marché aux Livres et aux Fleurs** combines books and flowers in the attractive setting of the courtyard of a 17th-century former stock exchange (Tue–Sun 1–7, Métro: Rihour). The **Marché de Wazemmes**, held in the surroundings of a church, is good for local fruit and vegetables, with antiques and North African items thrown in for good measure (place de la Nouvelle-Aventure, open Sun, Tue and Thu 7am–2pm, Metro: Gambetta). For the biggest second-hand market in the country, time your visit to coincide with the **Braderie de Lille** 24-hour rummage sale (first Sat–Sun in Sep). Around 200km (125 miles) of walkways are lined with stalls selling everything you could possibly imagine.

Strasbourg is famous for its **Christmas markets**, held in December, selling home-made toys and gingerbread. Its weekly market, the **Marché des Producteurs**, attracts growers and buyers from all over Alsace (place du Marché-aux-Poissons, Sat 7–1). Among the city's other shopping treats, sample the outstanding confectionery and cakes at **Patisserie Confiserie Kubler** (29, avenue des Vosges, Strasbourg, tel: 03 88 35 22 27, www.kubler.fr, open Tue–Sun 7:30–7) – the Verger d'Alsace cake, with apple and cinnamon mousse inside, is fabulous.

In Beaune, buy Burgundian cheeses at **Le Tast'Fromages** (23 place Carnot, tel: 03 80 24 73 51, 9–12, 2:30–7, Easter to Christmas Sun: 10–1). Choose from around 120 varieties, including the local Époisses au Marc de Bourgogne and Amour de Nuits-St-Georges.

Dijon is the place for mustard. **Moutard Fallot** is one of France's most respected producers and its mustards are widely available.

CHAMPAGNE

This is the Champagne region of France. Tour the vast cellars before a tasting session to select the best at **Champagne Taittinger** (9 place St-Nicaise, Reims, tel: 03 26 85 84 33, www.taittinger.com, open mid-Mar–mid-Nov daily 9:30–1, 2–5:30; closed weekends mid-Nov–mid-Mar). **Martel**, at 17 rue des Crénaux, offer a tour, showcasing their vintage Brut rosé (tel: 03 26 82 70 67; www.champagnemartel. com; daily 10–7).

Where to...
Be Entertained

There's a buzzing nightlife in Lille, Reims and Strasbourg, while in the smaller towns you'll find cafés that double as bars in the evenings. Look out for summer festivals – one of the best is Les Flâneries Musicales d'Été, held in venues across Reims in July and August. It celebrates classical music and blues with around 100 concerts in a festival started by the great violinist Yehudi Menuhin. Lille also has a great calendar of festivals, including an international film festival in November.

CINEMA

Le Metropole is a modern cinema in Lille, screening retrospectives, with films shown in their original languages and followed by discussions (26 rue des Ponts de Comines, tel: 08 92 68 00 73).

BARS

If you're in Reims head for the **Café de Paris**, a beautifully decorated bistro with a stained-glass ceiling and paintings on the walls. It serves a wide selection of Champagnes by the glass (14, place Myron Herrick, Reims, tel: 03 26 47 52 54, open Mon–Sat from 10am).

It seems that no French city is complete today without its own lively version of the Irish theme pub. The effect may be surreal, but for one of the best, check out **O'Bradys**, which stages live concerts on Fridays from 9pm (4, place de Bordeaux, Reims, tel:

03 88 25 59 91, open Mon–Wed 11am–2am, Thu–Fri until 3am). A different national theme is found at Lille's **Le Kremlin** bar (51 rue Jean-Jacques Rousseau, tel: 03 20 51 85 79, open Mon–Sat 6pm–1am). As the name suggests, it's a Russian bar, with 40 different vodkas on offer, under the watchful eye of a bust of Lenin.

One of the most pleasant bar-restaurants in Metz is **Brasserie Flo**. It is perfect for a drink before or after a show at the nearby Opera or Arsenal theatre, or for dinner (2 bi, rue Gambetta, tel: 03 87 55 94 95, www.flometz.com, open daily 7:30–10:30am, noon–3pm, 7pm–12:30am, closes at 11.30pm Sun–Mon).

NIGHTCLUBS

For a night out in Beaune, try **L'Opera Night** (rue de Beaumarché, Palais des Congrès, tel: 03 80 24 10 11, www.operanight.net, open Fri–Sat 11pm–6am). This a

nightclub complex, with a huge dance floor, music from the 1980s and '90s, a cocktail bar, and the smarter l'Armstrong bar.

In Reims, **Le Vogue** is an urban-techno club where you can dance to some of France's most famous DJs (93, Bd Général Leclerc, Reims, tel: 03 26 47 34 29, www.levogue.fr, open Thu–Sat 11pm–5am, free entry on Thu). **Le Guest Fabulous** club is another place to be seen in Reims (18 avenue de Paris, tel: 03 26 84 05 31, www.guestclub.fr, open Fri–Sat from 11:30pm).

La Laiterie is Strasbourg's home of underground culture (13 rue Hohwald, tel: 03 88 23 72 37, www.laiterie.artefact.org, open Tue–Sat 7:30–11:30pm). Check out the bar, theatre and concert hall.

In Dijon, Complex le Carre (10 rue Marguerite Youcenar, tel: 03 80 74 09 70, www.lecarre.fr) is a nightclub, bowling alley and restaurant, where you can turn early evening entertainment into late hours of dancing.

The Loire

Getting Your Bearings

The Loire is a wide, shallow river that threads slowly westwards through northern France to emerge at the sea beyond Nantes. Its valley and tributaries encompass the ancient provinces of Anjou, Touraine, Orléanais and Berry, making it the historic heart of the country. An end to centuries of struggle against invading English forces came in the mid-15th century, making way for a building boom on a scale of grandeur that is unique in France.

The majority of the magnificent Renaissance châteaux or palaces for which this area is so well known lie along the stretch of river between Angers in the west and Orléans in the east. They range from fairytale turretted piles to more intimate stately homes that are still inhabited, and any visit to the area should try to include a mixture of both.

There is fast *autoroute* access to the main cities, including centrally placed Tours. For exploring at leisure, the most scenic minor roads are to the south of the river.

N12
Mayenne
Laval
Craon
N162
N171
Châteaubriant
PAYS DE LA LOIRE
Nozay
N171
N171
E60
A11
Ange
Pontchâteau
Ancenis
Le Croisic
N23
St-Nazaire   La Loire
A87
Nantes
Vallet   E62
Mayenne
A33   N137
Pornic   Sèvre Nantaise   Cholet
Île de Noirmoutier
Challans
l'Île-d'Yeu

0		60 km
0		40 miles

Page 117: Château de Chenonceau on the River Cher
Left: The sumptuous interior of Château de Cheverny

Getting Your Bearings

★ Don't Miss

At Your Leisure

In Three Days

If you're not quite sure where to begin your travels, this itinerary recommends a practical and enjoyable three days exploring the Loire region, taking in some of the best places to see using the Getting your Bearings map on the previous page. For more information see the main entries.

Day 1

Morning
Start with the biggest and one of the most splendid of the royal châteaux, François I's **❶ Château de Chambord** (➤ 122–123). If you're there early you may be lucky enough to spot some of the park's famous **wildlife** (➤ 123). **Take a picnic** to eat in the grounds, or try the **restaurant** of the château for lunch (➤ 123).

Afternoon
Head the short distance south to see the more intimate **❻ Château de Cheverny** (➤ 128), a privately owned mansion, and still lived in by its owners. Then make your way northwest to the town of **Blois**, and **Le Bouchon Lyonnais** for supper (➤ 124).

Evening
Stay on in Blois and visit the **❷ Château Royal de Blois** (➤ 124) for a spectacular *son-et-lumière* performance.

Day 2

Morning
Visit the romantic and beautiful **❸ Château de Chenonceau** (below; ➤ 125), and take a short **trip on the river**, if there's time, before moving on to the beautiful **❽ Château d'Amboise** (➤ 128–129), with its grim history. Find a **café** in the small town for lunch.

Afternoon

Spend the afternoon sightseeing in **9 Tours** (➤ 129), with some **shopping** thrown in for good measure, or head north on the N138/E502 to **16 Le Mans** (➤ 131) for a sight of gleaming **racing cars** in the museum there.

Evening

Stay on in either **Le Mans** or **Tours** for the **nightlife** (➤ 134).

Day 3

Morning

Spend a morning discovering the delights of picturesque **4 Château d'Azay-le-Rideau** (above; ➤ 126–127), and visit the ancient **Église St-Symphorien** (➤ 127) in the nearby village. Try the cave-built **Les Grottes** (➤ 133) restaurant in **Azay-le-Rideau** for lunch.

Afternoon

Continue west along the Loire valley to the charming "Sleeping Beauty's Castle", **12 Château d'Ussé** (➤ 130), or while away the afternoon n the extensive gardens of **10 Château de Villandry** (➤ 129).

Evening

Take your pick of excellent **restaurants** in the area.

⓪ Château de Chambord

The biggest and architecturally one of the most splendid of the Loire châteaux, Chambord is at the top of many visitors' lists of favourites. Its vital statistics – including 440 rooms and a chimney for every day of the year – defy its purpose as an up-market royal hunting lodge: this was regal ostentation on a grand scale. The interior, stripped of most of its artefacts during the Revolution, is rather bare, but this successfully shows off some architectural oddities that make a visit worthwhile. The surrounding 5,440ha (13,440-acre) park is a setting for special events throughout the summer.

Building the Dream

François I commissioned the château in 1519, on a patch of marshy ground near the River Loire. He later demanded that the river be diverted to surround his palace, but had to make do with a moat instead, fed by a small tributary. Initial construction of the château took 12 years. His main architects were Jacques Sordeau and his nephew Pierre Neveu, and Jacques Coqueau.

However, the most famous name associated with the building of Chambord is that of **Leonardo da Vinci** (1452–1519), who François brought to live at nearby Amboise. The great master is widely credited with the design of the extraordinary Grand Escalier du Logis, an **open-sided double spiral staircase,** by which people could ascend and descend

The château and parkland appears almost dreamlike at dawn

FRANÇOIS I

- 1494 Born in Cognac.
- 1515 Succeeded his uncle, Louis XII, to the throne of France.
- 1519 Lost out in the election for Holy Roman Emperor to Charles IV of Spain, who became a lifelong enemy. Started building the château at Chambord.
- 1520 Met with Henry VIII of England at the Field of the Cloth of Gold, in Picardy, an event named after the lavish tents of the French.
- 1525 Captured in battle against Charles V and ransomed the following year at a cost of Artois, Burgundy, Flanders and various Italian territories.
- 1547 Died and was succeeded by his second son, Henri II.

at the same time without meeting each other, leading up, via the king's bedroom, to a **lantern tower**. It's the most complex and intriguing of 14 large and 60 small staircases in the building.

The **roofscape of Chambord** is its best-loved feature, a forest of turrets and towers, chimneys and columns. Balconies up here allowed the royal party a bird's-eye view of the hunting below.

Successive monarchs added to Chambord, most significantly the theatrical King's Bedroom of 1748, lined with **panelling from Versailles**. Long before that, royalty had lost interest, and Chambord was granted to a succession of owners until finally coming under state control in 1932.

A forest of turrets and chimneys adorns the château

TAKING A BREAK

A small **restaurant at the château** serves excellent food at reasonable prices. There are also plenty of places to picnic in the grounds.

🚼 222 C1 ✉ Château et Domaine National de Chambord, Maison des Réfractaires, 41250 ☎ 02 54 50 40 00; www.chambord.org 🕐 Apr–mid-Jul 9–6:15; mid July–mid-Aug 9–7:30; mid-Aug–mid-Sep 9–6:15 💶 Moderate, under-18's free, accompanied by an adult; under-25s members of the European Union free

CHÂTEAU DE CHAMBORD: INSIDE INFO

Top tips Guided **tours in English** around the château are available daily throughout July and August.
- The park, once a royal hunting forest, is still good for seeing deer, wild boar and other wildlife. Visit the park at **dawn or dusk** for the best chance of spotting them.

Don't miss In the **King's study** a window has been scratched with a message, using a diamond. It is believed that François himself wrote *"Souvent femme varie, bien fol est qui s'y fie"*, which translates as "Women are fickle and it's a fool who trusts them".

2 Château Royal de Blois

The magnificence of this royal palace hides an unrivalled tale of bloody intrigue, while its contrasting architecture reflects changes in fashion across the centuries. The earliest parts of the structure, built around a central courtyard, date from the 13th century. One outstanding feature is the spiral staircase, part of a decorative Italianate wing added by François I, and reminiscent of his work at Chambord (➤ 122–123).

Tours of the château take in the royal bedchamber where a foul murder took place in 1588 at the command of Henri II. The unfortunate victim was Henri, Duc de Guise, a serious political rival to the king's power in France.

As you explore the château and its surroundings, hang on to your entry ticket – it also gives entry to the superb **Musée des Beaux-Arts**, the Gaston d'Orléans wing, St-Calais chapel, the gem-cutters museum and the St-Saturnin churchyard on the opposite bank of the river. The Gaston d'Orléans wing was a later addition in the more reserved classical style, complete with high-pitched roof, by master architect François Mansard (1598–1666).

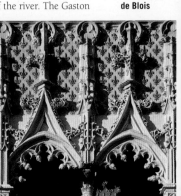

The statue of Louis XII adorning the Château Royal de Blois

For a different view of the château and its history, attend a *son et lumière* show in the courtyard. They're held every evening from the end of April through to mid-September, with commentary in English on Wednesdays.

TAKING A BREAK

A good value option serving local dishes of the region is **Au Bouchon Lyonnais** (25 rue des Violettes, Blois, tel: 02 54 74 12 87).

➕ 222 C1 ✉ place du Château, 41000 Blois ☎ 02 54 90 33 33; www.chateaudeblois.fr ⏰ Mid-Mar–Sep daily 9–6:30 (Jul–Aug until 7); Oct–mid-Mar 9–12, 2–5:30 💶 Moderate

3 Château de Chenonceau

With a three-storey gallery built out over the River Cher, Chenonceau is one of the most beautiful and romantic of the Loire châteaux, and its history is caught up with the lives of the strong women of the age. Tours reveal a richly furnished interior, as well as the kitchens and wine cellar, and there's plenty to see in the park, including the walled garden, a maze and a floral workshop.

There is plenty to explore at Chenonceau

Catherine de Briçonnet built the main structure in the early 16th century, and it was later given by Henri II to his charismatic mistress, Diane de Poitiers (1499–1566). She left her mark in the first **bridge** over the river, and the **parterre garden**, but was thrown out on Henri's death by his jealous widow, Catherine de Médicis. Catherine's contribution was to build the gallery above the bridge, and lay out the park, before passing it on her death to her daughter-in-law, Louise of Lorraine. Restoration in the mid-19th century was done by Madame de Pelouze.

For a water-borne view of the château, take a **boat trip on the river** from Chisseaux. Contact La Bélandre, tel: 02 47 23 98 64, www.lebelandre.com, operates Apr–Oct.

TAKING A BREAK

There's a choice of **two restaurant**s in the outbuildings, open mid-Mar to Nov.

✚ 222 C1 ✉ 37150 Chenonceau ☎ 02 47 23 90 07; www.chenonceau.com ⏰ 10 Feb–15 Mar 9:30–6; 16 Mar–31 Mar and 5 Nov–9 Feb 9:30–5; Apr–May 9–7; Jun and Sep 9–7:30; Jul–Aug daily 9–8; 1–27 Oct 9–6:30; 28 Oct–4 Nov 9–6 🎟 Moderate

4 Château d'Azay-le-Rideau

The small, white, L-shaped Château d'Azay-le-Rideau sits on an island in the River Indre. Its sumptuous Renaissance interior includes furniture dating from the 16th century, and paintings and tapestries that reflect gracious living for the wealthiest people at the time when these châteaux were built.

Italian and Gothic influences can be seen in a seamless blend of opulence, as you explore the salons, the great hall, the library and the dining room. The **grand staircase** has straight flights, considered an innovation in an age when spiral was the norm. A salamander, the royal symbol of François I, is carved above the main entrance, but this compliment to the King was not enough to save the château from a royal manipulation that saw its creator disgraced and exiled.

The château is surrounded by moats and gardens

A BLOODY REVENGE

In 1418, an entire garrison of 350 men was hanged here, and the village and fortress razed. It happened during the period of the Hundred Years' War, as French and English factions sought control of France. Azay-le-Rideau belonged to the Duke of Burgundy, but when the Dauphin – the future Charles VII – passed through the area he was insulted by the garrison. Charles promptly laid siege to fortress and village, and exacted his bloody revenge.

The interior contains furniture dating from the 16th century

Royal Connections

There was a castle on the site here until 1418, when it was wiped out by the future Charles VII, and it was exactly 100 years before Marcelin Berthelot, courtier to both Louis XI and Charles VIII, laid the plans for his new mansion.

The architects were Étienne Rousseau, Pierre Maupoint and Jacquet Thoreau. Berthelot's son Gilles, treasurer to François I, is credited with completing the job in 1524, but in fact it was Gilles's wife, the formidable Philippa Lesbahy, who supervised all the building and design work.

A Building Interrupted

Two of the proposed four sides of the château were complete when disaster struck: the king, feeling threatened by his most powerful ministers, engineered a financial scandal and Gilles Berthelot was forced to flee. All his possessions were confiscated, and he died in exile in Lorraine, in 1530, having never actually lived in the beautiful château he had created.

TAKING A BREAK

Visit the restaurant **Les Grottes**, built into the solid rock, in the village of Azay-le-Rideau (► 133).

🏠 216 B5 ✉ 37190 Azay-le-Rideau ☎ 02 47 45 42 04; www.azay-le-rideau.monuments-nationaux.fr 🕐 Apr–Jun and Sep 9:30–6; Jul–Aug daily 9:30–7; Oct–Mar 10–12:30, 2–5:30 💰 Moderate, under-18s free

---

CHÂTEAU D'AZAY-LE-RIDEAU: INSIDE INFO

Top tip Check locally for details of evening *son-et-lumière* shows in summer.

Hidden gem The village of Azay-le-Rideau has a second, less showy treasure, which is worth seeking out. It's the old, weathered **Église St-Symphorien**, parts of which date back to the 10th century. Look out for the carvings of rows of saints around the doorway.

At Your Leisure

The archways in the Abbaye de St-Benoît-sur-Loire, founded in the 17th century

🖪 St-Benoît-sur-Loire

In a landscape dominated by fine châteaux, the village of St-Benoît-sur-Loire provides a different perspective: its claim to fame is its **abbey church**, said to be one of the best Romanesque buildings in France. It was raised as the Abbaye de Fleury between c1067 and 1218, but pilgrims had been coming here since AD675 for the shrine of the Italian St Benedict. Known as the founder of Western monasticism, Benedict (c480–547) had been buried at Monte Cassino, near Naples, and his relics were presumably stolen and brought here.

The building is sublime, accessed via the tall stone archways of the belfry porch. Inside, look out for the carved choir screen, presented by Cardinal Richelieu in 1635, and the mosaic floor imported from Italy. The resident Benedictine monks offer fascinating guided tours between the daily services.

➕ 223 D2
Tourist Information Office
✉ 44 rue Orléanaise, 45730 ☎ 02 38 35 79 00

🖪 Château de Cheverny

Cheverny lies southeast of Blois, and is worth a visit as one of the most interesting privately owned châteaux in the region. The handsome exterior is regular and classical in style, the interior sumptuously decorated to reflect the first half of the 17th century, in the flamboyant style of Louis XIII, complete with tapestries and grand paintings. Despite all of this, it still manages to feel like somebody's home rather than a museum. You can explore the grounds in summer via electric buggy.
➕ 221 C1 ✉ 41700, Cheverny ☎ 02 54 79 96 29; www.chateau-cheverny.fr 🕐 Apr–Jun and Sep 9:15–6:15; Jul–Aug daily 9:15–6:45; Oct–Mar 9:45–5 💰 Moderate

🖪 Château de Chaumont

When Henri II died in 1559, his widow Catherine de Médicis evicted his powerful and charismatic mistress, Diane de Poitiers, from Chenonceau and banished her to this lesser château, where she might live out her days in seclusion. It's a massive, rather bleak castle, with huge pepper-pot corner and gateway towers, in a strategic location favoured by the counts of Blois since the 10th century. The grounds are the setting for a annual **garden festival** (mid-Jun to mid-Oct), when 25 or so themed gardens are created by France's top garden designers.
➕ 222 B1 ✉ 41150, Chaumont-sur-Loire ☎ 02 54 20 99 22; www.domaine-chaumont. fr 🕐 Jul–Aug 10–7; Sep 10–6:30; Oct 10–6; Nov–Mar 10–5 💰 Moderate

🖪 Château d'Amboise

Amboise is one of the royal châteaux of the Loire, built by Charles VIII (1470–98) in an elaborate Italianate style that set new trends in its day. It has a mixed history. In 1560 it was the focus of the bloody backlash against the Amboise Conspiracy, when 1,300 Protestants who had plotted to kidnap the young François II were hanged from the battlements. After that, royalty abandoned it, and only fragments of the structure survive today. The highlights are the little Gothic chapel of St-Hubert on the ramparts, and the broad spiral ramp inside the great drum tower.

The attractive town of Amboise, with its narrow streets, clusters around the château. Leonardo da Vinci (1452–1519) came to live here during the last four years of his life, with a pension from François I, and models created from his drawings are displayed in a **museum** here.

➕ 222 C1 ✉ 37400, Amboise ☎ 02 47 57 00 98; www.chateau-amboise.com ⏰ Feb 9–12:30, 1:30–5; Apr–Jun 9–6:30; Jul–Aug daily 9–7; Sep–1 Nov 9–6; 2–15 Nov and Mar 9–5:30; 16 Nov–31 Jan 9–12:20, 2–4:45 💶 Moderate

9 Tours

Tours is a busy city with an appealing old town and plenty of high-class shopping. The best streets for this are rue des Halles and rue Nationale. Great antiques shops line rue Colbert, and you'll find restaurants and art galleries along here, too.

There are street markets galore, including the **flower market** on Boulevard Béranger, held on Wednesday and Saturday. The **Musée des Beaux-Arts** by the Cathédrale St-Gatien is worth a look for its works by Mantegna, Rubens and Rembrandt (open Wed–Mon 9–12:45, 2–6).

➕ 222 B1

Tourist Information Office

✉ 78–82 rue Bernard Palissy, BP 4201, 37042 Tours Cedex 1 ☎ 02 47 70 37 37; www.ligeris.com ⏰ Mid-Apr to Sep Mon–Sat 8:30–7, Sun 10–12:30, 2:30–5; Oct to mid-Mar Mon–Sat 9–12:30, 1:30–6, Sun 10–1

10 Château de Villandry

Villandry is best-known for its 6ha (15 acres) of formal gardens, restored to their 16th-century glory by Joachim de Carvallo in the 20th century. They are laid out on three levels, with a **water garden** at the highest. There is a **decorative garden** in the middle with formal beds outlined by box hedges and punctuated with clipped bushes of yew, while at the lowest level, directly in front of the château itself, is the **potager** – a supreme example of a formal kitchen garden, where fruit trees and vegetables are set in rectangular beds according to the colour of their foliage.

Jean le Breton built the château and garden in 1532. Inside the château, look out for wonderful paintings by Goya and Velázquez.

➕ 222 B1 ✉ 37510 ☎ 02 47 50 02 09; www.chateauvillandry.com ⏰ 1–3 Jan daily 9:30–4.30; 6–28 Feb 9–5; 1–27 Mar 9–5:30; 28 Mar–30 Jun 9–6; Jul–Aug 9–6:30; Sep–Oct 9–6; 31 Oct–15 Nov 9–5; 18 Dec–31 Dec 9–4.30. Closed 4 Jan–5 Feb, 16 Nov–17 Dec 💶 Moderate

The beautiful decorative garden at Château de Villandry

⑪ Langeais

Approaching Langeais from the south, a suspension bridge over the Loire sweeps you into the village, which lies on the eastern edge of the Parc Naturel Régional Loire Anjou. Troglodyte dwellings are built into the rocks, and there's extensive parkland around the château to explore.

The castle dates from 1465 and was intended as a fortress to ward off the threat of invasion from Brittany at a time when Louis XI held court in Tours. Louis's son Charles VIII neutralized the threat in 1491 by marrying Anne of Brittany here. Behind the rather grim exterior is a richly furnished Renaissance interior.

✚ 222 B1

Château de Langeais

✉ Langeais, 37130 ☎ 02 47 96 72 60; www.chateau-de-langeais.com ⏱ Feb–Mar 9:30–5:30; Apr–Jun and Sep–12 Nov 9:30–6:30; Jul–Aug daily 9–7; 13 Nov–Jan 10–5 💶 Moderate

⑫ Château d'Ussé

Possibly the most romantic of the Loire châteaux, multi-turreted Ussé lies on the Indre, surrounded by the forest of Chinon. It is said to have inspired Charles Perrault to write the fairytale of *Sleeping Beauty* in 1697, and as a result is widely known as the Château de la Belle au Bois Dormant.

It was started in the late 15th century, and originally had four sides around the central courtyard – remodelling in the 17th century removed one to make the most of the views. The stunning formal gardens were designed by André Le Nôtre. The château is still in private hands, and access to the 18th-century interior, with its elegant furniture and costume displays, is by guided tour.

✚ 216 B5 ✉ 37420 ☎ 02 47 95 54 05; www.chateaudusse.fr ⏱ Mid-Feb–Mar daily 10–6; Apr–Aug 10–7; Sep–11 Nov 10–6 💶 Expensive

⑬ Chinon

The château on the high rocks at Chinon, on a bend of the River Vienne, was no Renaissance palace but rather a medieval stronghold. Today it is a ruin, still dominating the old town at its feet, with its narrow medieval streets and timbered houses, and wine cellars, or *caves*, which undermine the cliffs below. There are in fact two castles on the site, including Fort St-George, built by Henry II of England, who died here in 1189. The most significant event in Chinon's history came in 1429, when Joan of Arc came here to convince the Dauphin that she could retake Orléans from the English. The event is celebrated by a **museum** in the château's clock tower (open daily).

✚ 216 B5

Tourist Information Office

✉ place Hofheim, 37500, BP 141 ☎ 02 47 93 17 85; www.chinon-valdeloire.com ⏱ May–Sep daily 10–7; Oct–Apr Mon–Sat 10–12:30, 2:30–6

Aerial view of the turreted Château d'Usse

The royal tombs at Fontevraud; the last resting place of the Richard the Lionheart

🎖 Abbaye Royale de Fontevraud

Much of this great 11th-century abbey fell into decay after it was abandoned during the Revolution, and it served as a prison between 1804 and 1965. Restoration is ongoing, and one of its principal points of interest is the set of tombs in the church: it's the last resting place of Henry II of England, his wife Eleanor of Aquitaine and their Crusader son, Richard the Lionheart.

➕ 216 B5 ✉ BP 24, 49590 Fontevraud-l'Abbaye ☎ 02 41 51 73 52; www.abbaye-fontevraud.com 🕒 Jan–Mar, Nov–Dec daily 10–5; Apr–Jun, Sep–Oct 10–6; Jul–Aug 10–7 💶 Moderate, under-18s free

🎖 Angers

Angers is a good-sized town on the River Maine, with an attractive old quarter, the Doutre, that is pleasant to wander through. The **château**, built in the 15th century to fend off the Bretons, is boldly striped with the local black-coloured stone. Here you can see the surviving fragments of a remarkable tapestry, commissioned by the Duc d'Anjou in 1375 to hang in the local cathedral. The tapestry pieces illustrate scenes from the writings of St John the Divine. More modern tapestry can be seen at the **Musée de la Tapisserie Contemporaine**, at 4 boulevard Arago (tel: 02 41 24 18 45).

➕ 222 A1

FOR KIDS

- **Port St-Père**: Planète Sauvage is a brilliant drive-through safari-park between Nantes and Pornic (Port St-Père, 44170, tel: 02 40 04 82 82, www.planetesauvage.com, open Mar–mid-Nov daily).
- **Doue-la-Fontaine:** Zoo Doué has an interesting collection of animals, including lions and leopards (tel: 02 41 59 18 58, www.zoodoue.fr, open daily Feb–Oct).

Tourist Information Office
✉ 7 place Kennedy, 49051 ☎ 02 41 23 50 00; www.angers-tourisme.com 🕒 May– Sep Mon 10–7, Tue–Sat 9–7, Sun 10–6; Oct–Apr Mon 2–6, Tue–Sat 9–6, Sun 10–1

🎖 Le Mans

Visit this busy industrial town in June for all the excitement of the famous 24-hour motor race. If you can't make it, then you can visit the **Musée Automobile de la Sarthe**, in rue de Laigné instead (www.lemusee24h.com; open Jun–Aug daily 10–6; Mar–May, Sep–Dec Wed–Sun 11–5), to admire 11 previous race winners, plus around 140 other gleaming and desirable vehicles.

➕ 222 B2

Tourist Information Office
✉ Hôtel des Ursulines, rue de l'Étoile, 72000 ☎ 02 43 28 17 22; www.lemanstourisme.com 🕒 Jun–Sep Mon–Sat 9–6, Sun 10–12:30, 2–5; Oct–May Mon–Fri 9–6, Sat 9–12, 2–6, Sun 10–noon

Where to... Stay

Prices

Expect to pay per night for a double room

€ under €120   €€ €120–€220   €€€ over €220

Château de Marçay €€–€€€

This 15th-century château, set in verdant formal gardens, has been sympathetically renovated to offer luxury accommodation. Rooms are in the castle itself or in an adjacent wing. There's a gourmet restaurant, a good-sized pool and sundeck.

➕ 216 B5 ⊠ 37500 Marçay-Chinon
☎ 02 47 93 03 47;
www.chateaudemarcay.com ⊕ Closed late Nov and late Jan–Mar

Hôtel Abbaye de Fontevraud €–€€

For a stately treat, you can stay the night in one of France's most splendid abbeys. There are 52 well-appointed and elegantly furnished bedrooms, some of which open onto the attractive kitchen garden. Peace descends upon the place after the visitors have gone. There is an excellent restaurant in the cloister.

➕ 216 B5 ⊠ Le Prieuré de Saint-Lazare, rue St-Jean de l'Habit, 49590 Fontevraud l'Abbaye ☎ 02 41 51 73 16; www.hotelfp-fontevraud.com

Hôtel du Bon-Laboureur €–€€

A grand old 18th-century inn with an excellent restaurant, this hotel makes a good base for exploring the area around Chenonceau. Rooms are relatively small, but each is well equipped with TV and kitchenette. Air-conditioning is available in many. The restaurant is popular in its own right, so reserve early. There is also an outdoor pool.

➕ 222 C1 ⊠ 6 rue de Dr Bretonneau, 37150 Chenonceaux ☎ 02 47 23 90 02; www.bonlaboureur.com ⊕ Closed mid-Nov and Jan–mid-Feb

Hôtel Lion d'Or €€–€€€

Romorantin-Lanthenay is south of Orleans, away from many of the main sites of the Loire, but it's worth the diversion if you're looking for somewhere special, with an excellent restaurant. The hotel is in a Renaissance mansion, surrounded by immaculate gardens.

➕ 223 D1 ⊠ 69 rue Clemenceau, 41200 Romorantin-Lanthenay ☎ 02 54 94 15 15; www.hotel-liondor.fr ⊕ Closed mid-Feb–late Mar and late Nov

La Roseraie €

Another excellent choice in Chenonceaux, La Roseraie has the more intimate feel of a boutique hotel, with just 17 small, but well-equipped bedrooms. There's an outdoor swimming pool – perfect for relaxing after a busy day touring the chateaux. Enjoy wonderful cuisine in the restaurant, attached to the hotel, complete with terrace for alfresco summer dining.

➕ 222 C1 ⊠ 7 rue de Dr Breton-neau, 37150 Chenonceaux ☎ 02 47 23 90 09; www.charmingroseraie.com ⊕ Open Mar to mid-Nov

Le Prieuré €€–€€€

This attractive former priory at Chênehutte-les-Tuffeaux, located 7km (4.5 miles) northwest of Saumur, is a great place for families. The setting is a wooded hillside above the Loire, with an outdoor pool, tennis courts and a lawn for bowling. Parts of the building date back to the 12th century, and all rooms enjoy river views.

➕ 222 A1 ⊠ 49350 Chênehutte-les-Tuffeaux ☎ 02 41 67 90 14; www.prieure.com ⊕ Closed Feb

Where to...
Eat and Drink

Prices

Expect to pay per night for a meal, excluding drinks:

€ under €30   €€ €30–€60   €€€ over €60

Auberge des Matfeux €€–€€€

Set in an interesting 20th-century building, the Auberge offers excellent regional dishes, including many created with local ingredients. It serves wild-caught river fish if available; the signature dish is ravioli with langoustine. Chef Xavier Souffront is known for his innovative approach.

🚩 222 B2 ☒ 289 avenue Nationale, 72230 Arnage ☎ 02 43 21 10 71; www.aubergedesmatfeux.fr
🕐 Jul–Aug Sun–Thu 12–2:30, Sat 12–2:30, 7:30–9:30; Sep–Jun Sun–Tue 12–2:30, Wed–Sat 12–2:30, 7:30–9:30. Closed first two weeks in Jan

Auberge de Porc Vallières €–€€

A former pub on the banks of the Loire now offers a hearty menu of regional specialities; you'll find that herb-stuffed cabbage complements the meat dishes.

🚩 222 B1 ☒ 152 Vallières, 37230 Fondettes ☎ 02 47 42 24 04 🕐 Tue, Wed, Sun 12–2; Mon, Thu–Sat 12–2, 7–9

Grand St-Benoît €–€€

This restaurant overlooks a beautiful 12th-century church. Inside, exposed oak beams reveal its age, but the furniture is contemporary while the menu offers well-prepared regional dishes.

🚩 223 D2 ☒ 7 place St-André, 45730 St-Benoît-sur-Loire ☎ 02 38 35 11 92
🕐 Tue–Fri 12:15–1:45, 7:15–8:45, Sat 7:15–8:45, Sun 12:15–1:45. Closed end Aug–early Sep and late Dec–late Jan

Hotel Grand St-Michel €€–€€€

Enjoy beautiful views of the Château de Chambord from the dining room and terrace of this restaurant, in a building that once served as the kennels to the château's hunting pack. The food is unfussy, with a regional bias – try the duck breast in a green peppercorn sauce, or the duck pâté. This place is especially popular on Sundays and holidays, so be prepared to book ahead.

🚩 222 C1 ☒ place Saint Louis 41250 Chambord ☎ 02 54 20 31 31; www.saintmichel-chambord.com 🕐 Daily noon–2, 7–9. Closed late Nov–early Dec

Les Grottes €€–€€€

This charming restaurant at Azay-le-Rideau is worth visiting for its location alone, because it is built into two caverns carved straight from the cliff. In these unusual surroundings you can sample traditional regional specialities such as duck with apple, or sausage with scrambled egg. There are lots of excellent local wines on the list to choose from.

🚩 216 B5 ☒ 23 rue Pineau, 37190 Azay-le-Rideau ☎ 02 47 45 21 04 🕐 Mon, Wed–Sat 12–2:30, 7–9:30; Tue 7–9:30; Sun 12–2:30. Closed end Aug–early Sep, Dec–Feb

Licorne €€€

A starter such as prawn and basil ravioli in morel sauce should whet your appetite for the main course in this popular restaurant in Fontevraud, with its Louis XIV-styled interior. Other temptations might include sweet treats such as warm chocolate tart with a pear and lemon-butter sauce.

🚩 216 B5 ☒ Allée Sainte-Catherine, 49590 Fontevraud-l'Abbaye ☎ 02 41 51 72 49 🕐 May–Sep daily 12–2, 7–9; Oct–Apr Tue–Sun 12–2, 7–9. Closed Sun–Mon, Wed evenings in winter

Where to... Shop

There are plenty of places to shop in the area, including unusual gift ideas at the châteaux.

For a little souvenir of history, call in at **Tapisserie Langlois** in Blois (1 rue de la Voûte du Chateau, tel: 02 54 78 04 43, open Mon–Sat). Here, some of the best tapestries from the local châteaux are reproduced; prices range from €180–€3,000. One of the best château gift shops is at **Cheverny**, where you can buy anything from comic books to a replica suit of armour (Cour-Cheverny, tel: 02 54 79 96 29, open daily). And if you're looking for antique art treasures, try **Christian Dumartin**'s shop in the Manoir de Beauvais, Chinon (Ligre, tel: 02 47 98 36 63, open Mon–Fri 9–noon, 2–7, but check ahead).

The Loire region has good local markets. One of the best is the **Marché d'Orléans**, which sets up in different parts of the city on different days. Look for it on Tuesdays on Blossière (7–noon) and on Thursdays in place Dunois (3–7.30pm), and on Saturdays at Charpenterie Quai du Roi (6am–12.30pm). **Tours** has a daily market, with *charcuterie*, fruit and vegetables, and local crafts, seen at its best on Saturdays (place des Halles, 7am–2pm).

For top-range designer shopping, head for **rue Crebillon** in Nantes, and the boutiques of the **passage Pommeraye** arcade. If rustic craftwork is more to your taste, go to **Cooperative de la Vannerie** at Azay-le-Rideau, where local artisans sell their wares.

Where to... Be Entertained

At night, some of the châteaux have *son et lumière* (sound and light) shows depicting the history of the buildings. The most spectacular of these is at Puy du Fou, where at weekends a cast of hundreds takes part in historical re-enactments (Jun to mid-Sep, tel: 08 20 09 10 10, www.puydufou.com, expensive).

CINEMA

The **Gaumont Angers Multiplex**, in the St-Serge district of Angers, close to the university, shows new movies, with around half in English (avenue des Droits de l'Homme, tel: 08 25 87 88 78, www.cinemasgaumontpathe.com). Nantes holds the **Three Continents Film Festival** in late November,

with movies from Asia, Latin America and Africa (tel: 02 40 69 74 14; www.3continents.com).

MUSIC AND DANCE

Lasers blazing into the night sky announce the Loire's biggest dance venue, **Le Do Ré Mi**, at Beaulieu-sur-Layon, south of Angers, with a capacity of 3,000 (tel: 02 41 44 67 67, open Thu–Sat 11pm–dawn).

For a more intimate experience, try **L'Arc en Ciel** (rue Halle aux Toiles, 61000 Alençon, tel: 02 33 26 32 15, www.larcenciel-61.com), which holds regular theme nights. **Le Pyms**, in Tours, favours up-to-the-minute music (170 avenue de Grammont, tel: 02 47 66 22 22, www.lepyms.com, open Wed–Thu, Fri–Sat 10:30–5, Sun 11–5).

Southeast France

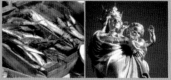

★ Don't Miss

Moulins

N7

Loire

Lapalisse

Montluçon

A71

E11

Vichy

Villefranche-sur-Saône

E21

Nantua

Bourg-en-Bresse

A40

AUVERGNE

Clermont-Ferrand

Riom

Roanne

N7

Lyon

E611

Belley

E15

Puy 7 7

E70

Thiers

de Dôme

Montbrison

Givors

8 ✈

E70

Issoire

Parc Naturel Régional du Livradois Forez

St-Étienne ✈

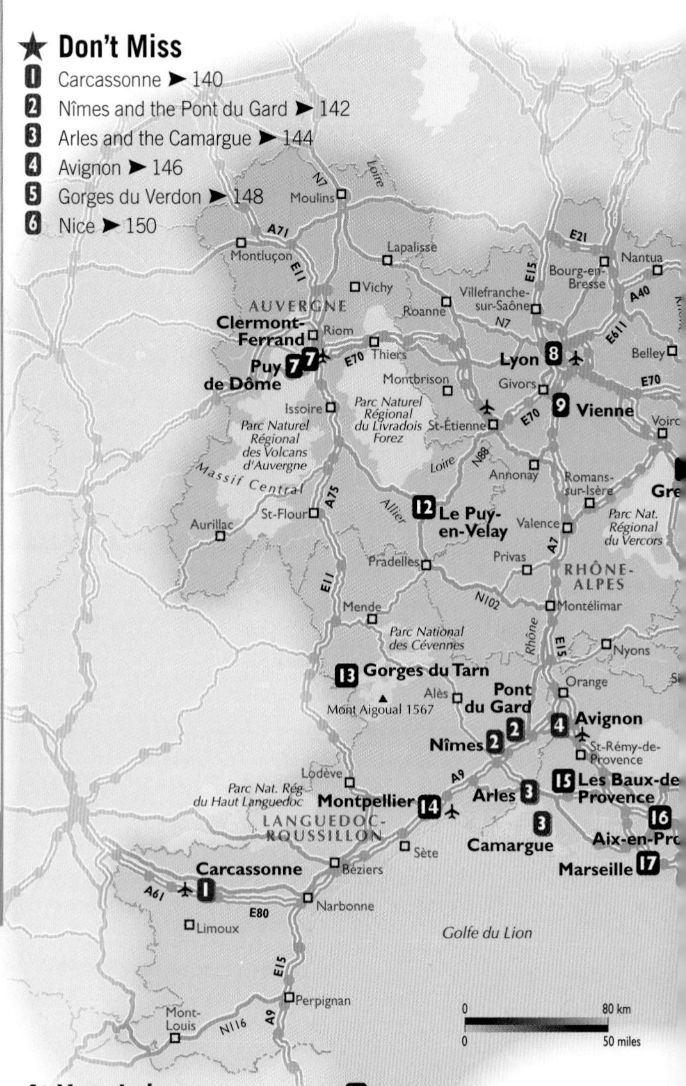

E70

9 **Vienne**

Parc Naturel Régional des Volcans d'Auvergne

Annonay

Romans-sur-Isère

Gre

Massif Central

A75

Loire

N88

12 **Le Puy-en-Velay**

Valence

Parc Nat. Régional du Vercors

Aurillac

St-Flour

Allier

Privas

RHÔNE-ALPES

Pradelles

N102

Montélimar

E11

Mende

N102

Rhône

E15

Nyons

Parc National des Cévennes

13 **Gorges du Tarn**

Alès

Orange

▲ Mont Aigoual 1567

Pont 2 2 4 **Avignon**

du Gard ✈ St-Rémy-de-Provence

Nîmes 2

Lodève

A9

15 **Les Baux-de-Provence**

Parc Nat. Rég. du Haut Languedoc

Montpellier 14 ✈

Arles 3

16

LANGUEDOC-ROUSSILLON

Sète

3

Aix-en-Pro

Camargue

Marseille 17

Carcassonne

A61 ✈ 1

Béziers

E80

Narbonne

Golfe du Lion

Limoux

E15

0 ──────── 80 km

Mont-Louis

N116

Perpignan

0 ──────── 50 miles

At Your Leisure

Getting Your Bearings

France's Mediterranean coastline is well known as the playground of the rich and famous. In fact, most of the chic resorts are to be found east of the cultural melting-pot of Marseille, stretching up to the tiny principality of Monaco. West of the city is a low-lying, sandy shore, with quieter villages and historic towns, and the wildlife-rich lagoons of the Camargue region.

Inland there's a great diversity of landscapes to discover, from the sometimes rugged hills and rolling farmland of Provence to the east, the wild high country of the Causses around the spectacular Gorges du Tarn in the west, and the dryer landscapes of the Cévennes in the middle. The fertile valley of the Rhône stretches northwards to the major hub of Lyon. On the eastern edge, the borders are with Switzerland and Italy, a mountainous country popular for winter sports.

The A7/E15 is the main driving route from the north, and the A9/E15 and A8 are the *autoroutes* along the coast – all can become jammed on white-hot holiday weekends. If you can take your time and spread your journey out, there's a more appealing network of minor roads to explore, and recent improvements to some of the narrowest sections of the A75, between Clermont-Ferrand and Montpellier, make that another good option.

Page 135: The harbour at Quartier du Port, Nice
Below: View over the lovely old port at Marseille

In Four Days

If you're not quite sure where to begin your travels, this itinerary recommends a practical and enjoyable four days exploring Southeast France, taking in some of the best places to see using the Getting your Bearings map on the previous page. For more information see the main entries.

Day 1

Morning
Explore the fascinating **medieval fortress** at ❶ **Carcassonne** (left; ➤ 140–141), and wander through the ancient streets of this captivating city before lunching in style on local specialities at **Le Languedoc** restaurant (➤ 141).

Afternoon
Head eastwards toward the Mediterranean on the A61/E80 autoroute to join the A9 coastal motorway to reach the cosmopolitan and buzzing city of ⓮ **Montpellier** (➤ 155). Spend the rest of the afternoon sightseeing in the city, on foot or, if you're feeling energetic, hire a bike.

Evening
Enjoy the restaurants and 24-hour nightlife of Montpellier, one of the Mediterranean's liveliest cities.

Day 2

Morning
Visit ❷ **Nîmes and the Pont du Gard** (➤ 142–143) for some of the best **Roman relics** in the area. Pick out a **café in Nîmes**, or dine at the shady **restaurant** by the aqueduct, to avoid the midday heat.

Afternoon
Drive southeast to ❸ **Arles and the Camargue** (➤ 144–145), for another stunning **Roman amphitheatre**. Have a cooling drink in a café here before continuing south into the marshlands of the **Camargue** delta, and the wildlife of the **Étang de Vaccarès** (➤ 144).

Evening
Make your way northeast of Arles to the remote village of ⓯ **Les Baux-de-Provence** (➤ 155), to watch the sunset.

Day 3

Morning

Start the day with an exploration of **4** **Avignon** (➤ 146–147), including the **Palais des Papes** and a quick dance on the **old bridge** (➤ 147). There's lots of choices of places to eat, or grab a **freshly filled baguette** and get on the road again.

Afternoon

Head east on the N100, then the D907 and D6 to **Moustiers-Ste-Marie** (right) and the start of the dramatic **5** **Gorges du Verdon** (➤ 148–149). At the eastern end link up with the N85 (Route Napoléon) southeast, and head into **21** **Grasse** (➤ 158–159), centre of France's perfume industry, for the refreshment of all your senses.

Day 4

Morning

Take the N7 coast road east along the Riviera via popular **19** **Cannes** (➤ 158) and less showy **20** **Antibes** (➤ 158) to the city of **6** **Nice** (➤ 150–151). Be seen to stroll along the **Promenade des Anglais**, and lunch on seafood, with views of the harbour, at **L'Âne Rouge** (➤ 151).

Afternoon

Cool off in the air-conditioned interiors of one or two of the best **museums and art galleries** (➤ 150,151).

Evening

Go a little further east to **22** **Monaco** (➤ 159), for an extravagant night out at **Monte Carlo's famous casino** (below; ➤ 164) – but don't break the bank.

O Carcassonne

Carcassonne is a fascinating city in two distinct parts. On the east bank of the River Aude lies the Cité, the largest medieval fortress in Europe, restored in the 19th century to spectacular glory. On the west bank lies the Bourg, or Ville Basse, a settlement founded in 1260 to a strict grid pattern, which owes its fortune to the arrival of the Canal du Midi in the 17th century. Together they make Carcassonne an intriguing and rewarding city to explore.

View towards Carcassonne, the largest medieval fortress in Europe

The 3km (2 miles) of **battlemented double ramparts** that surround the Cité are one of the most striking features. They are studded with more than 50 defensive towers and turrets, and are remarkably complete. Originally there were just two ways in and out: the western Porte d'Aude and the eastern Porte Narbonnaise. People still live within the defences, and there are lots of shops and restaurants to explore in the narrow streets around **place Marcou**.

The lower town centres on **place Carnot**, and was once also walled and moated. The town's battlements were pulled down and the ditches filled in after the Revolution, to be replaced with leafy boulevards. Its prosperity was built on textiles and wine, both trades aided by its strategic place on the canal. Stroll around the pedestrianized streets to admire

Carcassonne

The **market** (Tuesday, Thursday and Saturday mornings) has
been held here since medieval times, and is another strong
link in the town's history.

TAKING A BREAK

Treat yourself to a sustaining dish of the classic *cassoulet*
(meat and bean casserole), perhaps rounded off with a Grand
Marnier ice-cream, at the up-market **Le Languedoc** restaurant
at 32 allée d'Iéna (tel: 04 68 25 22 17).

+ 212 A2
Tourist Information Office
✉ 28 rue de Verdun ☎ 04 68 10 24 30; www.carcassonne.org ⏱ Apr–Jun
and Sep–Oct Mon–Sat 9–6, Sun 9–1; Jul–Aug daily 9–7

CARCASSONNE: INSIDE INFO

Top tips Access to the walls of the Cité is by **guided tour only** – enquire at the
tourist office for details (admission charge: moderate).
- Look out for **jousting tournaments** in the Cité in summer, which evoke an age
  of chivalry long gone. They're occasionally held in the grassy slips of the
  lices hautes, between the inner and outer ramparts.
- **Hire a boat** (15 quai de Riquet, Carcassonne, tel: 04 68 71 88 95) and
  spend an hour or so navigating the charming Canal du Midi.
- **A spectacular fireworks display** takes place on 14 July every year to celebrate the
  burning of the city, Embrasement de la Cité Médiévale.

2 Nîmes and the Pont du Gard

The Roman town of Nîmes and the spectacular aqueduct that was built to bring water to its citizens combine to form one of the great sights of France. They are 20km (12.5 miles) apart, so you can choose which to see first.

Around Nîmes

The buildings of the city's old quarter are interesting, but what makes this a "must see" site is **Les Arènes**, the 2,000-year-old amphitheatre. It's the best preserved Roman amphitheatre in the world, and still used for bullfights and other events. As a concession to modern requirements, an inflatable roof can be added in winter time. There are three tiers of stone seats inside, designed to seat around 20,000 spectators – be warned, there's no safety rail on the top tier.

Nîmes' Roman temple, the **Maison Carrée**, is less spectacular in scale, but still amazingly well preserved. There are some exquisite small mosaics in the interior. The whole structure dates from the first century BC. The temple is next door to the contemporary art gallery, more widely known as the **Carré d'Art**. It's a light and spacious modern building designed by English architect Sir Norman Foster in 1984, and displays a collection of modern art and temporary exhibitions.

The Pont du Gard

This huge, honey-coloured marvel strides across the River Gardon in three imposing tiers. Examine it closely from the bridge immediately beside it and you'll see there's no mortar holding it up, just the skill of the Roman engineers who constructed it around 19BC, using six-tonne stone

The first-century Roman arena in Nîmes

DID YOU KNOW?

Nîmes is the birthplace of a famouse hard-wearing cotton fabric that has become the essential ingredient of the world's favourite leisure-wear. The clothing is jeans, and the fabric, of course, is *serge de Nîmes*, better known as **denim**.

blocks. Projecting stones were built into the design, to hold scaffolding in place for repairs. The water channel is the top tier, part of an ambitious scheme to transport water from the spring near Uzès 50km (31 miles) to Nîmes, for drinking, bathing and fountains. Learn more about the building and 19th-century restoration in the exhibition centre, on the left bank.

TAKING A BREAK

Try the art-filled **Vintage Café** in Nîmes, between the arena and the Maison Carée (7 rue de Bernis, tel: 04 66 21 04 45).

✚ 213 D4
Tourist Information Office
✉ 6 rue Auguste, 30000 ☎ 04 66 58 38 00; www.ot-nimes.fr ⊙ Easter–Sep Mon–Fri 8:30–7, Sat 9–7, Sun 10–6; Jul–Aug Mon–Sat 9–7, Sun 10–6; Oct–Easter Mon–Fri 8:30–6:30, Sat 9–6:30, Sun 10–5

Les Arènes
✉ place des Arènes ☎ 04 66 21 82 56 ⊙ Jan–Feb and Nov–Dec daily 9–5; Mar, Oct 9–6; Apr–May and Sep 9–6:30; Jun 9–7; Jul–Aug 9–8 💷 Moderate

Maison Carrée
✉ place de la Comédie ☎ 04 66 21 82 56 ⊙ Jan–Feb and Nov–Dec daily 10–1, 2–4:30; Mar 10–6; Oct 10–1, 2–6; Apr–May and Sep 10–6:30; Jun 10–7; Jul–Aug 10–8 💷 Inexpensive

Musée d'Art Contemporain (Carré d'Art)
✉ place de la Maison Carré
☎ 04 66 76 35 70 ⊙ Tue–Sun 10–6 💷 Inexpensive

Pont du Gard
✚ 213 D4 ✉ Exhibition Centre, Pont du Gard, 30210 ☎ 08 20 90 33 30; www.pontdugard.fr ⊙ Site open 7am–1am all year; exhibition hall open Easter–Sep daily 9–7; Oct 9–6, Nov–Dec 9–5 💷 Exhibition hall: Moderate

---

NÎMES AND THE PONT DU GARD: INSIDE INFO

Top tips In midsummer the **heat can be blistering**, so it pays to plan your visit around a shady lunch stop in Nîmes, visiting the Pont du Gard either early in the morning or later in the afternoon, when the sun is not so fierce.

■ For an **overview of Nîmes,** head for the Magne tower in Jardin de la Fontaine.

■ The **entrance fee** to the Pont du Gard is €15 (for up five people, €10 Nov–Feb) and includes the museum, the cinema, the temporary exhibitions and Ludo, a discovery zone for kids. It also gives access to the parking areas on both sides of the river. You don't have to pay an admission fee to visit the bridge itself.

3 Arles and the Camargue

Roman Arles is the gateway to the mysterious and romantic natural wilderness of the Camargue, a marshy flatland famous for its exotic wildlife, its semi-wild white horses, its little black bulls bred for fighting and its annual gypsy festival. Thousands of pink flamingos come to feed in the shallow waters here, and evaporating sea water leaves vast crystalline saltpans. Roads are few, so prepare to extend your exploration on foot or – better – by guided boat trip.

Arles

This small town is one of the most appealing of Provence, with Roman public buildings – including a well-preserved 20,000-seat **amphitheatre** – rubbing shoulders with medieval houses and churches in the centre. It makes a good base for exploring the area. There are various excellent and worthy museums of antiquities in and around the town, but the most unusual and fun of all is the local folk museum, the **Musée Arlatan**. A Roman Festival is held here with events throughout the year (www.festival-arelate.com).

Beautiful carvings in Église St-Trophime, Arles

In 1888 Vincent Van Gogh (1853–90) left Paris and came to Arles, where he fell under the spell of the Provençal light and landscapes. He lived in a modest cottage known as the "yellow house" (destroyed by bombing in 1944), but at this productive time he painted masterpieces including the famous *Sunflowers* series. The end came the following year when, after a row with his friend Paul Gauguin over the founding of an artists' colony at Arles, and cutting off part of his own left ear, Van Gogh was committed to hospital.

The Camargue

Comparatively few roads penetrate this low-lying marsh, the delta of the Rhône, and its protected status means that visitor access is to some extent contained. The nature reserve centres on the shallow **Étang de Vaccarès**, and there's a superb visitor facility at **La Capelière**, with marked nature trails and information about the birds and plants of the area. South of here, the salt marshes give way to an expanse of sand dunes and ponds. It's great for bird-watching: look out for flamingos, avocets and egrets feeding in the shallows, bitterns and herons in the reedbeds, and ducks, geese and waders on the shore.

Wildlife lovers will enjoy the Pont de Gau ornithological park

TAKING A BREAK

After exploring the arenas in Arle, head to the rustic **La Mamma** restaurant (20 rue de l'Amphithéâtre, tel 04 90 96 11 60) to enjoy tasty but inexpensive Italian and regional cuisine.

✚ 213 E3
Tourist Information Office
✉ esplanade Charles de Gaulle, boulevard des Lices, 13200 ☎ 04 90 18 41 20; www.tourisme.ville-arles.fr ⏰ Jan–Easter and Oct–Dec Mon–Sat 9–4:45, Sun 10–1; Easter–Sep daily 9–6:45

Musée Arlaten
✉ 29–31 rue de la République ☎ 04 90 93 58 11 ⏰ Apr–May andSep 9:30–11:30, 2–5; Jun–Aug 9:30–11:30, 2–5:30; Oct–Mar 9:30–11:30, 2–4. Closed Mon Oct–Jun 🎟 Moderate

Réserve Nationale de Camargue
✚ 213 E3 ✉ Centre d'Information, La Capelière, 13200 Arles ☎ 04 90 97 00 97; www.reserve-camargue.org ⏰ Apr–Sep daily 9–1, 2–6; Oct–Mar Wed–Mon 9–1, 2–5 🎟 Inexpensive

ARLES AND THE CAMARGUE: INSIDE INFO

Top tips You are likely to **see much more** on a boat trip, horse ride or cycle tour than you will from a car. The village of **Saintes-Maries-de-la-Mer** is a good base for activities; contact the tourist office at 5 avenue Van Gogh, 13460, tel: 04 90 97 82 55, www.saintesmariesdelamer.com, open daily.
- The handsome, fortified 12th-century church in Saintes-Maries-de-la-Mer is the focus of the annual two-day **gypsy fair,** held on 24 to 25 May to celebrate the feast days of Marie Jacob, sister of the Virgin Mary, and Marie Salome, mother of the apostles James and John. Sarah, maid to both Maries, and the gypsies' patron saint, is buried within the church.

One to miss If you're expecting to see paintings by Van Gogh in Arles' **Fondation Van Gogh,** near the amphitheatre, then you'll be disappointed. However, the gallery has some interesting art by other modern painters, including Francis Bacon, which takes its inspiration from Van Gogh's works.

4 Avignon

The grandeur of Avignon's medieval walled city, dominated by a huge papal palace, makes it an intriguing place to visit. And for humble contrast, there's the remains of a venerable bridge made famous by the traditional song *Sur le pont d'Avignon*.

Remnants of a Golden Age

Avignon was thrust on to the world stage in 1309, when Pope Clement V decided to move here from Rome. For almost 70 years the town became the heart of the Christian world, and the enduring legacy of this exciting period, when culture and scholarship flourished, is the magnificent fortified palace, the **Palais des Papes**.

When the popes eventually returned to Rome in 1378 they took many of their treasures with them, and there is a bleak emptiness about the palace. Hints of past luxury can be seen in the frescoed walls and ceiling of the papal bedchamber, and the Gobelin tapestries of the banqueting hall.

Above: Pont St Benezet over River Rhône with the Palais des Papes behind

Opposite: fresco on the ceiling at the Palais des Papes

Around the town, you'll find the best shopping along rue de la République, while the cafés of the place de l'Horloge offer the chance to relax with a coffee and watch the world go by. There are museums to explore, and an essential stop is the **Pont St Bénézet** – the Pont d'Avignon immortalized in song. It was originally a wooden structure, built in 1177 by the young shepherd St Bénézet, and was rebuilt in stone after a siege in 1226. It was constantly buffeted by the strong flow of the Rhône, and in the mid-17th century, most was washed away. Now just four picturesque arches remain.

TAKING A BREAK

Enjoy tea and delicious cakes or perhaps a light lunch at **le Simple Simon**, a decorative English-style tea room and restaurant in the heart of the old town (26 rue Petite-Fusterie, tel: 04 90 86 62 70).

✚ 213 E4
Tourist Information Office
✉ 41 cours Jean-Jaurès, 80400 ☎ 04 32 74 32 74; www.ot-avignon.fr
🕐 Apr–Oct Mon–Sat 9–6, Sun 9:45–5; Nov–Mar Mon–Fri 9–6, Sat 9–5, Sun 10–noon. Opening hours are liable to change, so call ahead to verify times

Palais des Papes
✉ 6 rue Pente Rapide – Charles Ansidéi, BP 149 cedex 1, 84008 ☎ 04 90 27 50 00; www.palais-des-papes.com 🕐 Apr–Jun and Oct daily 9–7; Aug 9–9; Jul and Sep 9–8; Nov–Mar 9:30–5:45 💶 Moderate

AVIGNON: INSIDE INFO

Top tip The **Passion Pass**, available from the tourist information office, gives reduced price entry to the main sights.

Hidden gem The **Fondation Angladon Dubrujeaud,** on 5 rue Laboureur, is a privately owned art gallery with some treasures of 20th-century art, including works by Picasso and Cézanne (tel: 04 90 82 29 03, www.angladon.com, open Wed–Sun 1–6; also Tue May–Nov, moderate).

5 Gorges du Verdon

France's version of the Grand Canyon is the deepest and most dramatic river gorge in mainland Europe: an unmissable 21km (13 miles) of steep cliffs and precipitous vegetation punctuated by stupendous viewpoints. At the bottom run the clear green waters of the river that gives the chasm its name, and which run out into the artificial Lac de Ste-Croix, created in 1973.

The gorge was formed over millions of years by the River Verdon, and is one of the natural wonders of the world. Today it seems incredible that it was surveyed for the first time in 1905, by the great speleologist Édouard-Alfred Martel. Yet even now, geology dictates that the roads are few and modest in scale as the canyon narrows to 198m (650ft) across, and the steepness of the limestone cliffs at each side, up to 700m (2,296ft) high, makes them accessible only to very experienced climbers. The southern route from Moustiers-Sainte-Marie, the **Corniche Sublime** (D71), carved out in the 1940s, gives the best views, with the spectacular **Balcons de Mescla** viewpoint the highlight. Loop north via Trigance to return along the northern side and the **Route des Crêtes**.

The Verdon River threads through the gorge

Exploring in the Gorges

The river powers a hydro-electric plant, and is dammed below Moustiers, offering good opportunities for experienced canoeists. Short walks lead from many of the view-points, such as the zig-zag path from the Point Sublime, on the north side. Hardy walkers can tackle the challenging **Sentier Martel footpath**, which runs along the valley floor between Rougon and Meyreste and takes at least one day.

ÉDOUARD-ALFRED MARTEL

Martel (1859–1938) is known worldwide as the father of speleology – the science of cave exploration. From an early age, and despite training as a lawyer, Martel began a pioneering exploration of the underground caverns in the limestone landscape of the Causses. His three-day exploration of the Gorges du Verdon, previously believed impenetrable, was undertaken with two companions. Martel's journey was driven partly by curiosity, and partly by the need for research into water supplies, and in the 1950s the government considered blocking the whole valley for a reservoir, settling instead for the more limited Lac de Ste-Croix.

TAKING A BREAK

There are plenty of cafés in **Moustiers-Ste-Marie**, and there are also lots of *belvédères*, or viewpoints, where you can stop for a picnic and enjoy the panoramas.

🚩 214 A4
Tourist Information Office
✉ place de l'Église Moustiers-Sainte-Marie, 04360 (western edge of the canyon) ☎ 04 92 74 67 84; www.ville-moustiers-sainte-marie.fr 🕐 Mar and Oct daily 10–12:30, 2–5:30; Apr–Jun 10–12:30, 2–6; Jul–Aug Mon–Fri 9:30–7, Sat, Sun 9:30–12:30, 2–7; Nov 10–12, 2–5:30; Dec–Feb 10–12, 2–5

Adrenalin sports in the canyon

Musée de la Préhistoire des Gorges du Verdon
✉ route de Montmeyan, 04500 Quinson ☎ 04 92 74 09 59; www.museeprehistoire.com 🕐 Feb–Mar daily 10–6; Apr–Sep 10–7; Jul–Aug 10–8; Oct–mid-Dec 10–6 💶 Moderate

---

GORGES DU VERDON: INSIDE INFO

Top tips The roads that run along each side of the canyon are **narrow and winding**, and in places only just wide enough for two cars to pass – so take extra care while driving.

- The **Sentier Martel footpath** along the river has collapsed tunnels and is subject to sudden changes in water level. It is best walked in the safety of a group or with an experienced guide.
- If you don't feel like driving along the whole canyon, then **a short stretch of the Corniche Sublime** will give you a good taster of this natural phenomenon.
- **Faïence** is the local decorative earthenware pottery, and you'll see it on sale in villages around the Gorges, but especially on the streets and in the little shops of Moustiers-Ste-Marie.

Don't miss The stunning modern, boat-shaped **Musée de la Préhistoire des Gorges du Verdon,** designed by English architect Sir Norman Foster, is at Quinson, just west of Lac de Ste-Croix. It opened in 2001, and with its re-created cave, interactive displays and neolithic tools and other items found in the area, it's a fabulous museum dedicated to the people who inhabited the Gorges area around 400,000 years ago.

6 Nice

Nice, one of the biggest cities along the Mediterranean coast and the capital of the Riviera, fairly buzzes with life. There's an old Italian corner to discover, plus some of the top art galleries of the region, and if you're here in the two weeks before Lent, you're bound to get swept up by the colourful frenzy of the Mardi-Gras carnival.

Nice's history has been influenced by successive owners, including the Ligurians, the Greeks and the Romans, and only became part of France when the Italians (who called it Nizza) handed it over to the French in 1860. In the 19th century it became a chic winter resort, numbering Queen Victoria among its illustrious visitors.

Many splendid belle-époque buildings line the broad, noisy promenade des Anglais along the seafront, including the magnificent domed **Hotel Negresco**. The Paillon promenade divides the new town from the Italianate jumble of the old

TOP GALLERIES AT A GLANCE

Musée d'Art Moderne et d'Art Contemporain
This intriguing modern structure of four towers linked by bowed girders and glass holds a great collection of avant-garde and pop-art dating from the 1960s. Highlights include Andy Warhol's *Campbell's Soup Cans*.
✉ promenade des Arts ☎ 04 97 13 42 01; www.mamac-nice.org ⏰ Tue–Sun 10–6 💶 Free

Musée Henri Matisse
Matisse (1869–1954), who spearheaded the Fauvist movement in the early 20th century, moved to Nice in 1917, and is buried in the cemetery near by. This gallery, in a 17th-century villa in the gardens at Cimiez, contains the artist's breathtaking collection of his own sinuous sketches and brightly coloured gouache paintings.
✉ 164 avenue des Arènes de Cimiez ☎ 04 93 81 08 08; www.musee-matisse-nice.org ⏰ Wed–Mon 10–6 💶 Moderate

Musée Marc Chagall/Musée du Message Biblique
A museum specially designed to hold the French Surrealist artist's biblical works, with fabulous stained-glass panels, mosaics and paintings.
✉ avenue de Dr Ménard, Boulevard du Cimiez ☎ 04 93 53 87 20; www.musee-chagall.fr ⏰ May–Oct Wed–Mon 10–6; Nov–Apr Wed–Mon 10–5 💶 Moderate

Musée des Beaux-Arts
In a private mansion dating from 1876, near the western end of the beach, with paintings and sculpture, mainly 17th to 19th century. Highlights include works by Fragonard, Degas, Rodin and Dufy.
✉ 33 avenue des Baumettes ☎ 04 92 15 28 28; www.musee-beaux-arts-nice.org ⏰ Tue–Sun 10–6 💶 Free

The curve of the beach is backed by the promenade des Anglais

quarter, where you'll find interesting little shops and cafés and churches. The Cimiez hill was the centre of the Roman settlement, and you can explore a small oval **amphitheatre** here and a **museum** of excavated remains.

There are 19 different galleries and museums to discover in Nice – the panel opposite provides a quick guide to four of the best of them.

TAKING A BREAK

Dine on fabulous fresh seafood with a Mediterranean twist at the moderately priced **L'Âne Rouge**, overlooking the harbour (7 quai des Deux-Emmanuel, tel: 04 93 8949 63).

✚ 214 C3
Tourist Information Office
✉ 5 promenade des Anglais, 06000 ☎ 08 92 707 407; www.nicetourism.com
🕐 May–Sep Mon–Sat 9–8, Sun 9–6; Oct–Apr Mon–Sat 9–6

NICE: INSIDE INFO

Top tip With the **French Riviera Pass** you get entrance to the main sights and museums and discounts in many shops and restaurants. It's available for one, two or three days and is not limited to Nice. Check the website for details (www.frenchrivierapass.com).

Hidden gems Two of the lesser-known museums, but well worth seeking out, are the **Asian Arts Museum**, at 405 promenade des Anglais, and the **Anatole Jakovsky International Museum of Modern Art,** on avenue de Fabron, which houses naïve art from all over the world.

One to miss If you have to miss out on one of the galleries, skip the **Musée d'Art et d'Histoire,** on rue de France, which is limited to the story of Nice and only open at weekends.

At Your Leisure

7 Puy de Dôme and Clermont-Ferrand

The Massif Central is France's volcano belt and the best vantage point is from the summit of the 1,465m (4,806ft) Puy de Dôme, which can be ascended on foot or by bus. The 360-degree view from the top takes in the surrounding mountain chains and Clermont-Ferrand below. The capital of the Auvergne, Clermont-Ferrand is an industrial city built around a volcanic mound. On the top stands a Gothic cathedral of black lava, with a prominent spire. The city's other main sight is the Romanesque church of **Notre-Dame-du-Port**. Nearby is **Vulcania**, a theme park with games and displays on all things volcanic.

➕ 217 F2

Tourist Information Office

✉ place de la Victoire 63000 Clermont-Ferrand ☎ 04 73 98 65 00 🕐 May–Sep Mon–Fri 9–7, Sat–Sun 10–7; Oct–Apr Mon–Fri 9–6, Sat 10–1, 2–6, Sun 9:30–12:30, 2–6

Vulcania

✉ Route de Mazayes, St-Ours-Les-Roches, Clermont-Ferrand ☎ 04 73 19 70 00; www.vulcania.com 🕐 24 Mar–Jun and 25 Oct–14 Nov daily 10–6; Jul 10–7 (14 Jul–25 Aug Wed 10–11pm); Aug 10–7:30; Sep–24 Oct Wed–Sun 10–6 💶 Expensive

8 Lyon

France's third most populous city, Lyon is a gastronomic centre *par excellence*, and boasts a history that once saw it as the capital of the Roman Gallic empire.

Its centre lies along the narrow wedge, or Presqu'île, sandwiched between the rivers Saône and Rhône, with modern suburbs sprawling to the east. To the west lies the old Renaissance quarter known as **Vieux Lyon**, and this is a good place to start any exploration. The main streets – rue St-Jean and rue de Boeuf – run parallel with the Saône, and are characterized by the tall housesk, which rest on a warren of *traboules* – vaulted walkways and arcades filled with boutiques, galleries and cafés. For the quintessential Lyon experience, stop off at a *bouchon* bistro for a snack and watch the world go by. The **Cathédrale St-Jean** is also in this area, a remarkable building with four low, sturdy towers that mark the transition between Romanesque and Gothic architecture.

To catch up with the city's Roman history, take the funicular from near

The views from Puy de Dôme over France's volcano belt are superb

the cathedral up the Fourvière hill, where the landmark **Basilique Notre-Dame de Fourvière** was constructed in the 19th century on the site of the original forum. Just south of here, the underground **Roman museum** has intriguing remains, including a rare mosaic depicting a circus.

There are more great museums to explore around the centre, including a world-class art gallery, the **Musée des Beaux-Arts**, and various smaller museums dedicated to the silk industry, on which much of the city's wealth was founded. Four métro lines make it easy to get around.

➕ 218 C3
Tourist Information Office
✉ place Bellecour, 69002 ☎ 04 72 77 69 69; www.lyon-france.com ⏰ Daily 9–6

Cathédrale St-Jean ✉ place St-Jean
⏰ Mon–Fri 8–12, 2–7:30 (5pm Sat–Sun)

Musée de la Civilisation Gallo-Romaine
✉ 17 rue Cléberg ☎ 04 72 38 81 90
⏰ Tue–Sun 10–6 💰 Inexpensive, free on Thu

Musée des Beaux-Arts ✉ 20 place des Terreaux ☎ 04 72 10 17 40 ⏰ Sat–Mon, Wed–Thu 10–6, Fri 10:30–6; alternate galleries closed at lunchtime 💰 Moderate

9 Vienne
This ancient town lies about 20km (12.5 miles) south of Lyon, on the Rhône, offering a vivid picture of a

A cable car at Chamonix-Mont-Blanc, one of France's most popular ski resorts

major Roman settlement, built when the Roman empire was at the height of its powers. A *petit train* links the main sites in summer. The best remains are at the **Musée et Sites Archéologique de St-Romain-en-Gal**, where you can wander among the outlines of houses, streets, public baths and workshops, and admire the mosaics. The huge, stepped, semicircular amphitheatre, or **Théâtre Romain**, on rue du Cirque, was built in AD50 and thoroughly restored in the 20th century, and is a venue for summer concerts. Vienne flourished again as an ecclesiastical centre in the 12th century, but declined as Lyon expanded.

➕ 218 C2
Tourist Information Office
✉ cours Brilliet, 38200 ☎ 04 74 53 80 30; www.vienne-tourisme.com ⏰ Jul–Aug Mon–Sat 10–6, Sun 10–5; Sep–Jun Mon–Sat 9–noon, 1:30–6, Sun 10–12, 2–5

Musée et Sites Archéologique de St-Romain-en-Gal
✉ route D502 ☎ 04 74 53 74 01 ⏰ Mar–Oct Tue–Sun 10–6; Nov–Feb 10–5 💰 Inexpensive

10 Chamonix-Mont-Blanc
Situated beneath Western Europe's highest mountain, Mont Blanc, the town of Chamonix is well known as

a ski resort in winter. From spring to autumn its transport infrastructure offers an easy introduction to the French Alps. The two most popular excursions from the town are by cable car up to the 3,842m (12,605ft) **Aiguille du Midi**, from where there are 360-degree mountain views, and the rack-and-pinion Montenvers railway to see the **Mer de Glace** glacier and ice cave, which is freshly carved each year.

⊞ 219 F3
Tourist Information Office
✉ 85 place du Triangle de l'Amitié 74400 Chamonix-Mont-Blanc ☎ 04 50 53 00 24; www.chamonix.com ⊙ Mon–Sat 9–12:30, 2–6

⑪ Grenoble

Grenoble is a vibrant high-tech city built on a flat plain in the shadow of the Alps. The best way to see it is from the **cable car**, which goes from the centre of the old-town quarter, high over the River Isère and up to the 16th-century Fort de la Bastille (moderate, closed Jan). Its proximity to the mountains makes it an obvious year-round sporting destination for walkers, skiers, climbers and adrenaline enthusiasts, but Grenoble is also keen to promote its connections to the arts. It's proud of its links with the novelist Stendhal, who was born here in 1783, and has several excellent art museums, of which the **Musée de Grenoble** has the best collection, and the **Centre National d'Art Contemporain** the more eccentric.

⊞ 219 D2
Tourist Information Office
✉ 14 rue de la République, 38019
☎ 04 76 42 41 41; www.grenoble-tourisme.com ⊙ Mon–Sat 9–6:30 all year; also May–Sep Sun 10–1, 2–5; Oct–Apr Sun 10–1

Musée de Grenoble ✉ 5 place de Lavalette
☎ 04 76 63 44 44; www.museedegrenoble.fr
⊙ Wed–Mon 10–6:30 ⊞ Inexpensive

Le Magasin – Centre National d'Art Contemporain
✉ 155 cours Berriat ☎ 04 76 21 95 84 ;
www.magasin-cnac.org ⊙ Tue–Sun 2–7
⊞ Inexpensive, under-10's free

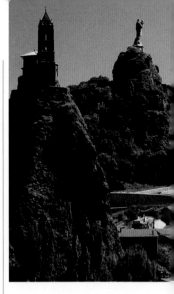

The town and cathedral of Le Puy-en-Velay are UNESCO World Heritage sites

⑫ Le Puy-en-Velay

In the Middle Ages this extraordinary town, in the south of the Auvergne region, was both a place of veneration in itself and a gathering point for departure on the arduous pilgrimage to Santiago de Compostela in Spain. Two monuments look down on it from their respective volcanic crags: the **Chapelle de Saint-Michel** and a giant iron statue of **Notre-Dame de France**, built out of iron from Russian cannons captured at the siege of Sebastopol. The town centre, including the **cathedral** with its 12th-century cloister, is protected as a UNESCO World Heritage Site.

⊞ 218 B1
Tourist Information Office
✉ 2 Place du Clauzel 43000 Le Puy-en-Velay
☎ 04 71 09 38 41; www.ot-lepuyenvelay.fr
⊙ Easter–Jun, Mon–Sat 8:30–12, 1:30–6:15, Sun 9:30–12:30, 2–6; Jul–Aug Mon–Sat 8:30–7, Sun 9:30–12:30, 2–6; Oct–Easter Mon–Sat 8:30–12, 1:30–6:15, Sun 10–12

⑬ Gorges du Tarn

The precipitous and winding limestone chasm along the River Tarn is one of the great beauty-spots of France. It is threaded through by the D907b, which strings together tiny medieval villages from Ispagnac in the northeast to Le Rozier in the southwest, including Ste-Énimie, St-Chély and Peyreleau.

Throughout its 50km (31-miles) length the gorge is never more than 500m (1,640ft) wide, sometimes narrowing to just 30m (98ft), and driving through it is a challenge in summer for the volume of slow-moving vehicles, and in winter for the Col de Perjuret, which can be blocked off by snow. Kayaking is one way to avoid the traffic, and boats are available for rent at several points along the route. Above the canyon stretch the limestone plateaux of the **Causses**, grazed by sheep and goats.

➕ 212 B4

Tourist Information Office

✉ Gorges du Tarn, Causse, Dourbie, 12640 Rivière sur Tarn ☎ 05 65 59 74 28; www.gorgesdutarn.com

🔟 Montpellier

White, modern architecture, wide squares, green parks and broad walkways are some of the distinctive features of this lively Mediterranean city. Its 120km (75 miles) of cycle routes make it a pleasure to explore, and bicycles and mopeds can easily be rented, with secure parking at over 1,000 points across the city. It's a city of 24-hour entertainment and arts festivals, which makes it popular with young people.

Place de la Comédie, in the old town, is the centre of the action, with the rue du Peyrou offering some of the best historical architecture and a triumphal arch. The **Musée Fabre** (currently closed) is one of the biggest art galleries in France, and well worth a visit for its touring exhibitions, as well as permanent collections of Flemish and Dutch art from the 16th to 17th centuries, neo-classical works, and paintings by 19th-century romantic artists, including Delacroix, Carot and Sisley.

➕ 212 C3

Tourist Information Office

✉ place de la Comédie, 30 allée Jean de Lattre de Tassigny, 34000 ☎ 04 67 60 60 60; www.ot-montpellier.fr 🕐 Mon–Fri 9:30–7:30, Sat 9:30–6, Sun 9:30–1, 2:30–6

Vélomagg (cycle rental)

✉ 27, rue Maguelone ☎ 04 67 22 87 82

Musée Fabre

✉ 39 boulevard Bonne Nouvelle, 34000 ☎ 04 67 14 33 00; www.museefabre. montpellier-agglo.com 🕐 Tue, Thu–Fri, Sun 10–6, Wed 1–9, Sat 11–6 💰 Moderate; free 1st Sun of the month

Montpellier's broad place de la Comédie

15 Les Baux-de-Provence

For the classic views of this ruined pinnacle fortress, be there at dawn or sunset if you can, when the low light turns the walls to gold. The panorama from the top across the surrounding Alpilles hills and to the plain below is stunning at any time, and shows what an excellent defensive position this was for the powerful and often brutal lords of Baux in the 12th to 15th centuries.

Beneath the walls of the citadel lies a small village, its pretty streets lined with arts and crafts shops and places to eat. It can get very busy here in summer, and when parking areas fill up the access road may be closed.

✚ 213 E3
Tourist Information Office
✉ Maison du Roi, 13520 ☎ 04 90 54 34 39; www.lesbauxdeprovence.com 🕐 May–Sep Mon–Fri 9–6, Sat–Sun 10–5:30; Oct–Apr Mon–Fri 9:30–5

16 Aix-en-Provence

There are more than 100 fountains in this gracious town, including one on the broad and bustling Cours Mirabeau that comes straight from the ground at a temperature of 36°C (96°F). The boulevard, with shady plane trees down the centre, is the heart of **Vieil Aix**, and a great place to pause for a coffee in one of the many cafés, watch the world go past and admire the grand 17th- and 18th-century mansions on the opposite side. Between here and the

Cathédrale St-Sauveur are some of the most interesting shops, selling antiques, haute couture and colourful Provençal handicrafts.

The cathedral has some tapestries and medieval art, but the artist celebrated in the town is Paul Cézanne, who was born in 1839 at 28 rue de l'Opéra. His most famous series of paintings depict the landscapes around Montagne Ste-Victoire, which lies to the east of Aix. You can view his preserved studio on rue Cézanne, but to see some of his paintings head to the **Musée Granet**.

✚ 213 F3
Tourist Information Office
✉ 2 place Général de Gaulle, 13100 ☎ 04 42 16 11 61; www.aixenprovencetourism.com 🕐 Apr–Sep Mon–Sat 8:30–8, Sun 10–1, 2–6; Oct–Mar Mon–Sat 8:30–7, Sun 10–1, 2–6

Musée Granet
✉ place St-Jean de Malte, quartier Mazarin ☎ 04 52 88 32 🕐 Jun–Sep 11–7; Oct–May 12–6 💷 Inexpensive

17 Marseille

The trading port of Marseille, a city of around one million people, has a reputation as a melting pot of cultures, with a significant population of North African immigrants.

Start any visit at the **Vieux Port** (Old Port), where thousands of boats jostle for space in the rectangular

One of more than a hundred fountains that grace Aix-en-Provence

Visit Château d'If by boat and enjoy
beautiful views over Marseille

basin. To the north is the colourful
le Panier district, heavily damaged
during World War II but scattered
with interesting historic buildings.
It leads up to the art gallery and
archaeology museum, **La Vieille
Charité**, in a 17th-century former
hospice, and the beautifully bold,
striped 19th-century **Cathédrale
de la Major**. To the east, the main
shopping streets are off the artery of
la Canebière, and you'll also find the
fascinating **Musée de l'Histoire
de Marseille** here. Restaurants are
plentiful in the area south of
the Vieux Port, the **Quartier de
l'Arsenal**, and this is where you
should go to taste the famous local
fish soup, *bouillabaisse*.

If you have time, the 15-minute
boat ride to the **Château d'If** is worth
it for the views and the thrill of seeing
the fortress there, linked to Alexandre
Dumas' 19th-century tale, *The Count
of Monte Cristo*.

➕ 213 F3

Tourist Information Office

✉ 4 la Canebière, 13001 ☎ 04 91 13 89 00;
www.marseille-tourisme.com 🕐 Mon–Sat 9–7,
Sun 10–5

La Vieille Charité

✉ 2 rue de la Charité ☎ 04 91 14 58 80;
www.vieille-charite-marseille.org 🕐 Jul–Sep
Tue–Sun 11–6; Oct–Jun 10–5 💰 Inexpensive

Musée de l'Histoire de Marseille

✉ cours Belsunce, Centre Bourse
☎ 04 91 90 42 22 🕐 Mon–Sat noon–7
💰 Inexpensive, under-5s free

The elegant tower of the Cathédrale
de la Major at Marseille

18 St-Tropez

St-Tropez is famous for fun, sun and celebrity glitz, its quay packed with yachts, its narrow streets with visitors enjoying the glamour and the *chic*. Despite all this surface luxury, what drew the rich and famous here in the first place can still be found in glimpses of the lovely old fishing village, in the **Vieille Ville**, with its small-scale, charming old houses.

The easiest way to get into the town, avoiding the worst of the traffic, is to park at Port Grimaud and catch the ferry across the bay.

➕ 214 B3
Tourist Information Office
✉ quai Jean-Jaurès (main part of harbour front) ☎ 08 92 68 48 28; www.saint-tropez.st
🕐 Jan–Mar 9:30–12:30, 2–6; Apr–Jun, Sep–Oct 9:30–12:30, 2–7; Jul–Aug daily 9:30–1:30, 3–8. Closed Nov–Dec

19 Cannes

Classy Cannes is unusual among Riviera resorts: it has a long sandy beach. Unfortunately, access to many parts is limited by private and hotel ownership, but there's a public beach at the western end of the town's great seafront promenade, **la Croisette**. Floodlit by night and lined with expensive shops, this is the place to see and be seen, or perhaps try your own hands in the concrete prints of the stars, set in the pavement outside the Palais des Festivals. There's more shopping along the rue d'Antibes.

The town is busy all year, but the social highlight is May, when Cannes transforms into Hollywood-on-Sea for the prestigious film festival.

➕ 214 B3
Tourist Information Office
✉ Palais des Festivals, 1 boulevard de la Croisette, 06403 ☎ 04 92 99 84 22; www.cannes.fr; www.festival-cannes.com
🕐 Jul–Aug daily 9–8; Sep–Jun 9–7

20 Antibes

Less showy than Cannes, Antibes still attracts its share of yachts. The most appealing parts of the town are in the old quarter, where Italianate buildings are crowded into the remains of a 17th-century defensive wall designed

Handprints of Hollywood's finest are set in concrete ouside the Palais des Festivals

by the military engineer Vauban. The chief reason, however, to visit Antibes is the **Musée Picasso**. Paintings, drawings, ceramics and sculptures, mostly dating to the three months in 1946 that Picasso spent here, are housed in a severe medieval fortress that once belonged to the Grimaldis of Monaco.

➕ 214 C3
Tourist Information Office
✉ 11 place Général de Gaulle, 06600 ☎ 04 92 90 53 00; www.antibesjuanlespins.com 🕐 Jul–Aug daily 9–7; Sep–Jun Mon–Fri 9–12:30, 1:30–6, Sat 9–12, 2–6

Musée Picasso
✉ Château Grimaldi ☎ 04 92 90 54 20
🕐 Mid-Jun–mid-Sep 10–6; Jul–Aug 10–8; mid-Sep–mid-Jun Tue–Sun 10–12, 2–6
💰 Expensive

21 Grasse

The lavender fields are one of the memorable sights of Provence, and the flowers they produce are a key ingredient in the modern perfume industry. Molinard, Galimard and Fragonard are the great perfumeries located in Grasse, the so-called Perfume Capital of the World, which supplies perfumes to all the biggest names, including Chanel and Dior. All three offer factory tours. Roses and jasmine, flowers essential to the industry, are celebrated with their own **festivals** in May and August. The **cathedral**, on place Godeau, is worth a quick look inside for the three early paintings by Rubens, dating from 1601.

🕂 214 B3

Tourist Information Office

✉ Palais de Congrès, 22 cours Honoré Cresp, 06130 ☎ 04 93 36 66 66; www.grasse.fr
🕐 Mid-Jun–mid-Sep daily 9–7; mid-Sep–mid-Jun 9–12:30, 2–6

22 Monaco

The Grimaldi dynasty's principality of Monaco covers just 2sq km (0.8 sq mile), and is known as the glitzy tax refuge of the super-rich. Since its origins as a medieval fortress, it has become a highly charged and spotlessly clean city, expanding upwards via skyscrapers and outwards on to artificial rocky platforms. Its unique status is due to its protection by Napoleon, who gets his own museum in the royal **Palais du Prince**. Witness the changing of the guard (daily 11:55). Members of the Grimaldi family, including movie star Princess Grace (1929–82), are buried in the **cathedral**. East of here is Monte Carlo, where the **Casino** raises a steady revenue (➤ 164).

🕂 214 C4

Tourist Information Office

✉ 2a boulevard des Moulins, 98000
☎ 377/92 16 61 16; www.visitmonaco.com
🕐 Mon–Sat 9–7, Sun 10–noon

FOR KIDS

■ **Gorges du Verdon**: Try the thrills and spills of white-water rafting or canoeing down the river from Aboard Rafting (Casteliane 18, place de l'Église, tel: 04 92 83 76 11, www.aboard-rafting.com, open Apr–Sep).

■ **Mougins, north of Cannes**: At Buggy Cross three tracks offer racing on quad bikes or mini-motorcycles, and vehicles for over-4s (located by the Automobile Museum, tel: 04 93 69 02 74, www.buggycross. fr, open Wed, Sat–Sun and during French school holidays).

Enjoying the sunshine at an outdoor café in Monte Carlo

Where to... Stay

Prices

Expect to pay per night for a double room
€ up to €120   €€ €120–€220   €€€ over €220

Abbaye de Sainte Croix €€–€€€

This restored 12th-century abbey sits in a prominent position with views of Provençal landscapes. The original Romanesque architecture shines through the simple yet luxurious décor of the 21 rooms and four suites. It's a wonderful retreat after sightseeing, with a pool and a gastronomic restaurant.
⊞ 213 E3 ⊠ Val-de-Cuech, 13300 Salon-de-Provence ☎ 04 90 56 24 55; www.hotels-provence.com ⓒ Closed Nov–end Mar

Hostellerie de Cacharel €€

Style and simplicity are the watchwords at this comfortable hostellerie, set in the middle of a wildlife-rich nature reserve in the Camargue, complete with its own stables. Flamingos feed in the surrounding ponds and marshes, and there's no television – this is a real get-away place. There's no restaurant either, but a dinner platter can be ordered in advance. The white-painted building is typical of the area, with beamed ceilings, big fireplaces and tiled floors, and furnishings in the 16 bedrooms are stylish and comfortable. There's also an outdoor swimming pool, which is a great place to relax in the summer.
⊞ 213 D3 ⊠ route de Cacharel, 13460 Saintes-Maries-de-la-Mer ☎ 04 90 97 95 44; www.hotel-cacharel.com

Hôtel Calendal €

A three-star hotel located close to the arenas in Arles, the Calendal makes a comfortable and inexpensive base for exploring the town and the wider area. There are 38 air-conditioned and well-appointed bedrooms, with wonderful views to the arenas or over a garden courtyard. Inside, you'll find the tiled floors and wrought iron typical of Provence. Breakfast can be eaten in the garden under the palm trees.
⊞ 213 E3 ⊠ 5 rue de Laure, 13200 Arles ☎ 04 90 96 11 89; www.lecalendal.com ⓒ Closed Jan

Hôtel de la Cité €€€

Hotels don't come much more sumptuous than this one in Carcassonne, and it's no surprise to learn that Queen Elizabeth II has stayed here. It's in the old part of the city, and one of the few places to retain its garden. There are 50 rooms and 11 themed suites, decorated in styles from Provençal comfort to neo-Gothic grandeur. Every service is discreetly available, including an outdoor pool.
⊞ 212 A2 ⊠ place Auguste-Pierre Pont, 11000 Carcassonne ☎ 04 68 71 98 71; www.hoteldelacite.com ⓒ Closed end Jan–mid-Mar

Hôtel Imperator Concorde €€–€€€

There's more than a touch of extravagance in this beautiful hotel, which overlooks the Jardin de la Fontaine and place Picasso in the heart of Nîmes. Its roadside setting is made up for by the wonderful gardens. There are 62 spacious rooms, well-designed and comfortable, with air-conditioning. Sip a cocktail before dinner with the ghosts of Ava Gardner and Ernest Hemingway, who both stayed here in the past. Breakfast is not included in the room price.

Where to... 161

Where to...
Eat and Drink

Prices

Expect to pay per person for a meal, excluding drinks

€ up to €30   €€ €30–€60   €€€ over €60

Chez Fonfon €€€

Escape the more touristy areas of the old port in Marseille, and come instead to the fishing port, now a conservation area, to taste *bouillabaisse*, the quintessential fish soup for which the city is famous. Chez Fonfon is a family-run place on the waterfront, well known to the locals for more than 50 years. Inside, the styling is cool, elegant Mediterranean, with green basket-weave chairs, tiled floor, and bright splashes of colour provided by Provençal fabrics. A bottle of house wine with your meal costs around €15.

🕂 213 F3 ⊠ 140 rue du Vallon des Auffes, 13007 Marseille ☎ 04 91 52 14 38; www.chez-fonfon.com 🕐 Mon 7:30–9:45, Tue–Sat 12–2, 7:30–9:45. Closed Mon Nov–May

Christian Étienne €€

The food does not come cheap at this beautiful Avignon restaurant, but the quality is excellent and the setting superb. It's housed in a wonderful 14th-century palace, complete with painted ceilings and frescos, and with a priceless view out from the terrace over the fabulous Palais des Papes. Truffles are a significant feature of the

---

🕂 213 D4 ⊠ quai de la Fontaine, 30000 Nîmes ☎ 04 66 21 90 30; www.hotel-imperator.com

Hôtel Negresco €€€

Prominently located on the famous promenade des Anglais, the black dome of the Negresco is a much-loved Nice landmark dating back to 1912. Inside, it's a luxurious palace to art, with works covering all periods from the Renaissance to the 21st century. Everything is on a grand scale, and guests staying in the 117 rooms and 24 suites have access to the hotel's own private stretch of Mediterranean beach.

🕂 214 C3 ⊠ 37 promenade des Anglais, 06000 Nice ☎ 04 93 16 64 00; www.hotel-negresco-nice.com

Le Mas d'Aigret €–€€

If you want to see the dawn rise over Les Baux, then you'll need to stay in the village, and this unusual hotel carved into the rocky hillside is a great place to be, with wonderful views. There are 16

air-conditioned bedrooms, simply but tastefully furnished, with cool, white-painted furniture and pretty floral bed-covers. Facilities at this three-star hotel include a well-appointed lounge, a bar and an outdoor swimming pool.

🕂 213 E3 ⊠ 13520 Les Baux-de-Provence ☎ 04 90 54 20 00; www.masdaigret.com

La Reine Astrid €€–€€€

For a touch of luxury in Lyon, head for this four-star hotel in a residential district, close to the Parc Tête d'Or. There are 88 suites (including three apartments), with one or two bedrooms each, richly furnished in shades of deep blue, red and gold. Suites are also equipped with a kitchen, and there's an appealing terraced restaurant on site, or you can easily walk the short distance to sample the local eateries. The hotel facilities include a lounge, a cocktail bar and a gym.

🕂 218 C3 ⊠ 26 boulevard des Belges, 69006 Lyon ☎ 04 72 82 18 00; www.warwickastrid.com

sophisticated menu and the black truffle omelette is not to be missed.

🕂 213 E4 ⊠ 10 rue de Mons, 84000 Avignon ☎ 04 90 86 16 50; www.christian-etienne.fr ⊙ Tue–Sat noon–1:15,7:30–9:15

La Brasserie des Brotteaux €€–€€€

This old brasserie in Lyon has been serving food since 1913. Inside you'll find antiques, bright tiles and lots of polished glass and mirrors. Eat outside or retreat into the air-conditioned interior. There's a choice of *prix-fixe* menus, salads, and, even, Aberdeen Angus beef.

🕂 218 E3 ⊠ 1 place Jules Ferry, 69006 Lyon ☎ 04 72 74 03 98 ⊙ Mon–Fri 7:30am–midnight, Sat 10–3, 6:30–midnight

L'Âne Rouge €€

Seafood is the flavour of every day in this elegant restaurant with a terrace overlooking the harbour. High-backed chairs offer every comfort inside as you dine, perhaps, on prawn tart, succulent lobster or scallops roasted with chorizo, tomatoes and thyme. Fish lovers can choose from a daily selection of fresh fish. You can also order luxury picnic baskets.

🕂 214 C3 ⊠ 7 quai des Deux-Emmanuel, 06300 Nice ☎ 04 93 89 49 63; www.anerougenice.com ⊙ Fri–Tue 12–2:30, 7:30–9:30, Wed 12:30–2:30, Thu 7:30–9:30. Closed 8 Feb–13 Mar

Le Clos de la Violette €€€

One of the most popular and famous restaurants of Southeast France is this formal, sober and elegant restaurant in the heart of Aix-en-Provence, which boasts a magnificent garden and a terrace. Chef Jean Marc Banzo specializes in high-quality, Provencal and Mediterranean cuisine, which changes with the seasons. *Terrine de foie gras de canard, langoustines à la plancha, risotto crémeux au parmesan* are all choices to go for.

🕂 213 F3 ⊠ 10 avenue de la Violette, 13100 Aix-en-Provence ☎ 04 42 23 30 71 ⊙ Tue–Sat 12–1:30, 7:30–9:30

Le Louis XV €€€

If you're feeling in extravagant mode, there's only one place to dine out in Monaco – this very special restaurant in the magnificent Hôtel de Paris. The hotel was built in 1864, and the plush Louis XV-style dining room is the perfect backdrop for food cooked by one of France's top chefs, Alain Ducasse. The menu reflects themes such as hunting or the farm, and does not disappoint. House wine starts at €90 a bottle.

🕂 214 C4 ⊠ Hôtel de Paris, place du Casino, 98000 Monaco ☎ 377 98 06 88 64; www.alain-ducasse.com ⊙ Thu–Mon noon–2, 7:30–9:30; Jul–Aug Wed 7:30–9:30. Closed Dec

L'Univers de Christian Plumail €€–€€€

One of the most chic addresses in Nice, chef Christian Plumail is climbing the ladder of gastronomic success with his superb restaurant. The clean lines of the dining room with its modern sculpture and art make the perfect canvas for the beautifully presented dishes which demonstrate the principles of classic French cuisine. The menu changes weekly, and there are also seasonal menus, which feature superb dishes to whet the appetite of the most exacting gourmand and draw on local seasonal produce.

🕂 214 C3 ⊠ 53 boulevard Jean Jaurès, 06300 Nice ☎ 04 93 62 32 22; www.christian-plumail.com ⊙ Mon 7:30–9:30, Tue–Fri 12–2, 7:30–9:30, Sat 7:30–9:30

Pierre Reboul €€–€€€

Located in the historic centre of Aix-en-Provence, between the Palais de Justice and le Cours Mirabeau, this modern restaurant with contemporary décor and comfortable ambience. Under the vaulted ceilings, chef Pierre Reboul serves up a Provençal cuisine using local ingredients.

🕂 213 F3 ⊠ 11 Petite Rue St-Jean, 13100 Aix-en-Provence ☎ 04 22 20 58 26; www.restaurant-pierre-reboul.com ⊙ Tue–Sat 12–1:30, 7:30–9:30

Where to... Shop

There's no shortage of great shopping in this affluent part of France, with boutiques and big names in the towns and cities. Look out for the giant shopping mall on the edge of Grenoble, Grand'Place, which has around 140 shops and restaurants (tel: 04 76 09 55 45, open Mon–Sat 9:30–8). Lyon has the Part-Dieu Shopping Centre, with branches of Galeries Lafayette and Carrefour supermarket (17 rue de Dr Bouchut, tel: 04 72 60 60 62, open Mon–Sat 9:30–8).

FASHION AND SCENT

Fashionistas head for Cannes, and the likes of Jacques Loup, which stocks the latest designs and hottest labels in shoes, clothes and accessories (21 rue d'Antibes, tel: 04 93 39 28 35, open Mon–Sat 9:30–8). St-Tropez also has a reputation for glamour.

Look out for family-run shops in the region. These include Bijoux Dumont in Arles, where Provençal jewellery in gold, silver and semi-precious stones is made (3 rue du Palais, tel: 04 90 96 05 66, open Tue, Thu–Sat 9–12, 3–7). Seek out the handmade Roman-style sandals at Rondini in St-Tropez, as worn by Picasso (16 rue Clémenceau, tel: 04 94 97 19 55, open daily 9:30–noon, 3–7). Chapelier Mouret, in Avignon, is a great hat shop (20 rue des Marchands, tel: 04 90 85 39 38, open Tue–Sat 9:30–12:30, 2–7).

Grasse is the centre of the perfume industry – check out the factory and shop of Fragonard, a perfumerie dating back to the 18th century (20 boulevard Fragonard, tel: 04 92 42 34 34, open Mon–Fri 8:30–12:30, 1:30–6).

FOOD AND DRINK

Provence is known for its sweet treats. The best place to buy the diamond-shaped marzipan sweets called *calissons* is Confiserie Entrecasteaux at Aix-en-Provence, where they've been made to the same family recipe for more than four generations (24 cour Sextins, tel: 04 42 27 15 02, open Mon–Sat 8–noon, 2–7).

Olive oil is also widely produced, and you can buy oil and related products such as soap at Nice's Moulin à Huile Alziari (14 rue St-François-de-Paule, tel: 04 93 85 76 92, www.alziari.com.fr, open Mon–Sat 8:30–12:30, 2:15–7).

Lyon has two great markets. The covered Les Halles has food and flowers (102 cours Lafayette, tel: 04 72 10 30 30), while the Marché de la Croix Rousse, held on the boulevard of the same name, also includes fabric, household goods, crafts and clothing (tel: 04 72 10 30 30, open Tue–Sun 7–1). Grenoble has several markets, including the Marché place aux Herbes for food (Tue–Sun 6–1), Marché Victor Hugo on place Victor Hugo for manufactured goods (Mon–Sat 10–8), and Marché de l'Abbaye on place de la Commune for food and crafts (Tue–Sun 6–1).

ARTS AND CRAFTS

Buy faience porcelain at Atelier St-Michel in Moustiers-Sainte-Marie, (tel: 04 92 74 67 73, daily 2–5:30 (telephone to visit in the morning)), and check out the art at La Provence par Marc Ferrero (6 rue de a Paix, 06360 Eze, tel: 04 92 10 82 92, www.ferrerogallery.com, open daily 10–7). Nice has an arts anc crafts market (Marché Saleya d'Artisanat d'Art, open Jun–Sep Tue–Sun 6pm–midnight).

Where to...
Be Entertained

MUSIC AND THEATRE

Nîmes' **Roman amphitheatre** hosts events from concerts to bull fights (les Arènes, tel: 04 66 58 38 15). The **Roman amphitheatre** in Lyon is the setting for concerts, dance, theatre and cinema in summer – bring a cushion to sit on (6 rue de l'Antiquaille, tel: 04 72 57 15 40, open mid-Jun to mid-Aug).

A more traditional venue for classical music and opera is **l'Opéra Nationale de Lyon** (place de la Comédie, tel: 0826 30 53 25), while Montpellier has the grandiose **l'Opéra Comédie** (11 boulevard Victor Hugo, tel: 04 67 60 19 99, www.opera-montpellier.com).

For jazz, the intimate **Pelle-Mêle** in Marseille is hard to beat (8 place aux Huiles, tel: 04 91 54

85 26, open 2 May–10 Oct daily 6pm–3am). Grenoble also has a jazz club, **La Soupe aux Choux**, north of the river, which caters for all tastes from modern to trad (7 route de Lyon, tel: 04 76 87 05 67, open Tue–Sat 6–1am, closed Aug).

Cannes' modern **Palais des Festivals et des Congrès** hosts the annual film festival in May, but is also a year-round venue for international concerts, ballet, theatre and exhibitions (1 boulevard de la Croisette, tel: 04 93 39 01 01).

In Nice, **Auditorium du Conservatoire à Rayonnement Régional** (127 avenue de Brancolar, tel: 04 97 13 50 00, www.crr-nice.org), a new building for the conservatoire, hosts free concerts Monday evenings Oct–Apr.

CINEMA

There are 11 cinemas to choose from at Marseille's **Les Trois Palmes** (2 boulevard Léon-Bancal, tel: 04 91 87 91 87). **Le Club** in Grenoble has six-screens and often shows movies in their original language (9 bis rue de Phalonstère, tel: 04 76 46 13 38). Lyon has the **UGC Astoria** and **UGC Ciné Cité**; both show films in their original language (Astoria, 31 cours Vitton; Ciné Cité, 80 quai Charles de Gaulle, tel: 08 92 70 00 00).

BARS, CLUBS, CASINOS

If you're looking for an authentic Marseille experience with plenty of atmosphere, try the **Bar de la Marine**, facing the old harbour (15 quai de Rive-Neuve, tel: 04 91 54 95 42, open daily 7pm–2am). For something more contemporary try **Le Trolleybus** (24 quai de Rive Neuve, Vieux Port, tel: 04 91 54 30 45, www.letrolley.com, open

Thu–Sat 9pm–3am) with several distinct and spacious venues set in the old 17th-century arsenal.

La Siesta at Antibes offers every sort of night-time entertainment, from a casino to several dance floors (route du Bord de Mer, tel: 04 93 33 31 31, daily 10pm–5am). At **La Calle Ocho**, in Nîmes, you can dance to the rhythm of salsa and Cuban music (2 boulevard Amiral Coubert, Nîmes, tel: 04 66 67 34 59, open daily 8:30pm–2am).

The **Casino de Monte-Carlo** is probably the most famous in the world, and has featured in James Bond movies (place du Casino, tel: 98 06 21 21). If you're still feeling lucky, head for the bright lights of Cannes and **Casino Les Princes** (50 boulevard de la Croisette, tel: 04 97 06 18 50, open daily 11am–4am, games room from 8pm), or chill out on the terrace of **Le Festival bar** (52 la boulevard de Croisette, tel: 04 93 38 04 81, open daily 9am–midnight, closed 20 Nov–26 Dec).

Southwest
France

Getting Your Bearings

Pine forest, dunes and long sandy beaches characterize the Atlantic coastline of France. What it lacks in fashionable cachet it makes up for in wide open spaces – in the excellent skiing in the Pyrénées in winter and the watersports offered along its inland lakes in summer – which make it a great family holiday destination.

The coastal flatlands, more rugged to the north of the Gironde estuary, more predictable to the south, stretch down to the Pyrénées. This mountain chain forms a natural boundary between France and Spain and is covered with pasture and forest at this western end. Mineral and thermal springs in the mountains' shadow, their potential first spotted by the Romans, have left a legacy of small resorts and spa towns, with the faded queen of them all, Biarritz, drawing a new young crowd to its surfing beaches today. The N117 is the main route for access across the south.

Inland, to the southeast of Périgueux, lies the lush Dordogne countryside, threaded with a slow-moving river and dotted with ancient villages.

The major cities of the region are the busy wine capital, Bordeaux, and modern, high-tech Toulouse, which are linked by fast a *autoroute*.

Cattle grazing in the Pyrénées (above); the sandy shore at Biarritz (opposite page);
Pont de Pierre Bridge over La Garonne at dusk (page 165)

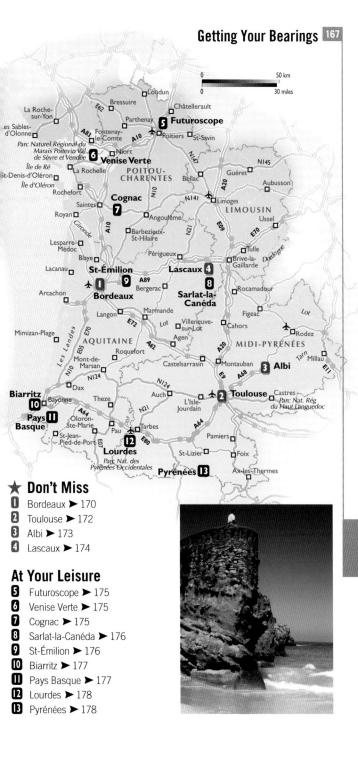

50 km
30 miles

Loudun
Bressuire
La Roche-sur-Yon
Châtellerault
Parthenay
5 Futuroscope
Les Sables-d'Olonne
Fontenay-le-Comte
Poitiers
St-Savin
Parc Naturel Régional du Marais Poitevin Val de Sèvre et Vendée
Niort
6 Venise Verte
NI45
Île de Ré
St-Denis-d'Oléron
La Rochelle
POITOU-CHARENTES
Guéret
Aubusson
Île d'Oléron
Rochefort
Bellac
Limoges
LIMOUSIN
Ussel
Cognac
7
Saintes
Angoulême
Royan
Gironde
Barbezieux-St-Hilaire
Tulle
Brive-la-Gaillarde
Dordogne
Lesparre-Médoc
Périgueux
Lascaux 4
Blaye
Lacanau
St-Émilion
9
A89
Bergerac
8
Rocamadour
Arcachon
Bordeaux
1
Marmande
Sarlat-la-Canéda
Figeac
Lot
Langon
Villeneuve-sur-Lot
Cahors
Rodez
Mimizan-Plage
Les Landes
AQUITAINE
Roquefort
Agen
MIDI-PYRÉNÉES
Montauban
Albi 3
Tarn
Millau
Mont-de-Marsan
Castelsarrasin
EII
Auch
Toulouse 2
Castres
Parc Nat. Rég du Haut Languedoc
Biarritz
10
Bayonne
Theze
Dax
L'Isle-Jourdain
Pays Basque 11
Oloron-Ste-Marie
Pau
Tarbes
Pamiers
St-Jean-Pied-de-Port
Lourdes 12
St-Lizier
Foix
Parc Nat. des Pyrénées Occidentales
Pyrénées 13
Ax-les-Thermes

In Four Days

If you're not quite sure where to begin your travels, this itinerary recommends a practical and enjoyable four days exploring Southwest France, taking in some of the best places to see using the Getting your Bearings map on the previous page. For more information see the main entries.

Day 1

Morning
Enjoy a morning exploring the wine city of **①Bordeaux** (➤ 170–171), and stock up on a few bottles. Climb the **Tour Pey-Berland** (➤ 170) for the views, and take your time over a bistro lunch at **Le Café des Arts** (➤ 171).

Afternoon
Head south through the pine forests of Les Landes to the holiday resort of **⑩Biarritz** (➤ 177), where you can relax on the **beaches**, or perhaps sample the pleasures of the **Musée du Chocolat**.

Evening
Unwind in a café or bar with a glass of wine, or treat yourself to a night out at the **ballet** (➤ 182).

Day 2

Morning
For a quick glimpse of the **⑪Pays Basque** (➤ 177–178), take minor roads inland and stroll around the pretty towns of **Sare** and **Ainhoa**. Take an early lunch in either one of them then pick up the A64/E80 motorway east for **②Toulouse** (➤ 172).

Afternoon
This magnificent city has plenty of landmark sites to fill an afternoon's sightseeing, including the splendid pilgrimage church of **St-Sernin** (left) and the high-tech **Cité de l'Espace space centre**.

Evening
There's plenty of **nightlife** to choose from in the city, from wine bars to an arts **cinema** (➤ 182).

Day 3

Morning
Take the A68 east and follow the trail of artist Toulouse-Lautrec in the old town of ❸ **Albi** (above; ➤ 173). Eat lunch in one of the cafés or bars on the main square, place du Vigan, then strike north via Cahors to **Rocamadour**.

Afternoon
Enjoy a walk around the Rocamadour (➤ 195–196), a stunningly beautiful and historic village built against a steep cliff.

Day 4

Morning
It's a short hop to ❽ **Sarlat-la-Canéda** (➤ 176), a golden stone town with a busy street market. For lunch in a restaurant here, try the local delicacies, such as *canard* (duck) and *foie gras*.

Afternoon and Evening
Book ahead to visit the famous re-created prehistoric caves at ❹ **Lascaux** (➤ 174), with their vivid paintings faithfully reproduced. Have dinner at the nearby **Restaurant la Vielle Auberge** (➤ 174).

❶ Bordeaux

This great city and port on the River Garonne is the capital of the world's biggest wine-producing area. A lively hub, with its own university, it has magnificent architecture and splendid open spaces, with attractions that include a 1,000-year-old church, a remarkable Palladian theatre and a rich variety of museums and galleries.

The Romans may not have been the first to settle here (there is evidence that Celtic tribes were here 300 years before), but they were the first to make a serious impact – and the vine cultivation that they introduced set the city on a course of prosperity that has never faltered.

Bordeaux's wealth over the centuries can be seen in its expansive layout, with wide boulevards and open squares. The biggest of these is the **esplanade des Quinconces**, a vast tree-lined space by the river, established in the early 19th century on the site of a former château.

For good shopping in the city, head straight for **rue Sainte-Catherine** and **cours Georges Clemenceau**.

Bordeaux Highlights

The medieval old town stretches west and south from place de la Bourse, on the river bank. The twin spires of the **Cathédrale St-André** are an unmistakable city landmark to the southwest. Parts date back to the 10th century, and

View of St-André from the tower of Pey-Berland

medieval sculptures adorn the huge space of the interior. Eleanor of Aquitaine, ex-wife of Louis VII and a powerful force in her own right, married the future Henry II of England here in 1152.

The bell tower next to the cathedral is the **Tour Pey-Berland**, 50m (165ft) high and topped with the figure of Notre-Dame-d'Aquitaine; the climb to the top is worth it for the views.

The tourist office shares the place de la Comédie with one of the city's most remarkable buildings, the **Grand Théâtre**. Dating from 1773, it was designed by Victor Louis (who restored the cathedral at Chartres, ► 65) in Greek Palladian style as a temple to the arts, with a facade incorporating

THE RELUCTANT MAYOR
In the esplanade des Quinconces, look out for a statue of **Michel Eyquem de Montaigne** (1533–92), the great essayist. He was celebrated in his day as an original thinker, which may have been a reflection on his experimental upbringing – until the age of six, he was encouraged to speak nothing but Latin. Having previously served as a city councillor, against his own wishes he was elected Mayor of Bordeaux in 1581, and served successfully for four years in all.

12 Corinthian columns and statues of the Muses. The magnificent gilded interior was restored in 1991, and the acoustics are excellent – catch a concert there if you can.

Bordeaux's compact **Musée des Beaux-Arts** is just west of the cathedral, in the peaceful setting of the gardens of the Palais Rohan. Among other highlights of the collection, look out for Van Dyck's formidable portrait of Marie de Médicis and Delacroix's *La Grèce sur les Ruines de Missolonghi*. For contrast, the **CAPC Musée d'Art Contemporain**, north of the esplanade des Quinconces, has breathed new life into a former warehouse, and buzzes with multimedia and other innovative exhibitions.

TAKING A BREAK
Le Café des Arts, at 138 cours Victor-Hugo, is a lively place for a meal or a snack, with bistro offerings such as salads, omelettes and scallops (tel 05 56 91 78 46).

✚ 216 A1

Tourist Information Office
✉ 12 cours 30 Juillet ☎ 05 56 00 66 00; www.bordeaux-tourisme.com
🕐 May–Jun and Sep–Oct Mon–Sat 9–7, Sun 9:30–6:30; Jul–Aug Mon–Sat 9–7:30, Sun 9:30–6:30; Nov–Apr Mon–Sat 9–6:30, Sun 9:45–4:30

Cathédrale St-André
✉ place Puy-Berland ☎ 05 56 52 68 10 🕐 Mon 1–7:30; Tue, Thu–Sun 10–12, 2–8; Wed 10–12, 2–7:30

Grand Théâtre
✉ place de la Comédie ☎ 05 56 00 85 95

Musée des Beaux-Arts
✉ 20 Cours d'Albret ☎ 05 56 10 20 56 🕐 Wed–Mon 11–6 💷 Inexpensive

CAPC Musée d'Art Contemporain
✉ 7 rue Ferrère ☎ 05 56 00 81 50 🕐 Tue–Sun 11–6, also Wed 11–8
💷 Free; temporary exhibitions moderate

BORDEAUX: INSIDE INFO

Top tips For information about **tours of the local vineyards,** including tastings (*dégustations*), call in at the Maison du Vin, opposite the tourist office.
■ **Guided tours** of the CAPC Musée d'Art Contemporain take place on the weekends at 4pm. Entry to the permanent collections at both the Musée des Beaux Arts and the CAPC Musée d'Art Contemporain is free.
■ A new **tram system** opened in February 2007, allowing ease of access from the town centre to the outlying suburbs. When crossing major highways on the routes, look out for trams in addition to cars and buses.

2 Toulouse

Toulouse, a major city on the banks of the Garonne, is a centre for high-tech industry with the largest aeronautical site in Europe – Airbus Industrie – and an adventure park themed around space exploration. The latter, the Cité de l'Espace, lies north of the centre and includes a planetarium and a full-sized Ariane rocket.

The city itself beats with a much older heart. It grew up at a key point on the pilgrimage route to Compostela in Spain, and the vast 11th-century **Basilique St-Sernin**, the biggest Romanesque church in France, dates back to that heady period. Note its distinctive pink, pillared spire. The construction of the Canal du Midi in the 18th century (➤ 141) brought further wealth to Toulouse, and the **town hall**, on the place du Capitole, is one of the best examples of architecture from this period. Relax in a café here, or explore the boutique-filled streets to the south.

The **Château d'Eau** at the southern end of the Pont Neuf is actually a redundant water tower from 1923 that has been converted to hold a photography museum and gallery (www.galeriechateaudeau.org, open Tue–Sun 1–7, inexpensive). Note the Toulouse en Liberté pass, available from the tourist office, which gives free entry to some museums and discounts at other attractions – good value if you plan to explore in detail.

TAKING A BREAK

Enjoy the atmosphere and dine on local specialities and delicious seafood in the stylish **Grand Café de l'Opéra**, the brasserie of a sumptuous hotel, at 1 place du Capitole (tel: 05 61 21 37 03; closed Aug).

There is plenty to see and explore at the Cité de l'Espace

🚑 211 F3
Tourist Information Office
✉ Donjon du Capitole ☎ 05 61 11 02 22; www.ot-toulouse.fr 🕐 Jun–Sep Mon–Sat 9–6, Sun 10:30–5:15; Oct–May Mon–Fri 9–6, Sat 9–12:30, 2–6, Sun 10–12:30, 2–5

Cité de l'Espace
✉ avenue de Jean Gonord ☎ 08 20 37 72 23; www.cite-espace.com
🕐 Summer daily 9–7; winter 9:30–5 💷 Expensive

Basilique St-Sernin
✉ place St-Sernin 🕐 Summer daily 8:30–6:30; winter 8:30–12:30, 2–6:30

3 Albi

This large brick-built town has two prominent claims to fame: a remarkable Gothic cathedral and a major museum to its most famous son, the painter Toulouse-Lautrec. There's good shopping around the central square, place du Vigan, and attractive formal gardens overlook the River Tarn.

The forbidding **Cathédrale Sainte-Cécile** dates from the 13th century, a time of bloody warfare between Catholics and Cathars. With its tall, narrow windows, which used to be used as arrow-slits, it is easy to see how the building once doubled as a fortress. The austerity of the exterior gives way to sumptuous Renaissance decoration on the interior, with elaborate frescoes over the ceiling and a vast, detailed 15th-century mural of the Last Judgement. The magnificent organ is claimed to be the biggest in France.

Homage is paid to Henri de Toulouse-Lautrec (1864–1901) in a **museum** in the former archbishop's palace, which also houses the tourist office. Toulouse-Lautrec was born into a wealthy aristocratic family, and suffered from various crippling genetic disorders from a young age. In 1884 he settled in Montmartre in Paris, where his stylish posters and paintings of the extraordinary, colourful characters all around him – barmaids, prostitutes, cabaret stars and race-goers – were to make him famous. Around 600 of his works are held here.

Detail of the ornate doorway at Sainte-Cécile Cathédrale

TAKING A BREAK

You'll find plenty of bars and cafés to choose from on the main square of Albi, **place du Vigan**.

✚ 212 A4
Tourist Information Office
✉ Palais de la Berbie, place Sainte-Cécile
☎ 05 63 36 36 00; www.albi-tourisme.fr
🕐 May–Jun, Sep Mon–Sat 9–12:30, 2–6:30, Sun 10–12:30, 2:30–5; Jul–Aug Mon–Sat 9–7, Sun 10–12:30, 2:30–6:30; Oct–Apr Mon–Sat 9–12:30, 2–6, Sun 10–12:30, 2:30–5

Cathédrale Sainte-Cécile
✉ place Sainte-Cécile 🕐 Jun–Sep daily 9–6:30; Oct–May 9–12, 2–6:30

Musée Toulouse-Lautrec
✉ Palais de la Berbie, place Sainte-Cécile ☎ 05 63 49 48 70; www.musee-toulouse-lautrec.com 🕐 Mar 10–12, 2–5:30; Apr–May daily 10–12, 2–6; Jun, Sep 9–noon, 2–6; Jul–Aug 9–6; Oct–Feb Wed–Mon 10–12, 2–5 💶 Inexpensive

4 Lascaux

A remarkable series of prehistoric paintings was discovered by accident at Lascaux, just south of Montignac, in the mid-20th century. While the originals have been sealed up again to preserve them from micro-organisms in the air, the paintings have been carefully re-created for visitors at nearby Lascaux II, and seeing them gives an insight into the concerns and skills of our early ancestors. Advance booking is essential.

Vivid bison, horses and deer in shades of ochre, brown and charcoal gallop across the uneven face of the stone, to stunning effect. The original artists mixed pigments, such as kaolin and haematite, to achieve different colours, and you can learn more about their techniques – replicated faithfully for the reconstruction – in the accompanying display. The purpose of the paintings remains obscure: was this simply artistic expression, or a series of messages or records about hunting in the area, or perhaps linked to some religious ceremony? We'll never know, but the impact of the images is remarkably fresh and immediate after around 17,000 years.

TAKING A BREAK

At the village of St-Genies, between Sarlat and Montignac, is the **Restaurant la Vieille Auberge**, which serves local food (le Bourg, tel: 05 53 28 90 38). Established in the late 19th century, it's now run by the great-great granddaughter of the original owner, and doubles as an art gallery.

🗺 216 C1
✉ Lascaux II, Montignac (enquiries via Semitour Périgord, BP 1024 Périgueux) ☎ 05 53 05 65 65; www.semitour.com ⏱ mid-Feb–Mar and Nov Tue–Sun 10–12, 2–5:30; Apr–Jun and Sep–Oct daily 9:30–5:30. Closed Jan to mid-Feb (hours may vary) 💷 Expensive

Bulls and horses run free on the stone walls of Lascaux II

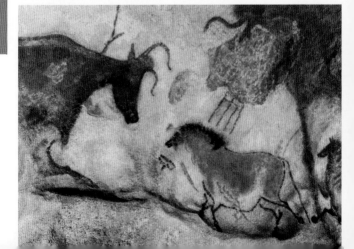

At Your Leisure

5 Futuroscope

A high-tech leisure park with eye-catching architecture, Futuroscope is a main attraction 11km (7 miles) north of Poitiers. Wonder at the giant, mirrored crystals apparently growing at an angle from the earth, and the huge sphere hovering above sheets of glass. These and more bizarre structures hold a variety of stylish and fun exhibits, from an auditorium of co-ordinated moving seats in front of semicircular 3D screens, to a 360-degree panorama to take your breath away. In the surrounding grounds you'll come across interactive water fountains and a "lake" that children can cross – on tricycles.

🛉 216 B4 ✉ BP 2000, 86130 Jaunay-Clan
☎ 05 49 49 11 12; www.futuroscope.com
🕐 Feb–Aug daily 10–dusk; Sep to mid-Nov 10–6 (hours may vary); mid-Nov–mid-Dec weekends only but closes in bad weather. Closed Jan ✋ Expensive

6 Venise Verte

"Green Venice", more properly known as the **Marais Poitevin**, is a marshy area on the western coast north of La Rochelle. Inland it is riddled with man-made waterways, and accessible only by boat. By the coast it is drier and more arid, with expansive salt

Futuroscope theme park near Poitiers

pans. It's great to explore on foot, by bicycle or from the water – hire a punt (*une plate*) in **Coulon**. Eels are a local delicacy.

🛉 215 C3
Tourist Information Office
✉ 31 rue Gabriel Audier, 79510 Coulon
☎ 05 49 35 99 29; www.marais-poitevin.fr
🕐 Mon–Fri 10–1

7 Cognac

This prosperous little town between Saintes and Angoulême is the centre of the worldwide cognac industry. You can visit one of the great **cognac houses**, where the brandy is distilled from the local grapes – Martell, Hennessy and Rémy Martin are some of the names to conjure with; the tourist office can supply details. Half-timbered buildings and stately Renaissance mansions rub shoulders in the old quarter, and you'll find the chic shops and restaurants around the central **place François I**.

🛉 216 A2
Tourist Information Office
✉ 16 rue du XIV Juillet ☎ 05 45 82 10 71; www.tourism-cognac.com 🕐 May–Jun and Sep Mon–Sat 9:30–5:30; Jul–Aug Mon–Sat 9–7, Sun 10–4; Oct–Apr Mon–Sat 10–5

8 Sarlat-la-Canéda

The lovely old town of Sarlat, with its honey-coloured stone, makes an excellent base for exploring the Dordogne region. You can sample its gastronomic pleasures, including *foie gras*, chestnuts, truffles and walnuts, in the many restaurants and small eateries, and wander at leisure through the streets of tall, distinguished-looking Renaissance town houses (known as *hôtels*) at its heart. They date mostly from the period 1450 to 1500, and their characteristic steep roofs are designed to support the heavy stone tiles. Don't miss the much-photographed **Maison d'Étienne de la Boétie**, birthplace of the 16th-century philosopher and poet, with its high gables and ornamental chimney stacks.

The **Saturday market** is a treat for the eye as well as the palate, and the **covered market** in the renovated old church of Ste-Marie, on Place de la Liberté stocks the best local produce.

➕ 217 D1

Tourist Information Office

✉ rue Tourny ☎ 05 53 31 45 45; www.ot-sarlat-perigord.fr ⏰ Apr, Oct Mon–Sat 9–12, 2–6, Sun 10–1; May–Jun Mon–Sat 9–6, Sun 10–1, 2–5; Jul–Aug Mon–Sat 9–7, Sun 10–1,

An old wooden-beamed shop in St-Émilion selling the locally produced wine

2–6; Sep Mon–Sat 9–1, 2–7, Sun 10–1, 2–5; Nov Mon–Sat 9–12, 2–5, Sun 10–1; Dec–Mar Mon–Sat 9–12, 2–5. Closed Sun.

9 St-Émilion

St-Émilion has everything a prestigious and historic wine-producing village should have: steep and narrow cobbled streets threading between handsome old stone houses, shady squares with good restaurants, side-streets with stylish little shops, and all surrounded by neatly combed fields of top-quality vines. The old town was not designed for cars, so it's best to park outside the medieval walls and explore on foot.

One of the strangest sights here is the **Église Monolithe**, an underground church that was carved out of the rock between the eighth and 12th centuries. It's opposite the tourist office on place des Créneaux, and visits are by guided tour only. The tours also take in the catacombs, and the grotto where Aemilianus, a Breton hermit who gives the town its name, came to live during the eighth century.

September marks the start of the grape harvest, and St-Émilion celebrates with a festival, the **Ban des Vendanges**. Events include wine tastings and a procession to the Tour du Roi, a tower from which a trumpet is blown to start the picking.

🚹 216 A1

Tourist Information Office

✉ place des Créneaux ☎ 05 57 55 28 28; www.saint-emilion-tourisme.com 🕐 Apr to mid-Jun and mid-Sep to Oct 9:30–12:30, 1:30–6:30; mid- to end Jun and early to mid-Sep 10–7; Jul–Aug daily 9:30–8; Nov–Mar 9:30–12:30, 1:30–6; Dec–Feb 10–12:30, 2–5:30 (hours may vary)

🔟 Biarritz

This faded beauty of a seaside resort was the holiday choice of the cream of European royalty in the late 19th century, and its casino and nightlife gave it a cachet with the smart set in the 20th century that lingers on. Now it's also popular with families, who come to enjoy the sands, and with surfers, who make the most of the roll of the Atlantic breakers (catch the July surf festival, the biggest in Europe). The magnificent old Hôtel du Palais still queens it over the **Grande Plage**, the most fashionable of the three beaches. Le Port-Vieux,

Enjoying the view over the Grande Plage at the resort of Biarritz

the smaller beach at the southern end, is where the whaling boats once sailed from. To the north, a lighthouse watches over all.

Back from the shore, you'll find elegant streets with chic shops and restaurants. The aquarium, the **Musée de la Mer**, is well worth a visit – there's also a shark pool and seals. Another popular attraction is the chocolate museum.

🚹 210 A3

Tourist Information Office

✉ square d'Ixelles ☎ 05 59 22 37 10; www.biarritz.fr 🕐 Mon–Fri 9–6, Sat 10–12, 2–5, Sun 10–1

Musée de la Mer

✉ Plateau Atalaye, Rocher de la Vièrge ☎ 05 59 22 33 34 🕐 Jun and Sep daily 9:30–7; Jul–Aug 9:30–midnight; Oct–May 9:30–12:30, 2–6; closed 1–21 Jan; feeding times 10:30 and 5 💷 Moderate

Musée du Chocolat

✉ 14 avenue Beau Rivage ☎ 05 59 23 27 72 🕐 Mon–Sat 10–12:30, 2–6:30; French school holidays daily 10–6:30 💷 Moderate

🔟 Pays Basque

The extreme southwest corner of France, Basque Country, is a small but exceptionally pretty region characterized by the Basque farmhouse – *etxe* – a large building with timberwork painted in ox-blood

Lourdes attacts millions of pilgrims and visitors each year

red or deep green. The two prettiest villages are **Ainhoa and Sare**, each a cluster of houses dating from the 17th and 18th centuries. St-Jean-Pied-de-Port, where pilgrims gather to cross the Pyrénées on the way to Santiago de Compostela in Galicia, also has great charm.

➕ 210 A3

Tourist Information Office

✉ 14 place De Gaulle 64220 Saint-Jean-Pied-de-Port ☎ 05 59 37 03 57; www.terre-basque.com ⏰ Jul–Aug Mon–Sat 9–7, Sun 10–1, 2–5; Sep–Jun Mon-Sat 9–12, 2–6

🄬 Lourdes

Each year this pilgrimage town attracts more than five million visitors seeking healing at the shrine of St Bernadette, the girl who saw visions in 1858. There are many sites for prayer, from the 20,000-capacity underground basilica to intimate churches. The tourist office has a map, including times of services.

➕ 210 C2

Tourist Information Office

✉ place Peyramale ☎ 05 62 42 77 40; www.lourdes-infotourisme.com ⏰ Jan–Feb, Nov–Dec Mon–Sat 9–12, 2–5:30; Mar, Oct Mon–Sat 9–12, 2–6; Apr–Jun, Sep Mon–Sat 9–12.30, 2–6:30, Sun 10–12:30; Jul–Aug Mon–Sat 9–7, Sun 10–6

🄬 Pyrénées

The Pyrénées forms a continuous barrier for more than 400km (250 miles) across southern France, from the Atlantic to the Mediterranean. The high passes on the French side form part of the Tour de France and are worth driving between spring and autumn for their views, but check the road ahead is open before beginning any ascent. Two easily accessible beauty spots are the **Cirque de Gavarnie** – a rock amphitheatre – and the **Pont d'Espagne**. A cable car takes day-trippers from the ski resort of La Mongie up to an observatory on the Pic du Midi de Bigorre (2,872m/9,423ft).

➕ 211 D2 to F1

Tourist Information Office

National Park information offices in St-Lary, Luz-Saint-Sauveur, Gavarnie, Cauterets, Arrens-Marsous, Laruns and Etsaut

☎ www.parc-pyrenees.com

FOR KIDS

- **Futuroscope**, near Poitiers: ➤ 175.
- **Biarritz**: Musée de la Mer ➤ 177. There's also an aquarium at **La Rochelle** (Bassin des Grands Yachts, tel 05 46 34 00 00, www.aquarium-larochelle.com, open daily, expensive).
- **Bordeaux**: Bring your skates to take part in the in-line skating night, in the downtown pedestrian area (first Sun of the month, free).
- **Near Tarbes**, north of Lourdes: Ferme Équestre Lou Cassou is a family-run stables that offers rides, lessons for children, and accommodation (16 rue des Forges, 64460 Labatut-Figuieres, tel: 05 59 81 98 60, www.loucassou.com, open Tue–Sun).

Where to...
Stay

Prices

Expect to pay per night for a double room

€ under €120 €€ €120–€220 €€€ over €220

Hôtel des Beaux-Arts €–€€

Views of the river and the Pont Neuf make the Hôtel des Beaux-Arts worth a visit. The building dates from the 18th century, but the three-star facilities are up-to-date, with satellite TV and mini-bars. There are 19 air-conditioned rooms, and the nearby Dix-Neuf restaurant is part of the same owner-group.

♦ 211 F3 ⊠ 1 place du Pont Neuf, 31000 Toulouse ☎ 05 34 45 42 42; www.hotelsdesbeauxarts.com

Hôtel le Postillon €

Its friendly atmosphere and very reasonable prices mean that this popular hotel is always busy, so book ahead. It's family-run, with 28 air-conditioned bedrooms – ask for one with a balcony overlooking the courtyard. There is no restaurant, but there are plenty of cafés and restaurants to choose from close by.

♦ 210 C3 ⊠ place de Verdun, 10 cours Camou, 64000 Pau ☎ 05 59 72 83 00; www.hotel-le-postillon.fr

Hôtel Parc Victoria €€€

This small but elegant 19th-century mansion is now a comfortable country house hotel. The 19 rooms and suites are well-appointed, spacious and homely. After a busy day exploring, guests can relax in the gardens and swimming pool.

♦ 210 A3 ⊠ 5 rue Cepé, 64500 St-Jean de Luz ☎ 05 59 26 78 78; www.parcvictoria.com ⊕ Closed mid-Nov to mid-Mar

Hôtel St-James €€–€€€

Drive southeast of Bordeaux for around 15 minutes to the village of Bouliac. This modern hotel, part of the superb Relais & Château group, has an attached bistro – Le Café de l'Espérance – that's worth a stop in its own right, plus two further restaurants. There are 15 air-conditioned rooms and 3 suites to choose from, furnished with top-quality audio systems and views over the outdoor pool to Bordeaux itself.

♦ 216 A1 ⊠ 3 place Camille-Hostein, 33270 Bouliac ☎ 05 57 97 06 00; www.saintjames-bouliac.com

Le Domaine Rochebois €€–€€€

Vitrac is 8km (5 miles) south of Sarlat-la-Canéda, and this medium-sized hotel in the Dordogne makes a good base from which to explore the region. The attractive building is neo-classical in style, and the views from the 10 air-conditioned bedrooms are of the gardens and the Dordogne Valley. Four stars mean the hotel has plenty of facilities, including an outdoor pool, tennis court and billiards, but there is no restaurant.

♦ 217 D1 ⊠ route de Montfort, 24200 Vitrac ☎ 05 53 31 52 52; www.rochebois.com ⊕ Closed Nov–May

L'Hôtel de Toiras €€–€€€

Set on the waterfront of this chic marina town, this former ship-owners mansion has been tastefully renovated and opened as a hotel in 2004. Rooms are small but luxuriously appointed, and there's a quiet interior courtyard where you can relax. The hotel restaurant is one of the best in town.

♦ 215 C3 ⊠ 1 quai Job-Foran, 17410 St-Martin-de-Ré ☎ 05 46 35 40 32; www.hotel-de-toiras.com ⊕ All year

Where to...
Eat and Drink

Prices

Expect to pay per person for a meal, excluding drinks

€ under €30   €€ €30–€60   €€€ over €60

La Corderie Royale €€–€€€

On the banks of the Charente River in Rochefort-sur-Mer this stylish restaurant takes its name from the historic rope factory in town. Enjoy the views as you tuck into seafood or perhaps beef in a cream sauce.

➕ 215 C3 ⊠ rue Audebert, 17300 Rochefort-sur-Mer ☎ 05 46 99 35 35; www.corderieroyale-hotel.com ⏰ Apr–Nov daily 12–1:30, 7:30–9:30; Dec–Jan and Mar Tue–Sat 12–1:30, 7:30–9:30, Sun 12–1:30. Closed mid-Dec–mid-Jan and Feb

Le Franchouillard €€

Sample regional specialities on a regularly changing *France à la carte* menu at this restaurant in the pedestrianized heart of Bordeaux. Clientele include young people, who come for the atmosphere. Be prepared for the highlight of the evening, at 11:30pm, when music sheets are handed out for a singalong with classic French songs.

➕ 216 A1 ⊠ 21 rue Maucoudinat, 33000 Bordeaux ☎ 05 56 44 95 86; www.lefranchouillard.com ⏰ Mon–Sat 12–3, 6–1am

Les Pyrénées €€–€€€

Enjoy superb regional cuisine, infused with the flavours of the Pyrénées, at this family-run Michelin-starred restaurant in St-Jean-Pied-de-Port. Lamb and truffles are two local delicacies, but you'll also find plenty of fresh fish.

➕ 210 A2 ⊠ 19 place de Général-de-Gaulle, 64220 St-Jean-Pied-de-Port ☎ 05 59 37 01 01 ⏰ Mon–Sat 12–2:30, 7–10. Closed last 3 weeks Jan, mid-Nov to mid-Dec, Mon pm Nov–Mar, Tue pm mid-Sep to mid-Jun

Marie Colline €€€

If you're visiting Cahors, this vegetarian restaurant is a great place to stop for lunch. There is usually a choice of two daily specials, along with a much wider selection of different dishes and desserts. Look out for *gratin au chèvre* (melted goat's cheese) and *clafoutis aux fruits* (a cake made with red fruits).

➕ 211 F5 ⊠ 173 rue Georges Clemenceau, 46000 Cahors ☎ 05 65 35 59 96 ⏰ Tue–Fri 12–2. Closed Aug

Michel Sarran €€€

One of Toulouse's best restaurants is Michel Sarran's elegant manor house with its contemporary décor. It has two dining rooms, each with a feeling of intimacy. Sarran is one of France's most celebrated chefs, and his creative cuisine comes at a price to match his reputation.

➕ 211 F3 ⊠ 21 boulevard Armand Duportal, 31000 Toulouse ☎ 05 61 12 32; www.michel-sarran.com ⏰ Mon–Fri 12–1:45, 8–9:45. Closed Wed lunch, Sat, Sun and 23–30 Dec

Restaurant de Fromages Baud et Millet €€

This family-run restaurant in the Bordeaux region is a little temple to the cheese-makers' art and definitely deserves a visit. There are more than 200 varieties of cheese on offer, and the patron can enthuse about each one. There's an all-you-can-eat cheese board on the menu, plus a selection of mouth-watering traditional cheese-based dishes, such as *raclette* (melted cheese with potato, pickles and onions).

➕ 216 A1 ⊠ 19 rue Huguerie, 33000 Bordeaux ☎ 05 56 79 05 77 ⏰ Mon–Sat 10–11:30

Where to...
Shop

There's plenty to shop for in this region, with excellent food markets in the rural towns, fashion in the seaside resorts and cities, and mouthwatering chocolate and pastries everywhere. Bordeaux is at the heart of France's wine growing industry, and Cognac is famous for its eponymous brandy.

FOOD AND DRINK

Bordeaux has several markets, of which the most popular must be Marché des Quays beside the Garonne River, the haunt of local producers and artisans (quai Chartron, open Sun 7–2). The Marché St-Michel is a fun flea-market, which competes on Sunday mornings, expanding four times a

year to become a huge bric-a-brac sale (place Canteloupe et Meynard, Sun 7–4). The Place des Capucins on cours de la Marne is the place for local delicacies such as cheese, *foie gras* and the creamy little cakes called *canelé* (Tue–Sun 9–1).

The Dordogne region is famous for its *foie gras* and other dishes from geese and ducks (such as *confit* and terrines), its truffles and its walnuts. Seek them out amid the other delicious treats on offer in the markets of Périgueux (place du Coderc and place de la Clautre, Wed and Sat 9–noon), Sarlat-la-Canéda (town centre, Sat 8:30–6 and Wed 8:30–1) and Ribérac (place du Marché, Fri 9–noon). If you'd rather buy from a delicatessen, try Rougié Sarlat, in Sarlat, which has been going

strong since 1875 – most products are canned (avenue du Périgord, tel: 05 53 31 72 45, open Mon–Sat 10–1, 2–6).

Cahors' open-air Marché Traditionnel is also worth a detour, with gastronomic delights including goat's cheese, *foie gras* and local wines (place de la Cathédrale, Wed and Sat 8am–12.30pm).

Toulouse has a covered market (place Victor Hugo, Tue–Sun 8–1), and a popular Sunday morning flea-market around the Basilique St-Sernin (8–1).

Chocoholics should make their way to renowned Chocolaterie Letuffe at Angoulême, where chocolate artistry reaches new heights and the *guinettes* (cherry and cognac) are to die for (10 place Francis-Louvel, tel: 05 45 95 00 54). L'Artisan Chocolatier in Albi is also a chocolate favourite, with great cakes and pastries (4 rue du Docteur Camboulives, tel: 05 63 38 95 33, open Tue–Sat 9–12.30, 2.30–7:30).

GIFTS AND SOUVENIRS

You can find unusual gifts at Violettes & Pastels in Toulouse, a shop partly dedicated to the violet and its many uses (10 rue St-Pantaléon, tel: 05 61 22 14 22, www.violettesetpastels. com, open Tue–Sat 10–7).

The city of Limoges is famous for its porcelain, and a great selection can be found at La Chainette (27 boulevard Louis Blanc, tel: 05 55 34 58 61, open Mon–Sat 10–12, 2–7).

Contemporary works of art are exhibited and sold at the Galerie des Remparts in Bordeaux (63 rue des Remparts, tel: 05 56 52 22 25, open Tue–Sat 10:30–1, 2:30–7, closed Aug).

If you're looking for antique furniture, try the Village Notre-Dame in Bordeaux, where around 30 dealers and experts are under one roof (61–67 rue Notre-Dame, tel: 05 56 52 66 13, open Mon–Sat 10–12:30, 2–7 all year; also Oct–Apr Sun 2–7).

Where to...
Be Entertained

Inevitably, the main centres for entertainment are also the major cities, including Bordeaux and Toulouse, with resorts along the coast from Biarritz in the south to La Rochelle in the north offering a wide variety of summertime options for everyone.

MUSIC, DANCE, THEATRE

Traditional **folk dancers** take to the old streets of the wine town of Bergerac at around 9pm on some weekday evenings in summer (usually Tue, Jul–Aug) – look out for them setting off from the square in front of the church of St-Jacques.

Biarritz has its own ballet company, **Ballet Biarritz**, in a venue operated by choreographer Thierry Malandain, with performances year-round (Gare du Midi, 23 avenue Foch, tel: 05 59 24 67 19, www.balletbiarritz.com).

There are several large venues for concerts, musicals and theatre, including the architecturally splendid neo-classical **Grand Théâtre** on place de la Comédie (tel: 05 56 00 85 95), and the sleek, modern **Espace Culturel du Pin Galant**, west of the city (34 avenue de Maréchal de Lattre de Tassigny, Mérignac, tel: 05 56 97 82 82).

Toulouse's National Orchestra performs regularly in the **Halle aux Grains** (place Dupuy, tel: 05 61 61 13 13, www.onct.mairie-toulouse. fr). The grandiose **Théâtre du Capitole** is the city's main theatre venue, with opera, concerts and ballet as well (1 place du Capitole, tel: 05 61 22 31 31/63 13 13).

CINEMAS

The ten-screen **UGC Ciné Cité** in Bordeaux, at 15 rue Georges Bonnac shows the latest movies in their original language (tel: 08 92 70 00 00).

In Toulouse, the **Cinémathèque** at 69 rue Taur shows art-house and foreign-language films (tel: 05 62 30 10, www. lacinemathequedetoulouse.com).

BARS, CLUBS AND CASINOS

For a relaxing evening head for the **Frog & Rosbif**, a small chain of pubs with microbrewery attached. You'll find branches in the former women's prison in Bordeaux (23, rue Ausone, tel: 05 56 48 55 85) and in Toulouse (14 rue de l'Industrie, 31000 Toulouse, tel: 05 61 99 28 57, www.frogpubs.com, open Mon–Fri 5.30–2am, Sat 1pm–3am, Sun 1pm–2am).

The **Opus Café**, near Place Wilson in Toulouse, has French and international rock acts six nights a week (24 rue bachelier, tel: 05 61 62 37 46, www.opus-cafe.net, Mon–Wed midnight –5am, Thu–Sat 11–dawn).

In Biarritz, **Casino de Biarritz** (1 avenue Edouard VII, tel: 05 59 22 77 77, www.lucienbarriere.com, open daily) is a fine period building where you'll need to dress up to gamble your money.

SPA

For something totally different, treat yourself to a spot of "vinotherapy" at **Martillac**, a 15-minute drive south of Bordeaux. It is a unique spa where wine and wine by-products are the basis of different treatments, from a Sauvignon massage to a Premier Grand Cru facial (**Les Sources de Caudalie**, Chemin de Smith Haute-Lafitte, Martillac, tel: 05 57 83 83 83, www.sources-caudalie.com).

Walks and Tours

1 MONTMARTRE AND SACRÉ-CŒUR

Walk

DISTANCE 2 miles/3km TIME 2.5–3 hours
START POINT Place Blanche ⊞ 208, off A5 END POINT Place des Abbesses 208, off A5

Explore the back streets of Paris's historic hilltop "village", with its leafy cobbled streets and steep stairways lit by iron lamps, its quaint whitewashed cottages and country gardens, its picturesque café-lined squares and its sweeping panoramas, and you will soon understand why so many generations of artists, writers and poets have fallen in love with this atmospheric neighbourhood.

1–2

From **place Blanche** climb up **rue Lepic** past tempting delicatessens and cafés. Turn left at the top and branch right, still on rue Lepic. Van Gogh lived in an apartment at **No 54** from 1886 to 1888, taking his inspiration from the windmills and gardens of Montmartre.

2–3

Continue to climb rue Lepic, following the road round to the right. Note the steep flights

Moulin de la Galette in Montmartre

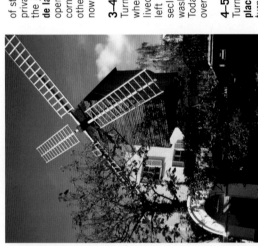

of steps on your left leading up to countrified private villas, and high above you (opposite the junction with rue Tholozé), the **Moulin de la Galette**, once the venue for a notorious open-air cabaret. A few steps beyond (on the corner with rue Girardon), Montmartre's only other remaining windmill – **Moulin Radet** – is now part of a restaurant.

3–4

Turn left here, and cross **avenue Junot**, where artists Utrillo and Poulbot once lived at **Nos 11 and 13**. Soon after, turn left into **square Suzanne-Buisson**, a lovely secluded park where St Denis allegedly washed his decapitated head in a fountain. Today a statue of the saint marks the spot, overlooking a boules pitch.

4–5

Turn right at the statue, descend into **place Casdesus**, in rue Simon-Dereure and turn right up several steps into **allée des**

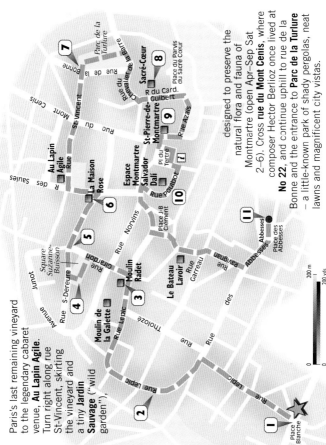

Brouillards. Here, the 18th-century Château des Brouillards on your right was once used as a shelter for homeless artists. Painter Pierre-Auguste Renoir lived and worked in one of the houses on the left from 1890 to 1897.

Paris's last remaining vineyard to the legendary cabaret venue, **Au Lapin Agile.** Turn right along rue St-Vincent, skirting the vineyard and a tiny **Jardin Sauvage** ("wild garden"),

5–6

At the end of allée des Brouillards, carry straight on up the cobbled **rue de l'Abreuvoir,** once a country lane used by horses and cattle en route to the watering trough (*abreuvoir*), which stood on the site of No 15. **Number 14** was formerly the Café de l'Abreuvoir, frequented by many great artists in Montmartre's heyday. Continuing up the hill to **No 12,** which Impressionist painter Camille Pissarro rented from 1888 to 1892. Note the charming sundial on the wall of **No 4,** with a picture of a rooster promising *Quant IV sonnera, je chanterai* ("When four strikes, I'll crow"). The restaurant at No 2, **La Maison Rose** (The Pink House), made famous in an early Utrillo canvas, makes a pleasant place for a lunch stop.

6–7

Turn left immediately after La Maison Rose and head steeply down **rue des Saules,** past

designed to preserve the natural flora and fauna of Montmartre (open Apr–Sep Sat 2–6). Cross **rue du Mont Cenis,** where composer Hector Berlioz once lived at **No 22,** and continue uphill to rue de la Bonne and the entrance to **Parc de la Turlure** – a little-known park of shady pergolas, neat lawns and magnificent city vistas.

of more than 300 works by the eccentric Spanish Surrealist artist, who died in 1989.

10–11

Follow **rue Poulbot** round to rue Norvins. Turn left, then almost immediately left again, and head downhill, passing the grassy square of place Jean-Baptiste Clément on your left. Turn right at the T-junction into **rue Ravignan**, and follow the road round to the left into place Émile Goudeau, past Le Bateau-Lavoir on your right. Leave the square down a small flight of steps. Cross over rue Garreau and continue downhill on rue Ravignan. A left turn at the next T-junction will take you straight to the art nouveau Métro stop at **place des Abbesses**.

TAKING A BREAK

Avoid the pricey, tourist cafés in place du Tertre. Try **La Maison Rose** (tel: 01 42 57 66 75) on rue de l'Abreuvoir or a picnic in the **Parc de la Turlure**.

WHEN?

Avoid this walk on Sundays, when the district is always jam-packed with locals and visitors.

7–8

Stroll through the park, leaving it by rue du Chevalier de la Barre round the back of the **Sacré-Cœur**, and carrying on into **rue du Cardinal Guibert**, which runs alongside the basilica to its entrance on place du Parvis du Sacré-Cœur. (Note that the entrance to the crypt and dome is in rue du Cardinal Guibert.)

8–9

On leaving the Sacré-Cœur, head right along **rue Azaïs**, admiring the distant views of Paris as you go. A right turn up rue St-Eleuthère will lead you to the church of **St-Pierre-de-Montmartre**, consecrated in 1147.

9–10

As you leave the church, continue straight ahead into **place du Tertre**, once a delightful 18th-century village square, now a veritable tourist honeypot, but worth a visit. Leave the square via **rue du Calvaire**. A right turn just before a descending flight of steps will lead you across cobbled place du Calvaire to rue Poulbot and the **Espace Montmartre Salvador Dalí** (tel: 01 42 64 40 10, www.dalipalis. com, open daily 10–6, 8pm Jul and Aug; moderate), which houses a permanent display

The neo-Byzantine Sacré-Coeur

2

CAP FRÉHEL AND THE CÔTE D'EMERAUDE

Drive

Pristine sandy beaches, a medieval bastion set on high cliffs, fabulous views from a historic lighthouse, and the inland contrasts of the Forêt de la Hunaudaye are just some of the riches on offer on this easy day's route. The Côte d'Émeraude, or Emerald Coast, is a rugged corner on the northern coastline, just west of St-Malo, which gives way to the pink sandstone cliffs and sandy bays of the Côtes d'Armor to the west.

DISTANCE 92km (57 miles) **TIME** 2–3 hours, but allow most of a day to enjoy the beaches along the route **START/END POINT** Lambale 🔖 221 D3

1–2

Start near the splendid Gothic church in the hillside village of **Lamballe**. This area is known throughout France as the home of the national stud farm, or *haras national* (tel: 02 96 50 06 98, www.haraspatrimoine.com, tours daily Jul–Aug daily, Sep–Jun Wed, Sat and Sun afternoons). Head east out of the village on the D28, then bear right on to the D52a, signposted to Plédéliac. Turn left on to the D55 and continue for 4km (2.5 miles), to reach the ruined **Château de la Hunaudaye** (tel: 02 96 34 82 10, open mid-Jun–mid-Sep daily 10:30–6:30). It dates from the 12th century, and became a victim of the Revolution. Look out for the spiral stair in the keep.

2–3

Turn left and left again along the D28, passing through the **Forêt de la Hunaudaye** to the tiny village of St-Aubin. Continue on the D52 and

Looking along the rocky coastline at Cap Fréhel

turn right. Follow the D13 and D43 towards Plébouille and the coast, and continue north beside the Baie de la Frénaye to the rocky tip. A massive 14th-century castle, **Fort la Latte**, built high on a lump of rock and surrounded by thick stone battlements, guards the end. To the west, the spectacular views are to the point of Cap Fréhel, while the Emerald Coast spreads down to the east.

3–4

Return to the main road, turn right and drive around the coast for 4km (2.5 miles) to reach **Cap Fréhel**, a dramatically sculpted headland 70m (230ft) above sea level. According to local lore, the giant Gargantua created the rocky point by throwing a lump of stone over his shoulder. The first lighthouse was built on this spot in the 7th century but the elegant square lighthouse seen today dates from the mid-19th century. It is open to visitors in summer (Easter–Jun Sat–Sun 2–5:30; Jul–Aug daily 2–5:30). Continue on the sinuous D34,

through heathland, to **Sables-d'Or-les-Pins**.
Pléhérel-Plage is a wonderful beach, but strong currents make it extremely unsafe for swimming.

4–5

Continue on the D34 and detour right on to the D786 to explore the fishing port and resort of **Erquy**, which is set on a curving bay. Scallops are the local speciality, and there are plenty of tempting eating places along the seafront. The harbour is sheltered by the protective arm of the Cap d'Erquy, and is home to both a sailing school and a dive centre.

5–6

Continue on the D786 towards Le Val-André, and after about 3km (2 miles) pass the medieval pink-sandstone **Château de Bienassis** (tel: 02 96 72 22 03; open 8 May–21 Jun Sun 2–5; 21 Jun–20 Sep

daily 2–5, but hours may vary), rebuilt in the 17th century with pepperpot towers.

6–7

Stay on the D786 to **Le Val-André**, one of the best beaches in Brittany. Take the D34 to **Planguenoual**, then the D59 back to **Lamballe**.

Street scene at the hillside village of Lamballe

3 THROUGH THE VOSGES ON THE ROUTE DES CRÊTES

Drive

DISTANCE 120km/75 miles **TIME** Allow a full day
START/END POINT Gérardmer 📖 225 E2

This drive takes in some of the best scenery in the Parc Naturel Régional des Ballons des Vosges, an area of mountains and spectacular natural beauty near the German border, southwest of Strasbourg. Its start and end point is the lakeside town of Gérardmer, where the pine forests are popular with walkers, and it includes the famous Route des Crêtes.

1–2

Leave **Gérardmer** on the D417, towards Colmar. After 2km (1.2 miles), pass the Hôtel de la Pierre Charlemagne on the right, and a parking area on the left signed La Cercenée, just before a roundabout (traffic circle). Go all the way round the roundabout and back towards Gérardmer, to swing right into **La Cercenée** parking area. Cross the D417 at the pedestrian crossing to reach the **Saut des Cuves**, where the Vologne river rushes through an unfenced narrow, rocky gorge. You can

view the cascade from the footbridge above. Return to the car park, where signboards give information about further walking routes in the area – with around 16,000km (9,940

View over the beautiful wooded landscape of Vosges miles) of mapped trails through the Forêt de Gérardmer, there's plenty of choice.

and small ski resort on a saddle linking Lorraine and Alsace, turn right onto the D430, the **Routes des Crêtes.** This winding, scenic road along the mountaintops (*crête* means crest) was constructed during World War I to enable north–south troop movements to remain mostly out of sight of the Rhine valley below. A short way from the Col de la Schlucht you come to the **Jardin d'Altitude du Haut-Chitelet,** which specializes in alpine plant species from across the globe (open in high season only).

4–5

A turn to your left takes you to the summit of Mount Hohneck (1,362m/4,468ft). from which there are all-round views over the Vosges to the north, south and west and the Rhine valley into Germany to the east.

A little further on, the Routes des Crêtes is at its most spectacular as it passes high above the upper Vallée de la Thur, down to the right. Eventually you reach the only settlement of any size on the high part of the route, the winter sports resort of **Le Markstein.** Go straight over the crossroads just after the town, still the Route des Crêtes, but now the D431. Ahead of you, a white ball, a civil aviation

2–3

Turn right out of the car park, and immediately left alongside the Hôtel de la Pierre Charlemagne on to the C12 Route du Saut des Cuves, towards **Xonrupt-Longemer.** Pass through the village, joining the D67a towards Longemer.

3–4

The route passes **Lac de Longemer,** then the smaller **Lac de Retournemer.** Both are surrounded by meadows and pine forests, with the Schlucht and Hohneck mountains ahead. At the junction with the D34D, turn left and then right when you meet the D417. Shortly before you reach the **Col de la Schlucht** (1,139m/3,737ft), a pass

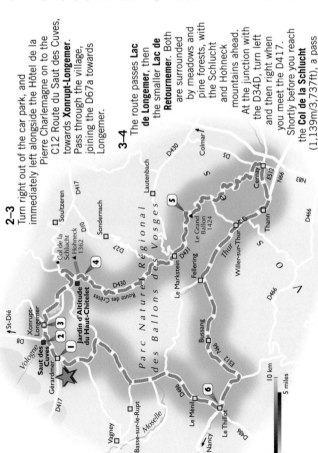

radar installation, crowns the top of Le Grand Ballon, which, at 1,424m (4,672ft), is the highest mountain in the Vosges. The road passes about 100m (300ft) below the summit. Enjoy the view from the roadside, which, on a clear day, takes in the Alps, or walk up to the top from the car park (allow at least 45 minutes for the round trip).

5–6
Just below the summit of the road, look out for a World War I **monument** dedicated to the Diables Bleus (Blue Devils). Further on, 30,000 men lost their lives in the fighting at Le Vieil Armand. Continue along the D431 to **Cernay,** then follow the N66 along the Thur valley and through Wiler-sur-Thur to **Bussang,**

a high point of the Vosges. Its main claim to fame is its Théâtre du Peuple (People's Theatre), a summer theatre in a gorgeous woodland setting that has been going strong since 1895. Continue in the same direction on the N66 and at **Le Thillot** take the D486 to return to **Gérardmer.**

Skiing in the Ballons des Vosges

TAKING A BREAK
There are lots of good picnic stops along the route – but expect to share them with plenty of other visitors in summer. You will find a good choice of **cafés and restaurants** along the route to suit all pockets and tastes – try to pick one with good views.

WHEN?
This drive is spectacular at any time of year, and the Route des Crêtes is popular, so be prepared for heavy traffic through the summer months. In winter, there may be ice and snow, and possible road closures, at high points along the route, so check locally for information before you set out.

4 EXPLORING INLAND FROM THE CÔTE D'AZUR

Drive

DISTANCE 150km/93 miles **TIME** Allow a full day for this drive, and be aware that the roads inland from the coast are often winding and slow. **START/END POINT** Menton ⊞ 214 C4

This picturesque circular route into the countryside which lies behind the principality of Monaco contrasts some of the prettiest – and busiest – villages and towns of the French Riviera with the peace and natural beauty of the Parc National du Mercantour.

1–2

Start from **Menton**, a pretty, and a pretty Italian town on the French side of the border. There's a **museum** by the waterfront dedicated to the poet, playwright and film director Jean Cocteau (1889–1963), **Musée Jean-Cocteau**, which is worth a quick look if you have time (Tel: 04 93 57 72 30, open Wed–Mon 10–12, 2–6; inexpensive, under-18's free). Pick up the road in the town centre signed **Autoroute (Nice, Italia)** and **Sospel**. Follow signs

The attractive bustling harbourside town of Menton is close to the Italian border

Breil-sur-Roya

IT

E80 A10

MONACO

MC

Cap Martin

Menton

Roquebrune

Beausoleil

Monte Carlo

La Turbie

Èze

St-Jean-Cap-Ferrat

Nice

Col de Turini 1607

Parc National du Mercantour

Sospel

D2566

Castillon

D2204

Col de Braus 1002

D21

L'Escarène

La Trinité

Drap

St-André

Tourrette-Levens

D19

N202

Var

Levens

Duranus

Vésubie

St-Jean-de-la-Rivière

Belvédère du Saut des Français

Lucéram

Peïra-Cava

Moulinet

D70

La Bollène-Vésubie

Lantosque

D2565

0 8 km
0 5 miles

4–5

Continue north from Peïra-Cava to the next viewpoint, **Col de Turini**. The mountain pass stands at 1,607m (5,272ft), and this is a good place for a break and refreshment at the hotel **Les Trois Vallées**.

5–6

Turn left on to the **D70**, following signs for La Bollène-Vésubie and Nice. Descend with care, and after about 10km (6 miles), just after the Chapelle-St-Honorat tunnel, look out for a small **chapel** on the left, on a bend. There are fabulous views from the parking area here.

for Sospel on the winding **D2566**, passing under the A8 and through Castillon-Neuf. At **Sospel,** go over the railway crossing and turn left, following signs for Moulinet and Col de Turini. The bridge at Sospel, with its central tower, was rebuilt in the 20th century after the 11th-century original was blown up during World War II.

2–3

Bear left at a bend on to the **D2204**. The road climbs to Col St-Jean, with views back down to Sospel. Go over **Col de Brau** 1,002m (3,288ft) and descend through hairpin bends almost into L'Escarène. Just after a railway bridge turn right, signposted to Lucéram and Peïra-Cava. Continue on this road to reach the attractively jumbled medieval *village perché* (hilltop village) of **Lucéram.**

3–4

Go through Lucéram, and when you reach the next junction, on a steep hill, bear left, following the signs for Turini. There are many more hairpin bends to negotiate before you reach the superb viewpoint of **Peïra-Cava.** To the east, the view is of the Parc National du Mercantour.

6–7

Continue on this road through La Bollène-Vésubie (intersection) turn left on to the **D2565**, signed for Nice and St-Martin-Vésubie (Vésubie is the name of the river that runs through here). This brings you to the valley floor. Follow signs for Lantosque and Nice, going straight on at first, then left along the main road. After 1km

A square tower crowns the medieval ramparts of the hillside village of Levens

(0.6 mile) divert right to go through **Lantosque** village, then rejoin the main road. Continue southwards through **St-Jean-de-la-Rivière**. About 1km (0.6 mile) beyond St-Jean fork left on to the **D19**, signed **Nice par Levens**. This road becomes narrower as it ascends the valley. Go through a tunnel just before Duranus and look for a viewpoint, on the right, which the **Saut des Français** looks out from sheer cliffs. Stay on the road into **Levens**, an appealing old town with two 18th-century chapels standing on two sides of the square, and a grand gateway – the remnant of a castle that has long-since disappeared.

7–8

Leave Levens on the **D19**, following signs for Nice, and passing Tourette-Levens. Soon after St-André the road passes under the A8. Turn left at traffic lights here, signed to Sospel. Cross a river and go straight over another set of traffic lights, passing under the A8 again. Take the next right turn, signed Route de Turin, cross the river and a level (grade) crossing, then turn left at traffic lights, signed La Trinité and Drap. At the roundabout (traffic circle), take the road signed for La Turbie and Laghet, and follow the **D2204a** up a winding

valley to **Laghet**. Here, a hairpin bend takes the road sharply right.

Pass under the A8 once more, and turn left at the next junction, an *autoroute* slip road, following signs to Menton. Turn left at the next junction, signed for La Turbie and Monaco, and stay on this road to the ancient Roman village of **La Turbie**. Its outstanding monument is the Trophée des Alpes, a triumphal arch built by Augustus Caesar around 6BC. After La Turbie, bear left past a hotel, signed Roquebrune and Menton, and turn right at traffic lights at the bottom of the hill, signed Nice and Beausoleil. At the next set of lights turn left, signed to Cap Martin. As it leaves the heart of the village, the road veers sharp left – go straight ahead here, signed for Mayerling and Cap Martin, to reach the sea. Follow the coast road back to **Menton**.

TAKING A BREAK

Les Trois Vallées hotel-restaurant stands at the high point of this tour, at the Col de Turini (tel: 04 93 04 23 23). There is also a choice of bars and restaurants in **Sospel**.

ROCAMADOUR

Walk

DISTANCE 1km (0.6 mile) **TIME** 1.5 hours
START POINT Upper car park (free), by the château **END POINT** 211 F5

Rocamadour is one of the top tourist sites of the Dordogne – a lovely old village pressed against the cliffs with a castle perched dramatically at the top.

1–2

From the **top car park**, take the signposted path to explore the **ramparts** of the castle. From here there are fabulous views over the village. Walk down the steeply winding **Chemin de Croix**, with the Stations of the Cross marked at each bend. Rocamadour was originally settled by a hermit, Amadour, and after his preserved body was discovered in the 12th century, the rock became a centre of pilgrimage. Pass through a tunnel under the basilica and continue to the **Cité Religieuse.**

2–3

There are seven chapels to explore here, but the most important one is to the left

Rocamadour is built against the cliff face

of the basilica, the **Chapelle de Notre-Dame**, Flamboyant Gothic style, which was beautifully restored in the 19th century, and contains a small 12th-century walnut statue of the Black Madonna – no one knows whether she was made black or became so over the centuries as the result of candle smoke.

To the right of the door to the church is a 13th-century fresco of the "Dance of Death". Look out, too, for a sword sticking out of the cliff face. This is supposedly, Durandal, the sword wielded by Roland, a legendary knight in the service of Charlemagne. Walk down the 223 steps of the **Grand Escalier** to explore the village at the bottom of the rock.

The Black Madonna statue in the Chapelle de Notre-Dame at Rocamadour

3–4

Turn left along the **main street**, which is lined with souvenir shops. Pass the tourist office (tel: 05 65 33 22 00, www.rocamadour.com) next to the Hôtel de Ville. Just before one of the original town gates, the Porte Salmon, turn right down a lane and go down a flight of steps. This brings you out at the **lower car park**, by the river. From here, take the lift and funicular through the rock (inexpensive, under-8's free), and back up to the **top car park**.

4–5

For an 8km (5-mile) extension from the lower car park, follow the **dragonfly signposts**, crossing the River Alzou by the stone bridge, and taking the lane to the left. After 150m (165 yards), a little path on your right leads to the **Fontaine de la Fillole**. Climb the hill among trees and, once on the plateau, continue past the farm of **Fouysselaze**, on your right.

5–6

When the path meets the **tarmac road**, turn right and follow this past the farm entrance and a wall on the right. Skirt a large hollow on the right, the Cloup de Magès. On your left is a **dolmen**, around 4,000 years old.

Leave the road and take the **GR46 footpath** to Rocamadour. Cross the D32 and follow a sign for the Fontaine de Berthiol. Cross the Alzou by the little bridge near the Moulin de Roquefraîche, go straight over a small crossroads, and enter the village via **Porte Basse**. Go through Porte Hugon to return to the **lower car park**.

Other Ways to See Rocamadour

At night, the town is illuminated, and there is a 30-minute **guided tour**. Contact the tourist office for more detailed information (tel: 05 65 33 22 00, inexpensive).

Between Easter and September, the **Petit Train** (Little Train) operates between the lower parking areas and the shops and restaurants (inexpensive). There is also a **funicular lift**, between the Cité Religieuse and the top car park (inexpensive, under-8's free). Frequencies vary according to the season.

TAKING A BREAK

There are plenty of **bars and restaurants** to choose from in the lower part of the town.

Practicalities

BEFORE YOU GO

WHAT YOU NEED

		UK	Germany	USA	Canada	Australia	Ireland	Netherlands	Spain
● Required ○ Suggested ▲ Not required △ Not applicable	Some countries require a passport to remain valid for at least six months beyond the date of entry – contact their consulate or embassy or your travel agent for details.								
Passport (or National Identity Card where applicable)		●	●	●	●	●	●	●	●
Visa (for stays of less than 3 months)		▲	▲	▲	▲	▲	▲	▲	▲
Onward or Return Ticket		▲	▲	▲	▲	▲	▲	▲	▲
Tetanus and Polio Vaccinations		▲	▲	▲	▲	▲	▲	▲	▲
Health Documentation		●	●	●	●	●	●	●	●
Travel Insurance		○	○	○	○	○	○	○	○
Driving Licence (national)		●	●	●	●	●	●	●	●
Car Insurance Certificate		○	○	n/a	n/a	n/a	○	○	○
Car Registration Document		●	●	n/a	n/a	n/a	●	●	●

WHEN TO GO

Paris

High season   Low season

JAN	FEB	MAR	APR	MAY	JUN	JUL	AUG	SEP	OCT	NOV	DEC
7°C	7°C	10°C	16°C	17°C	23°C	25°C	26°C	21°C	18°C	12°C	8°C
45°F	45°F	50°F	61°F	63°F	73°F	77°F	79°F	70°F	64°F	54°F	46°F

Sun   Sunshine and showers   Wet   Cloudy

Its size and geography mean that France has a varied climate. The north is often rainy, with mild winters and cool summers, while the south has hot, dry summers and warm, wet winters. Summer winds in the south can be refreshingly cool and gentle, but the notorious, persistent Mistral winds can blow for days, particularly in March and April. Paris can be hot and sticky in August, and many city-dwellers take their holidays elsewhere at this time. The high mountains dictate their own summer weather: While the Vosges and the Northern Massif can be hot, the Massif Central is generally stormy, the Cévennes wet and the southern Massif dust-dry. Winter brings its own delights, with excellent winter sports in the Alps and the Pyrénées Jan–Mar, and the atmospheric Christmas markets of Strasbourg and elsewhere.

GETTING ADVANCE INFORMATION

Websites
- French Tourist Office: www.franceguide.com (also for US visitors)
- Paris Tourist Office: www.parisinfo.com
- French Tourist Office www.tourist-office.org

In the UK
French Tourist Office
Lincoln House, 300 High
Holborn WC, London 1V 7JH
☎ 09068 244123

GETTING THERE

By Air France has major international airports at Paris, Marseille, Toulouse, Strasbourg, Lyon and Bordeaux, plus around 170 smaller connecting airports. International flights from within Europe also land at smaller airports such as Montpellier.
From the UK, carriers include France's international airline, Air France (tel: 0844 490 787 in UK; 3654 in France; www.airfrance.com), as well as British Airways (tel: 0870 850 9850; www.ba.com), easyJet (www.easyjet.com) and Ryanair (tel: 0871 2560 000; www.ryanair.com). Flying time varies from about 1 to 2.5 hours.
From the US and Canada, numerous carriers operate direct flights, including American Airlines (tel: 1 800 433 7300 in US; www.aa.com), Delta (tel: 1 800 241 4141 in US; www.delta.com) and Air Canada (tel: 1 888 247 2262 in Canada; www.aircanada.com). Flying time varies from 12 hours (US west coast) to 7.5 hours (Montréal).

By Rail Paris is the main railway hub, with six major railway stations, each handling traffic to different parts of France and Europe. SNCF, the national carrier, operates high-speed trains (TGV) to Paris from main stations throughout France. The Eurostar passenger train service (tel: 08705 186186 in Britain, www.eurostar.com) from London St Pancras International via the Channel Tunnel to Paris Gare du Nord takes 2 hours 15 minutes.

By Sea Several ferry companies operate regular services from England and Ireland to north and northwest France. Crossing times from England vary from 35 minutes to 9 hours, and from Ireland around 14 to 18 hours.

TIME

France is on Central European Time, one hour ahead of Greenwich Mean Time (GMT +1). From late March, when clocks are put forward one hour, until late October, French summer time (GMT +2) operates.

CURRENCY AND FOREIGN EXCHANGE

Currency France is one of the 16 European countries to use a single currency, the Euro (€). Euro coins are issued in denominations of 1, 2, 5, 10, 20 and 50 cents and €1 and €2. Notes (bills) are issued in denominations of €5, €10, €20, €50, €100, €200 and €500.

Exchange You can exchange travellers' cheques at some banks and at bureaux de change at airports, main railway stations and some department stores, and exchange booths. All transactions are subject to a commission charge, so you may prefer to rely on cash and credit cards. Travellers' cheques issued by American Express and VISA may also be changed at many post offices.

Credit cards are widely accepted in shops, restaurants and hotels. VISA (Carte Bleue), MasterCard (Eurocard) and Diners Club cards with four-digit PINs can be used in most ATM cash dispensers. Some smaller shops and hotels may not accept credit cards – always check before you book in.

In the US
French Tourist Office
825 Third Avenue, 29th
floor (entrance on 50th St),
New York NY10022
☎ 514 288 1904

In Canada
French Tourist Office
1800 avenue McGill College,
Suite 1010,
H3A 3J6 Montreal
☎ 514-288-2026

In Australia
French Tourist Office
Level 13, 15 Bligh Street
Sydney, NSW 2000
☎ (02) 9231 5244

WHEN YOU ARE THERE

NATIONAL HOLIDAYS

1 Jan	New Year's Day
Mar/Apr	Easter Sunday and Monday
1 May	May Day
8 May	VE (Victory in Europe) Day
6th Thu after Easter	Ascension Day
May/Jun	Whit Sunday and Monday
14 Jul	Bastille Day
15 Aug	Assumption Day
1 Nov	All Saints' Day
11 Nov	Remembrance Day
25 Dec	Christmas Day

Banks, museums, shops and restaurants close.

ELECTRICITY

The power supply in France is 220 volts. Sockets accept two-round-pin (or increasingly three-round-pin) plugs, so an adaptor is needed for most non-Continental appliances. A transformer is needed for appliances operating on 110–120 volts.

OPENING HOURS

- ○ Shops
- ● Offices
- ● Banks
- ● Post Offices
- ● Museums/Monuments
- ● Pharmacies

8 am 9 am 10 am noon 1 pm 2 pm 4 pm 5 pm 7 pm

- ☐ Day
- ☐ Midday
- ☐ Evening

Shops Many shops close 12–2pm, Sunday and Monday, but may open longer hours, especially in summer.
Banks Some open extended hours, including Saturday morning, but may close Monday. Banks may close at noon on the day before a national holiday.
Museums Museums usually close at least one day a week, and this varies across France.

TIPS/GRATUITIES

Restaurant, café and hotel bills must by law include a service charge so a tip is not expected, although many people do leave a few coins in restaurants.

Taxis	€2
Tour guides	€5
Porters	€2
Usherettes	small change
Hairdressers	€5
Lavatory attendants	small change

SMOKING

As in the rest of Europe, smoking is banned by law in all indoor public places throughout France, including restaurants, cafés and bars. Some restaurants, airports and other buildings, however, have enclosed ventilated cubicles for the use of smokers.

TIME DIFFERENCES

GMT	France	Spain	USA (NY)	USA (West Coast)	Sydney
12 noon	1 pm	1 pm	7 am	4 am	10 pm

STAYING IN TOUCH

Post Post offices are
identified by a yellow or
brown "La Poste" or "PTT"
sign, and post boxes are
usually square and yellow.
Most post offices open
from 9–12 and 2–5, and
they usually have an ATM.

Public telephones All
telephone numbers in
France comprise ten digits.
There are no area codes,
simply dial all ten digits of
the number. Paris numbers
all begin with 01.
In addition to coin-operated
models, an increasing

number of public phones take phone-cards (*télécarte*).
These are sold in units of 50 and 120 and can be
bought from France Telecom shops, post offices,
tobacconists and at railway stations. Cheap call rates
generally apply Mon–Fri 7pm–8am, Sat–Sun all day.

International Dialling Codes
Dial 00 followed by

UK:	44
USA / Canada:	1
Irish Republic:	353
Australia:	61
New Zealand:	64

Mobile providers and services A foreign mobile phone
with GSM technology will work almost anywhere in
France. Before you travel, check with your service
provider that you have roaming enabled and find out
what the charges are for use abroad. Alternatively, buy
a French pay-as-you-go SIM card or, if your phone is
non-GSM, you could rent a phone for your stay.

Wi-Fi and Internet Every major city in France has at
least one Internet café and, even in small towns,
you can usually find a public-sponsored cyberbase,
although you might have to reserve computer time.
WiFi hotspots, meanwhile, are spreading rapidly and,
in cities and areas frequented by business travellers,
most hotels offer free wireless Internet access.

PERSONAL SAFETY

Petty crime, particularly theft
of wallets and handbags, is
fairly common in the major
cities. Be aware of scruffy,
innocent-looking children:
they may be working the
streets in gangs, fleecing
unwary tourists. Report any
loss or theft to the *Police
Municipale* (blue uniforms).
To be safe:
- Watch your bag on the
  Métro, in busy tourist areas
  and in museum queues.
- Lock your car and do not
  leave anything valuable
  inside.
- Keep valuables in your
  hotel safe (*coffre-fort*).
- Avoid walking alone in dark
  city streets at night.

Police assistance:
☎ 17 from any phone

EMERGENCY NUMBERS	
POLICE 17	
FIRE 18	
AMBULANCE 15	
INTERNATIONAL EMERGENCY 112	

HEALTH

 Insurance Citizens of EU countries receive reduced-cost emergency health care with relevant documentation (European Health Insurance Card), but private medical insurance is still advised, and is essential for all other visitors.

 Dental Services As for general medical treatment (see above, Insurance), nationals of EU countries can obtain dental treatment at reduced cost. Around 70 per cent of standard dentists' fees are refunded, but private medical insurance is still advised for all.

 Weather July and August are likely to be sunny and hot. When sightseeing, cover up, apply a good sunscreen, wear sunglasses and drink plenty of fluids.

 Drugs Pharmacies – recognized by their green cross sign – possess highly qualified staff able to offer medical advice, provide first-aid and prescribe a wide range of drugs, although some are available by prescription (*ordonnance*) only.

 Safe Water Tap water is safe to drink, but never drink from a tap marked *eau non potable* (not drinking water). Bottled water is also widely available.

CONCESSIONS

Students/Youths Holders of an International Student Identity Card (ISIC) are entitled to discounted admission to museums, attractions and sights, air and ferry tickets and meals in some student cafeterias. Holders of the International Youth Travel Card (or GO 25 Card) qualify for similar discounts as ISIC holders (www.isic.tm.fr).

Senior Citizens If you are over 60 you can get discounts (up to 50 per cent) in museums, on public transport and in places of entertainment. You will need a *Carte Senior* which can be purchased from the *Abonnement* office of any main railway station. You may get a discount if you show your passport (www.senior-sncf.com).

TRAVELLING WITH A DISABILITY

Many older facilities and attractions lack amenities for people with disabilities, although most hotels with two or more stars have lifts (elevators). Few Métro stations have lifts, but RATP and SNCF run an Accompaniment Service (RATP, tel: 08 10 64 64 64; SNCF, tel: 08 90 64 06 50, www.voyages-sncf.com/guide/voyageurs-handicapes). The service is not free and you will need to book in advance.

CHILDREN

Children are welcomed in most hotels and restaurants. Many sights and attractions offer reductions; entrance to museums for under-18's is generally free. Baby-changing facilities are excellent in newer museums and attractions, but limited elsewhere.

TOILETS

Modern unisex, self-cleaning, coin-operated toilets are found on the streets of most major cities. In smaller towns and villages, free public toilets can normally be found by the market square or near tourist offices. Cleanliness varies, and some older or more remote establishments may have a squat toilet. Café toilets are for the use of customers only.

EMBASSIES AND HIGH COMMISSIONS

UK	**US**	**Australia**	**Canada**	**New Zealand**
☎ 01 44 51 31 00	☎ 01 43 12 22 22	☎ 01 40 59 33 00	☎ 01 44 43 29 00	☎ 01 45 01 43 43

SURVIVAL PHRASES

Yes/no **Oui/non**
Hello **Bonjour/bonsoir**
Goodbye **Au revoir**
How are you? **Comment allez-vous?**
Please **S'il vous plaît**
Thank you **Merci**
Excuse me **Excusez-moi**
I'm sorry **Pardon**
You're welcome **De rien/avec plaisir**
Do you have...? **Avez-vous...?**
How much is this? **C'est combien?**
I'd like... **Je voudrais...**

DIRECTIONS

Is there a phone box around here? **Y a-t-il une cabine téléphonique dans le coin?**
Where is...? **Où se trouve...?**
...the nearest Métro **le Métro le plus proche**
...the telephone **le téléphone**
...the bank **la banque**
...the toilet **les toilettes**
Turn left/right **tournez à gauche/droite**
Go straight on **allez tout droit**
The first/second (on the right) **le premier/ le deuxième (à droite)**
At the crossroads **au carrefour**

IF YOU NEED HELP

Could you help me, please? **Pouvez-vous m'aider?**
Do you speak English? **Parlez-vous anglais?**
I don't understand **Je ne comprends pas**
Could you call a doctor quickly, please? **Voulez-vous vite appeler un médecin, s'il vous plaît?**

RESTAURANT

I'd like to book a table **Puis-je réserver une table?**
A table for two please **Une table pour deux personnes, s'il vous plaît**
Do you have a fixed price menu? **Vous avez un menu prix fixe?**
Could we see the menu please? **Nous pouvons avoir la carte?**
Could I have the bill please? **L'addition, s'il vous plaît**
A bottle/glass of... **Une bouteille/un verre de...**

MENU READER

apéritifs appetisers
boissons alcoolisées alcoholic beverages
boissons chaudes hot beverages
boissons froides cold beverages
carte des vins wine list
coquillages shellfish
fromage cheese
gibier game
hors d'oeuvres/entrées starters
légumes vegetables
plats chauds hot dishes
plats froids cold dishes
plat du jour dish of the day
pâtisserie pastry
plat principal main course
potages soups
service compris service included
service non compris service not included
spécialités régionales regional specialities
viandes meat courses
volaille poultry

NUMBERS

0 **zéro**	11 **onze**	30 **trente**	101 **cent un**
1 **un**	12 **douze**	31 **trente et un**	110 **cent dix**
2 **deux**	13 **treize**	32 **trente-deux**	120 **cent vingt**
3 **trois**	14 **quatorze**	40 **quarante**	200 **deux cents**
4 **quatre**	15 **quinze**	50 **cinquante**	300 **trois cents**
5 **cinq**	16 **seize**	60 **soixante**	400 **quatre cents**
6 **six**	17 **dix-sept**	70 **soixante-dix**	500 **cinq cents**
7 **sept**	18 **dix-huit**	80 **quatre-vingts**	600 **six cents**
8 **huit**	19 **dix-neuf**	90 **quatre-vingt-dix**	700 **sept cents**
9 **neuf**	20 **vingt**	100 **cent**	800 **huit cents**
10 **dix**	21 **vingt et un**		900 **neuf cents**
	22 **vingt-deux**		1,000 **mille**

FOOD A–Z

agneau lamb
ail garlic
ananas pineapple
anguille eel
banane banana
beurre butter
bifteck steak
bière (bière pression) beer (draught beer)
boeuf beef
boudin noir/blanc black/white pudding
brochet pike
cabillaud cod
calmar squid
canard duck
champignons mushrooms
chou cabbage
choucroute sauerkraut
chou-fleur cauliflower
choux de Bruxelles Brussels sprouts
citron lemon
civet de lièvre jugged hare
concombre cucumber
confiture jam
coquilles Saint-Jacques scallops
cornichon gherkin
côte/côtelette chop
côtelettes dans l'échine spare ribs
couvert cutlery
crevettes grises shrimps
crevettes roses prawns
croque monsieur toasted ham and cheese sandwich
cru raw
crustacés seafood
cuisses de grenouilles frogs' legs
cuit (à l'eau) boiled

eau mineral gazeuse/non gazeuse sparkling/still mineral water
écrevisse crayfish
entrecôte sirloin steak
entrées first course
épices spices
épinards spinach
épis de maïs corn (on the cob)
escargots snails
farine flour
fenouil fennel
fèves broad beans
figues figs
filet de boeuf fillet
filet mignon fillet steak
filet de porc tenderloin
fines herbes herbs
foie gras goose liver
fraises strawberries
framboises raspberries
frit fried
friture deep-fried
fruit de la passion passion fruit
fruits de la saison seasonal fruits
gaufres waffles
gigot d'agneau leg of lamb
glace ice-cream
glaçons ice cubes
grillé grilled
groseilles redcurrants
hareng herring
haricots blancs haricot beans
haricots verts French beans
homard lobster
huîtres oysters
jambon blanc/cru/fumé ham (cooked/Parma style/smoked)
jus de citron lemon juice

jus de fruits fruit juice
jus d'orange orange juice
lait demi-écrémé/entier milk semi-skimmed/full-cream
langouste crayfish
langoustine scampi
langue tongue
lapin rabbit
lentilles lentils
lotte monkfish
loup de mer sea bass
macaron macaroon
maïs sweetcorn
marron chestnut
menu du jour/à la carte menu of the day/à la carte
morilles morels
moules mussels
mousse au chocolat chocolate mousse
moutarde mustard
myrtilles bilberries
noisette hazelnut
noix walnut
noix de veau fillet of veal
oeuf à la coque/dur/au plat egg soft/hard-boiled/fried
oignon onion
origan oregano
pain au chocolat croissant with chocolate centre
part portion
pêche peach
petite friture fried fish (whitebait or similar)
petits (biscuits) salés savoury biscuits
petit pain roll
petits pois green peas
pintade guinea fowl

poire pear
pois chiches chick peas
poisson fish
poivre pepper
poivron green/red pepper
pomme apple
pommes de terre potatoes
(pommes) frites chips
poulet (blanc) chicken (breast)
prune plum
pruneaux prunes
queue de boeuf oxtail
ragoût stew
ris de veau veal/sweetbread
riz rice
rôti de boeuf (rosbif) roast beef
rouget red mullet
saignant rare
salade verte lettuce
salé/sucré salted/sweet
saumon salmon
saucisses sausages
sel salt
soupe à l'oignon onion soup
sucre sugar
thon tuna
thym thyme
tripes tripe
truffes truffles
truite trout
truite saumonée salmon trout
vapeur (à la) steamed
venaison venison
viande hachée minced meat/mince
vin blanc white wine
vin rosé rosé wine
vin rouge red wine
vinaigre vinegar
xérès sherry

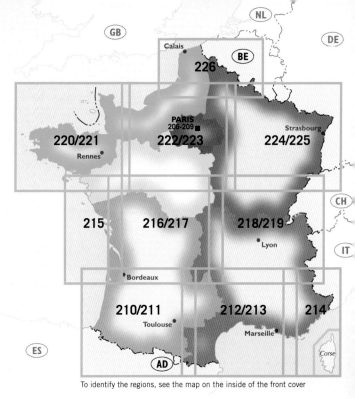

To identify the regions, see the map on the inside of the front cover

Streetplan

‒‒‒ Main road / minor road

▪ Featured place of interest

ℹ Tourist information

● Métro station

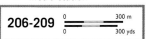
206-209 | 0 — 300 m / 0 — 300 yds

Regional Maps

▬▬ Major route

▭▭▭ Motorway (Expressway)

▭▭ National road

▭▭ Regional road

‒‒‒ International boundary

‒‒‒ Regional boundary

National park

▫ City / Town

▪ Featured place of interest

▪ Place of interest

✈ Airport

210-226 | 0 — 25 km / 0 — 15 miles

214 | 0 — 50 km / 0 — 25 miles

Atlas

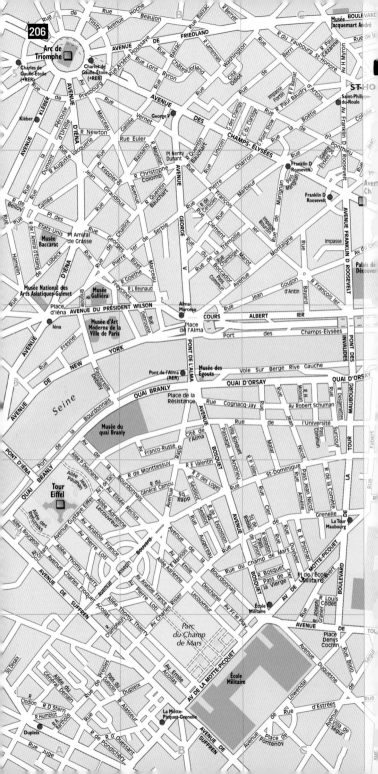

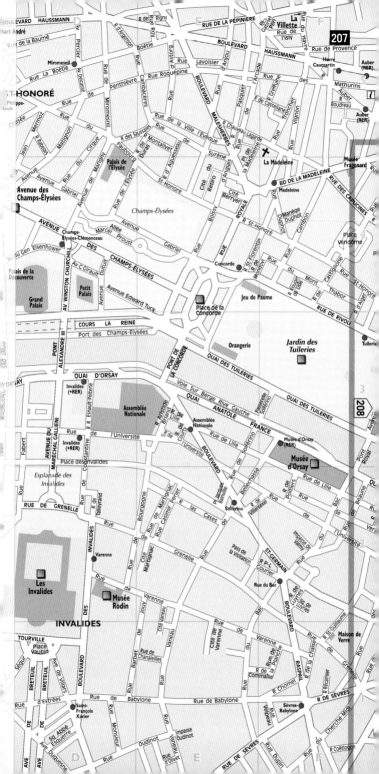

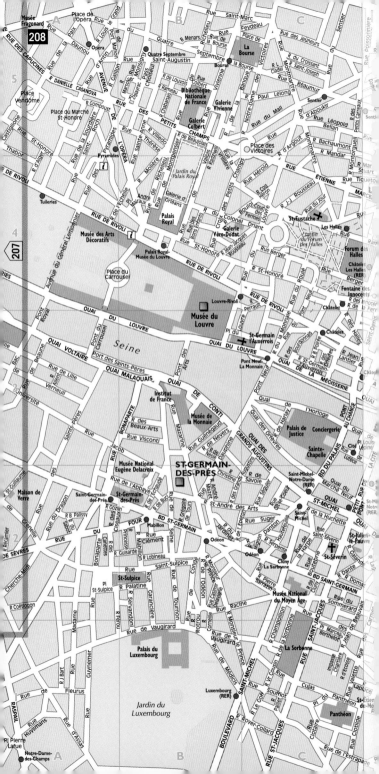

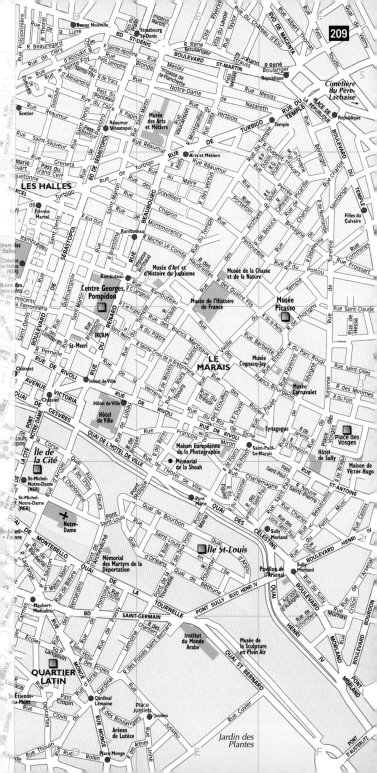

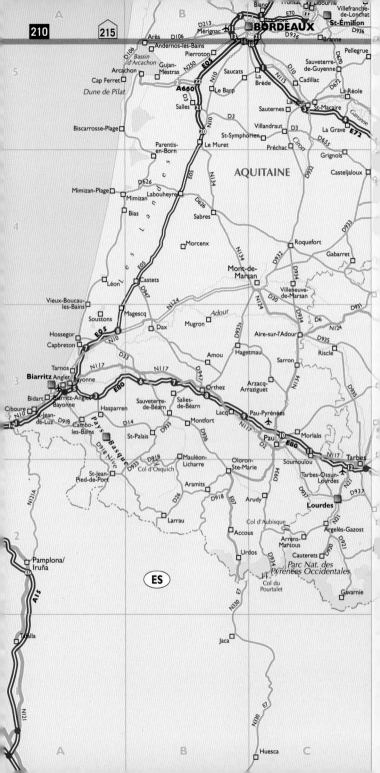

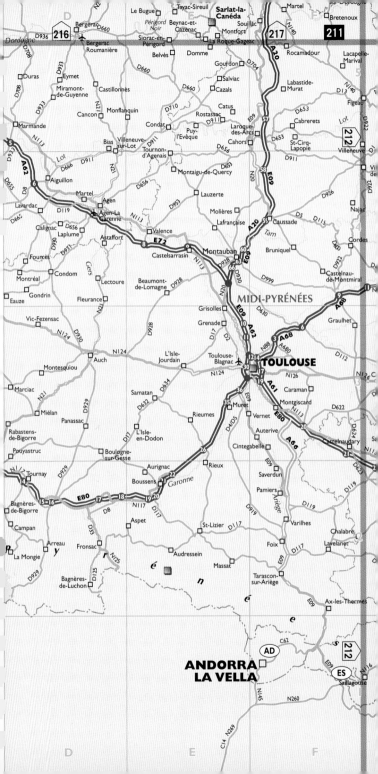

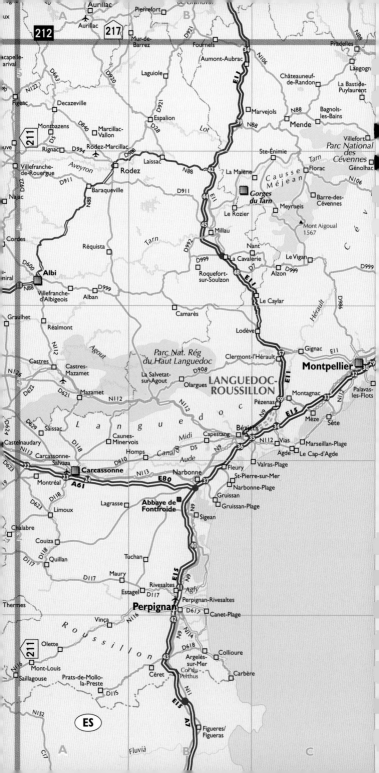

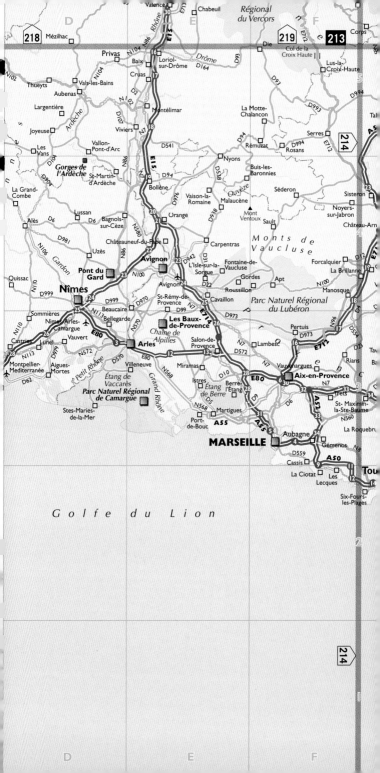

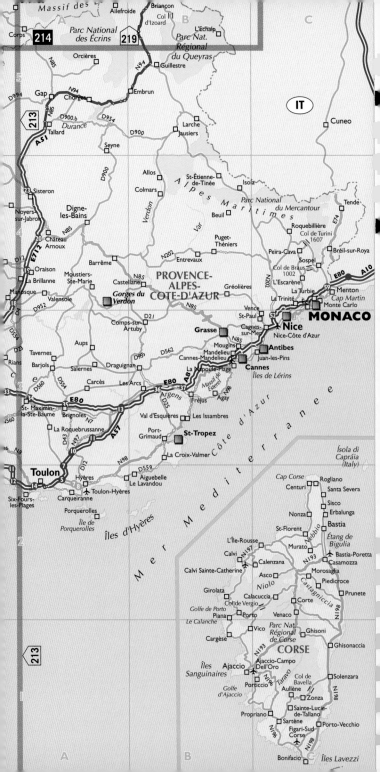

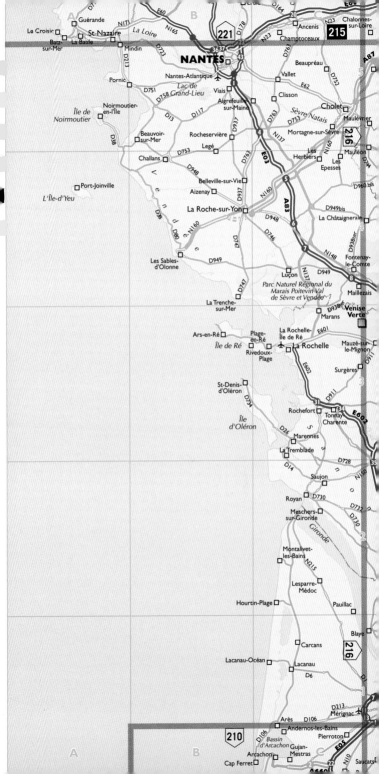

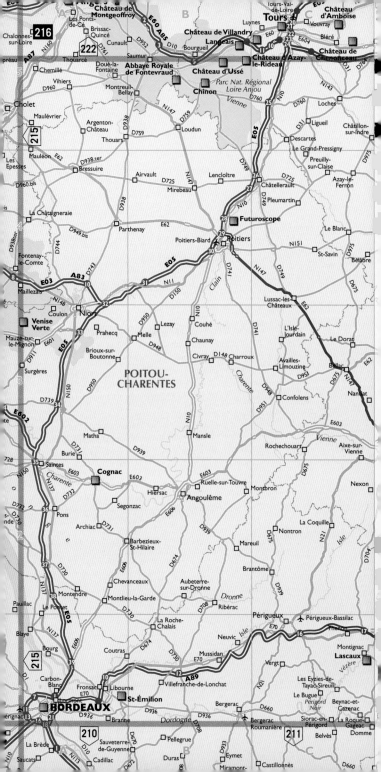

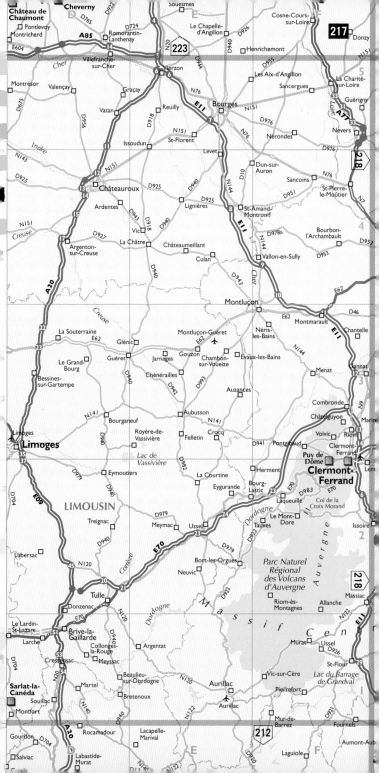

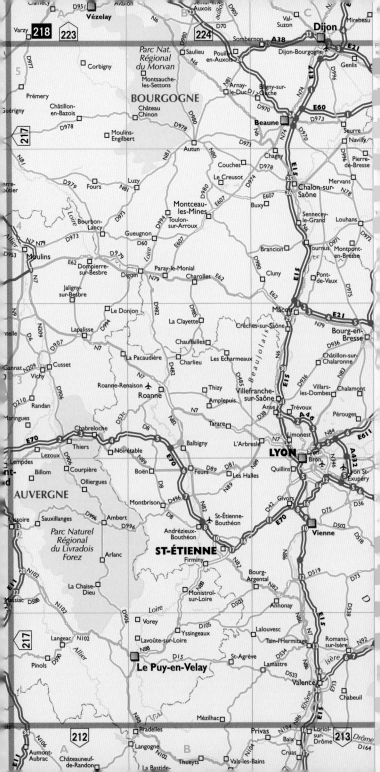

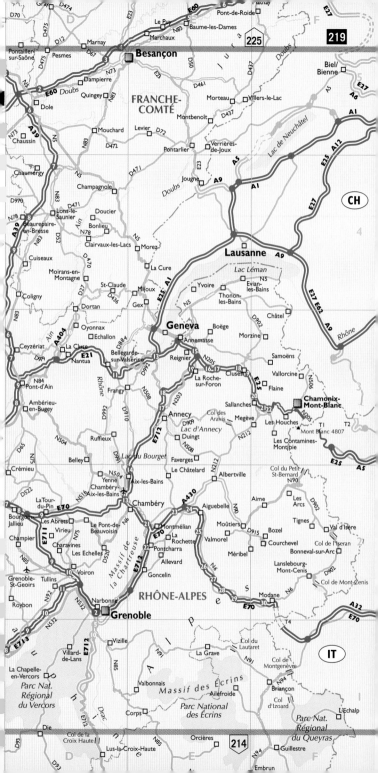

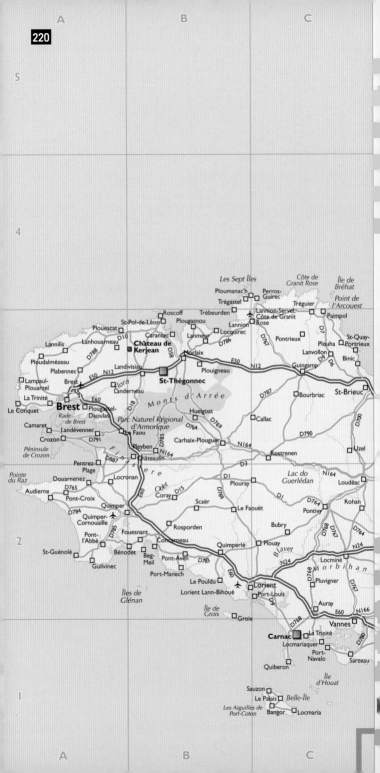

A **B** **C**

5

4

Les Sept Îles
Côte de
Granit Rose
Île de
Bréhat

Ploumanac'h
Perros-
Guirec
Point de
l'Arcouest

Trégastel
Tréguier

Trébeurden
Lannion-Servel,
Côte de Granit
Paimpol

Roscoff
Plougasnou
Lannion
Pontrieux
St-Quay-
Portrieux

St-Pol-de-Léon
Carantec
Lanmeur
Locquirec
Plouha

Plouescat
Lanhouarneau
D10
Château de
Kerjean
D58
Morlaix
D786
Lanvollon
Binic

Lannilis
Landivisiau
Plouigneau
E50
N12
Guingamp

Ploudalmézeau
D788
E50
N12
St-Thégonnec
D787
Bourbriac
St-Brieuc

Plabennec
Landerneau
Elorn
Monts d'Arrée
D700

Brest
Le Conquet
La Trinité
E60
Plougastel-
Daoulas
Huelgoat
D764
D769
Callac
D790

Camaret
Rade
de Brest
Parc Naturel Régional
d'Armorique
Carhaix-Plouguer
N164
D3
Rostrenen
Uzel

Crozon
Landévennec
D791
le Faou
D785
N164
Pleyben
Châteaulin

Péninsule
de Crozon
D887
Locronan
Odet
D1
Plouray
Lac do
Guerlédan
N164
Loudéac

Pointe
du Raz
Pentrez-
Plage
Douarnenez
D765
Coray
D15
Scaër
Le Faouët
D1
D764
Rohan

Audierne
Pont-Croix
E60
Quimper
Rosporden
D768
D767
D764

D784
Quimper-
Cornouaille
Fouesnant
Concarneau
Bubry
Pontivy

Pont-
l'Abbé
D785
Bénodet
Beg-
Meil
Quimperlé
Plouay
Blavet
N24
Locminé
Morbihan
D767

St-Guénolé
Guilvinec
Pont-Aven
D783
E60
N24
D768
Pluvigner

Îles de
Glénan
Port-Manech
Le Pouldu
Lorient
Lorient Lann-Bihoué
Port-Louis
Auray
E60
N166

Île de
Groix
Groix
D768
Vannes

Carnac
La Trinité
Locmariaquer
Port-
Navalo
Sarzeau

Quiberon
Île
d'Houat

Sauzon
Le Palais
Belle-Île
Les Aiguilles de
Port-Coton
Bangor
Locmaria

A **B** **C**

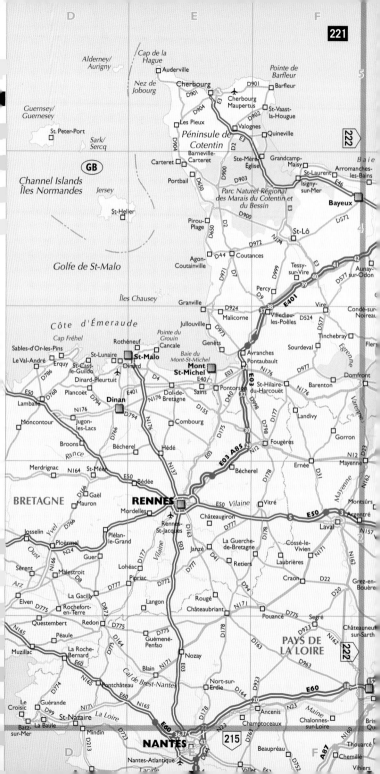

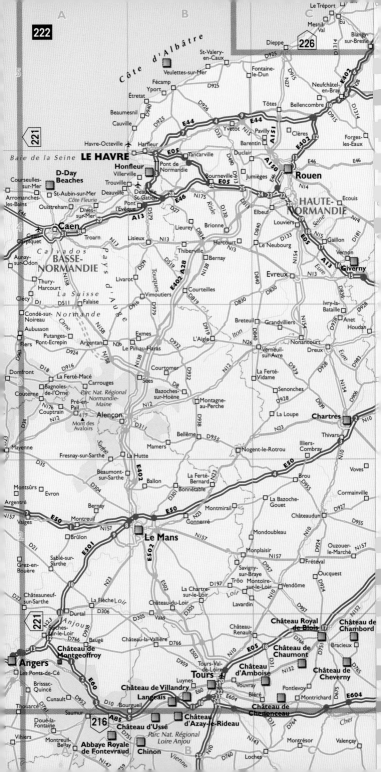

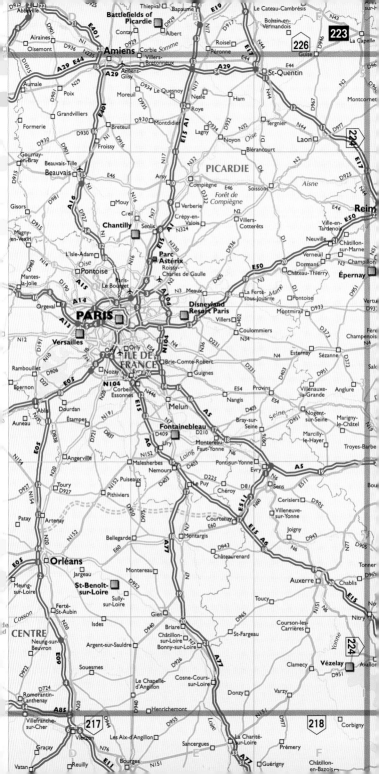

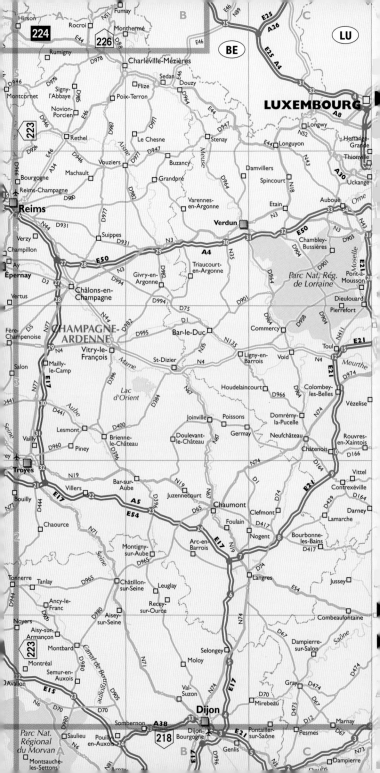

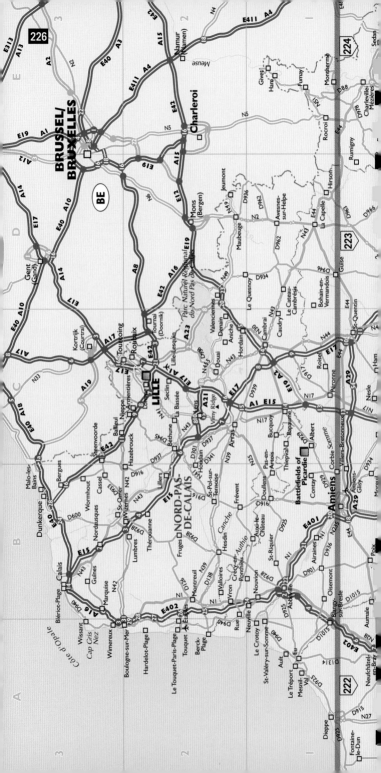

The Automobile Association would like to thank the following photographers, companies and picture libraries for their assistance in the preparation of this book.

Abbreviations for the picture credits are as follows: (t) top; (b) bottom; (l) left; (r) right; (c) centre; (AA) AA World Travel Library.

2i AA/Clive Sawyer; 2ii AA/Neil Setchfield; 2iii AA/Karl Blackwell; 2iv AA/Ian Dawson; 2v AA/T Oliver; 3i Ian Dagnall/ Alamy; 3ii AA/James A Tims; 3iii CW Images/Alamy; 3iv AA/Max Jourdan; 5l AA/Clive Sawyer; 5bc AA/Yadid Levy; 5br AA/Clive Sawyer; 6-7 James Osmond Photography/Alamy; 8 Musee de Toulon, France/Lauros/Giraudon/The Bridgeman Art Library; 9 Mary Evans Picture Library/Explorer/ADPC; 10 French Photographer,(19th century)/Private Collection/ The Bridgeman Art Library; 11 AA/Clive Sawyer; 13 AA/Michael Short; 14 AA/Rick Strange; 15l AA/Yadid Levy; 15r AA/ Clive Sawyer; 16 Tom Mackie/Alamy; 17 John Kellerman/Alamy; 18l Stephane Ouzounoff/Photolibrary; 18r Photos 12/ Alamy; 19 AA/Karl Blackwell; 20 AA/Clive Sawyer; 21 AA/Karl Blackwell; 22 Musee Marmottan, Paris, France/Giraudon/ The Bridgeman Art Library; 23tr Musee Toulouse-Lautrec, Albi, France/ Lauros/Giraudon/The Bridgeman Art Library; 24bl Jean-Pierre Muller/AFP/Getty Images; 24br AA/Max Jourdan; 25 Rex; 26 Yoshikazu Tsuno/AFP/Getty Images; 27l AA/Neil Setchfield; 27bc AA/Karl Blackwell; 27br AA/Roger Day; 39l AA/Karl Blackwell; 39bc AA/Karl Blackwell; 39br AA/Wyn Voysey; 40 AA/Karl Blackwell; 42 AA/Karl Blackwell; 43t Hemis/Alamy; 43b Louvre, Paris, France/Giraudon/ The Bridgeman Art Library; 44-45 AA/Karl Blackwell; 46 AA/Karl Blackwell; 47 AA/Max Jourdan; 48 AA/Max Jourdan; 49 AA/Clive Sawyer; 50 Sid Frisby/Alamy; 51 Peter Barritt/Alamy; 52 AA/Karl Blackwell; 54 AA/Karl Blackwell; 55 AA/Karl Blackwell; 56 AA/Max Jourdan; 58 AA/Max Jourdan; 59 AA/Max Jourdan; 60 AA/Karl Blackwell; 61t AA/Karl Blackwell; 61b AA/Karl Blackwell; 63t AA/Karl Blackwell; 63b AA/Karl Blackwell; 64 AA/David Noble; 65 AA/Max Joudan; 66 Jon Arnold Images Ltd/Alamy; 73l AA/Ian Dawson; 73bc AA/Alex Kouprianoff; 73br AA/Clive Sawyer; 74 Jon Arnold Images Ltd/Alamy; 75t Hemis/Alamy; 75b AA/Clive Sawyer; 76 Julia Gavin/Alamy; 77t Jon Arnold Images Ltd/Alamy; 77b AA/ Alex Kouprianoff; 78-79 Jon Arnold Images Ltd/Alamy; 79t AA/Ian Dawson; 80 AA/Ian Dawson; 81 Robert Harding Picture Library Ltd/Alamy; 82 Sami Sarkis France/Alamy; 83 nagelestock.com/Alamy; 84 Wilmar Photography/Alamy; 85 Stockfolio®/Alamy; 86 DC Premiumstock/Alamy; 87 AA/Ian Dawson; 88 AA/Alex Kouprianoff; 93l AA/T Oliver; 93bc AA/Michael Short; 93br AA/Jon Wyand; 95tl Peter Huggins/Alamy; 95tr Yadid Levy/Alamy; 96 Tibor Bognar/Alamy; 97 Stockfolio®/Alamy; 98 AA/Roger Day; 99 AA/Roger Day; 100 Directphoto.org/Alamy; 101 JTB Photo Communications, Inc./Alamy; 102 Art Kowalsky/Alamy; 104 AA/Jon Wyand; 105 Hemis/Alamy; 106 AA/Michael Short; 107 PCL/Alamy; 108 John Kellerman/Alamy; 109 Olaf Doering/Alamy; 110 AA/Barrie Smith; 111 The Art Archive/Alamy; 112 isifa Image Service s.r.o./Alamy; 117l Ian Dagnall/Alamy; 117bc AA/Rob Moore; 117br AA/Rob Moore; 118 Hemis/Alamy; 120 Hemis/ Alamy; 121 D A Barnes/Alamy; 122 JLImages/Alamy; 123 Hemis/Alamy; 124 Mark Zylber/Alamy; 125 Jon Arnold Images Ltd/Alamy; 126 Hemis/Alamy; 127 JTB Photo Communications, Inc./Alamy; 128 AA/J Edmanson; 129 Images Etc Ltd/ Alamy; 130 Hemis/Alamy; 131 AA/Rob Moore; 135l AA/James A Tims; 135bc AA/Clive Sawyer; 135br AA/Clive Sawyer; 137 AA; 138 Howard Sayer/Alamy; 139 AA/Clive Sawyer; 140-141 Tom Mackie/Alamy; 142 Richard Wareham Fotografie/ Alamy; 144 AA/Clive Sawyer; 145 AA/Yadid Levy; 146 Brian Jannsen/Alamy; 147 Gail Mooney-Kelly/Alamy; 148 AA/ Clive Sawyer; 149 AA/Clive Sawyer; 151 AA/James A Tims; 152 Jaubert Bernard/Alamy; 153 Tommaso Di Girolamo/ Photolibrary; 154 ImagesEurope/Alamy; 155 guichaoua/Alamy; 156 AA/Clive Sawyer; 157t AA/Clive Sawyer; 157b AA/ Clive Sawyer; 158 AA/Clive Sawyer; 159 AA/Clive Sawyer; 165l CW Images/Alamy; 165tc AA/Neil Setchfield; 165tr AA/ Paul Kenward; 166 Nicolas Thibaut; 167 AA/Pete Bennett; 168 AA/Neil Setchfield; 169 Nicolas Thibaut/Photolibrary; 170 Leslie West/Photolibrary; 172 AA/Neil Setchfield; 173 Nicolas Thibaut/Photolibrary; 174 AA/Adrian Baker; 175 Peter Horree/Alamy; 176 AA/Barrie Smith; 177 nobleIMAGES/Alamy; 178 AA/Barrie Smith; 183l AA/Max Kouprianoff; 183tc AA/ Philip Enticknap; 183tr AA/Alex Kouprianoff; 184 AA/Max Joudan; 186 AA/Karl Blackwell; 187 AA/Alex Kouprianoff; 188 AA/Alex Kouprianoff; 189 ImagesEurope/Alamy; 191 Hemis/Alamy; 192 AA/Clive Sawyer; 194 AA/Tony Oliver; 195 allOver photography/Alamy; 196 AA/Neil Setchfield; 197l funkyfood London-Paul Williams/Alamy; 197tc AA/Max Jourdan; 197tr AA/Max Jourdan; 201t AA/Karl Blackwell; 201c AA/Clive Sawyer; 201b AA/Karl Blackwell.

Every effort has been made to trace the copyright holders, and we apologise in advance for any accidental errors. We would be happy to apply any corrections in the following edition of this publication.

SPIRALGUIDE
Questionnaire

Dear Traveller

Your comments, opinions and recommendations are very important to us. Please help us to improve our travel guides by taking a few minutes to complete this simple questionnaire.

You do not need a stamp (unless posted outside the UK). If you do not want to remove this page from your guide, then photocopy it or write your answers on a plain sheet of paper.

Send to: The Editor, Spiral Guides, AA World Travel Guides, FREEPOST SCE 4598, Basingstoke RG21 4GY.

Your recommendations...

We always encourage readers' recommendations for restaurants, night-life or shopping – if your recommendation is used in the next edition of the guide, we will send you a FREE AA Spiral Guide of your choice. Please state below the establishment name, location and your reasons for recommending it.

_____

_____

_____

_____

_____

Please send me AA Spiral _____
(see list of titles inside the back cover)

About this guide...

Which title did you buy?

_____ **AA Spiral**

Where did you buy it? _____

When? m m / y y

Why did you choose an AA Spiral Guide? _____

_____

_____

_____

Did this guide meet your expectations?

Exceeded ☐   Met all ☐   Met most ☐   Fell below ☐

Please give your reasons _____

_____

_____

_____

_____

continued on next page...

Were there any aspects of this guide that you particularly liked?

_____
_____
_____
_____
_____

Is there anything we could have done better?

_____
_____
_____
_____

About you...

Name (Mr/Mrs/Ms) _____

Address _____

_____ Postcode _____

Daytime tel no _____ email _____

Please *only* give us your email address and mobile phone number if you wish to hear from us about other products and services from the AA and partners by email or text or mms.

Which age group are you in?

Under 25 ☐   25–34 ☐   35–44 ☐   45–54 ☐   55–64 ☐   65+ ☐

How many trips do you make a year?

Less than one ☐   One ☐   Two ☐   Three or more ☐

Are you an AA member? Yes ☐   No ☐

About your trip...

When did you book? m m / y y   When did you travel? m m / y y

How long did you stay? _____

Was it for business or leisure? _____

Did you buy any other travel guides for your trip? ☐ Yes ☐ No

If yes, which ones? _____
_____

Thank you for taking the time to complete this questionnaire. Please send it to us as soon as possible, and remember, you do not need a stamp (unless posted outside the UK).